IT WASN'T ME! ALL RIGHT?

IT WASN'T ME! ALL RIGHT?

Robert Rooney

Copyright © 2019 Robert Rooney

The moral right of the author has been asserted.

Apart from any fair dealing for the purposes of research or private study, or criticism or review, as permitted under the Copyright, Designs and Patents Act 1988, this publication may only be reproduced, stored or transmitted, in any form or by any means, with the prior permission in writing of the publishers, or in the case of reprographic reproduction in accordance with the terms of licences issued by the Copyright Licensing Agency. Enquiries concerning reproduction outside those terms should be sent to the publishers.

Matador
9 Priory Business Park,
Wistow Road, Kibworth Beauchamp,
Leicestershire. LE8 0RX
Tel: 0116 279 2299
Email: books@troubador.co.uk
Web: www.troubador.co.uk/matador
Twitter: @matadorbooks

ISBN 978 1785898 983

British Library Cataloguing in Publication Data.
A catalogue record for this book is available from the British Library.

Printed and bound in the UK by TJ International, Padstow, Cornwall
Typeset in 11pt Aldine401 BT by Troubador Publishing Ltd, Leicester, UK

Matador is an imprint of Troubador Publishing Ltd

For Eileen

Dedication

This is dedicated to a number of people. In my teaching career I have known a lot of good teachers. They far outnumber the smallish number of bad ones. I have also been privileged to work with some excellent teachers. Within that group there were five outstanding ones; teachers who actually not only loved their job but fitted into it apparently effortlessly, as effortless as all their preparation and hard work allowed. They were both gifted and blessed. Even the prospect of brain surgery attempted by a cretinous gorilla could not force me to identify them.

You get to know a lot about someone whenever you see them teach. After twenty years of marriage I got to know my wife again when she was directed to teach in our new amalgamated school. Seeing her professionalism and her genuine caring, compassion and effectiveness as a teacher and a human being caused me to fall in love all over again! And that, in a strange way, is what good teaching is all about. We come to recognise genuine goodness; to discover and cultivate hitherto hidden abilities; to accept that within 'achievement' there are infinite possibilities of progression; to discover our own faults and limitations; to strive for the possibilities of change and to exalt in the differing personalities of those around us. Education is a two-way process and I learnt a lot from pupils about myself in particular and life in general.

The main dedication goes to all those pupils who gave me so much over the period covered. This was a period when in Northern Ireland we lived through what is almost euphemistically referred to as 'the Troubles'. That term fails to express the reality of a time when life was cheapened; violence, cruelty and savagery often ruled and few of us were untouched by the loss of life. We have moved on but it is still a place full of memories and ghosts. Outside of home, the classroom was my sanctuary during that time and the pupils my benefactors.

Chapter One

'The beginnings and endings of all human undertakings are untidy.'
John Galsworthy

He whipped the belt from his trousers and twisting the buckle end round his fist like a professional street fighter snarled, 'OK! Right…have a go… have a fair dig!'

The invitation was obviously inviting me to partake in some sort of physical brawl but in a gentlemanly and acceptable manner, as indicated by the adjective 'fair'.

My brain was screaming. This shouldn't be happening. I had been a teacher for three weeks. How did I find myself in a corridor facing 'Piggy', a huge sixteen-year-old with a belt in his hands, screaming obscenities, black hair licked down with Brylcreem, his eyes darting like demented fireflies, inviting me 'to take him on'?

I would like to think I remained calm and outwardly showed all the composure and confidence instilled in me by a year's post-graduate immersion in the educational philosophies of Karl Barth, Piaget and Steiner. In reality, their considered and doubtless worthy musings were as useful as a recipe for the perfect soufflé might be to a chef whose kitchen is on fire.

The truth was I was scared, not so much physically, but emotionally I was as solid and determined as a terminally ill jellyfish.

The door of my classroom was still open and I was aware of the excitement of my class of eleven-year-olds and their unspoken wondering about who was going to emerge victorious. Apart from a solitary, 'Piggy's going to do him!' there were only gasps of expectation at what promised to be a real bit of craic.

How had this happened?

What was I to do? He had kicked open the door of my classroom, strutted in, thrown a sheet down on the desk and said, 'Green said you've to sign this.'

I couldn't let that go, just when I had managed some sort of discipline in the class. I stood up and shouted, 'Get out and don't ever come into my room like that without knocking the door.'

'I did knock the door!' he shouted back.

'You're a liar,' I responded in stentorian if careless tones.

His face contorted, he squinted his eyes, black hair falling over his forehead. 'I did knock the *fucking* door.'

There was an almost collective gasp and I was aware that every eye in my class was looking at me and waiting expectantly for my reaction. This was in an era when that particular expletive had little currency in the general population and was almost unheard of in a school.

When he failed to respond to 'Get out' I was reduced to trying to push him out of the class. It was like trying to move a mountain of jelly. He was undoubtedly strong and well-muscled but trying to grab any part of him was akin to wrestling with a giant squid. After what seemed an interminable time I managed to push him out the door and into the corridor where the invite was issued. The more angry and confused I became, he became more determined and I even sensed a condescending sneer of contempt at such an unworthy adversary.

'Piggy' was a different proposition physically to any of my charges. Standing at well over six feet tall, his jet-black hair hung loosely over a size sixteen neck with fists that looked roughly the same width. He had an emerging black moustache and a lower thrusting lip that made Frankenstein's surgical mouth look like an invitational kiss. Heavily built, he worked after school in the local abattoir… presumably challenging the local bulls to 'a fair dig'.

There was, short of a desire to end up in hospital, no way to try and pin him down. I was in a tumble-dryer of emotions: confusion, embarrassment and inadequacy. Luckily the shouting had attracted the attention of Piggy's teacher who had materialised beside me. Looking totally unconcerned he quietly, almost laconically, said, 'Put your belt back on Henry. If your trousers fall down you'll get your death of cold and possibly six months for indecent exposure. Come on back in… you're going to miss your turn at draughts.'

Piggy's rant was lowered to a murmur as he turned and followed him meekly into the class, but not so meekly that before disappearing into the room he turned and gave me a two-fingered salute.

*

St Cuthbert's was what in those unenlightened days would be described as a school for slow learners. That was to describe the pupils but, as I was to discover, could be applicable in some respects to at least a few of the staff. I had been appointed as a class teacher for fourteen eleven-year-old boys whose experience with their previous teacher appeared to be more or less anarchistic. A number of the staff regarded me with a mixture of pity and unconvincing encouragement. There had been an air of anarchy and total indiscipline in the particular class when I took over but things had gradually got better. They were an eclectic mix in many ways and if some of them were a little outside the range of anything I had ever experienced, then that could be coped with.

I was enjoying the work after having spent a summer in London employed ('working' would be a fanciful and inaccurate verb) in a brewery. Contractually I was obliged to be engaged in productive labour from 7.00 in the morning to 4.00 in the evening. I discovered quite early that this was a theoretical construction and, with the constraints imposed by the unions, a day meant that I was more likely to expire from boredom than any work-related condition. To have a working day which began at 9.30 am and finished at 3.10 pm was not only preferable but would enable my beer-saturated body to recover. That my social life back home was vastly improved, with parties on an almost nightly basis, meant that my daytime occupation only helped my very happy state of mind. To my surprise I began to thoroughly enjoy the challenge and found that with the energy and naivety of youth, I was good at it. The class was coming around to what was reasonable behaviour, extending to all the little courtesies and respect. We said 'Good morning' and 'Thank you', and were behaving like good little subjects of a fading empire should.

There were of course the odd exceptions during the day, as when Kevin would refuse to do any work and content himself with rocking in his chair repeating the mantra, 'He's mad, he's mad... our teacher's bloody mad!'

Or 'Jimbo' would fly into a rage and kick anything or anybody and scream 'I'm going to friggin' kill somebody.'

I discovered quite early that you always grabbed Jimbo from behind. His back kick was considerably less forceful than his front.

Apart from the odd incident I felt in total control and I

could feel the growing warmth and fondness my pupils felt for me. But Piggy's incident left me shaken and wondering if this type of teaching was really for me. Could I ever expect to become the sort of teacher that got someone like Piggy, in that sort of a mood, to retreat quietly like an obedient sheepdog?

His teacher was probably the best teacher I ever knew. He had an ability and a warmth that made him an outstanding teacher for the type of pupils he taught; sixteen-year-old boys from, in many cases, poor homes and whose parents had been denied any participation in the good life; boys who in many cases were destined to end up on the dole. Many of them were quite intelligent but because of some problem, emotional or intellectual, they were determined as unsuitable for mainstream education. If life and employment prospects after school were hard for a lot of youngsters it was doubly so if you were a poor Belfast Catholic with a CV that stated you were 'a slow learner'.

Yet this teacher had an ability to give them a sense of worth and a dignity that they received from few others. He was the reason I ended up in that school. He was my father.

As we drove home that afternoon he failed to mention the incident as if it had somehow lost its importance. I, on the other hand, had thought of little else.

'What was I to do?'

I started feeling I had to justify the debacle. I related the entire incident to him. He was silent. I was conscious he didn't want to patronise or embarrass me, or worse, belittle the incident.

'Well, what would you have done?'

Quietly he painted a completely different denouement which materialised in my mind as he spoke.

Piggy kicked the door in, strode across the room and, smirking, threw the sheet down in front of me. 'Green says you've to sign this.'

'Sure,' I smiled agreeably, ignoring the class. Looking at him admiringly, I queried, 'You've a terrific build… do you do a bit of boxing or weight lifting? Boy, I wish as I had a build like yours. What's your name anyway?'

'Henry,' he replied. 'Naw! I don't do any boxing but I can handle myself all right.'

Looking at him I paused and then confidentially beckoned to him to let me whisper in his ear, 'Listen, maybe you could do me a favour? You see this crowd of boys – they haven't a clue how to behave; maybe they will when they grow up like you but right now I'm trying to get them to understand basic manners. You know, saying "Sir", knocking doors, saying "Thank you". The sort of things someone like you has to do when they go for a job. When are you leaving school anyway?'

'In June.'

'Right! Well, what do you think… could you give me a hand? Maybe if you went outside again and then pretended you had forgotten something, knocked the door and came in with the sheet of paper they would all say to themselves, "Well if a big fella like Henry does that it must be all right for us".'

And he would have done it and done so willingly. He would have impressed the hell out of this new teacher, shown a class how to behave, gained a lot of kudos and ended up with a high sense of self-importance. I would have shown my class how I 'forced' even Piggy to obey my new rules and how the biggest guy in the school was some sort of a buddy to me. Everyone's a winner.

Now that's what should have happened.

My father had obviously entered the lists on my behalf when, the next morning, there was a loud knock at my door. After my 'Come in', Piggy entered and walked up to the desk where he stretched out his hand and said, 'Sorry about the wee bit of bother yesterday, Sir.'

I shook his hand warmly. 'No bother, we all do stupid

things.' Turning to the class I preached, 'See, that's how you act when you do something wrong. You be a man and apologise.'

I put my arm on Henry's shoulder and smiling broadly said, 'You know, big man, it's a good job we didn't have that fair dig… I would have had to kill you!'

'Aye! Right, in your dreams,' he laughed. As he was leaving he turned, 'See you at dinner time, Sir.'

We left the best of friends. I was learning and I was learning fast. I'd also established (rather cleverly I thought) that Henry was in the wrong but that if people apologised, matters could be sorted. I was later to learn how important it was for staff also to follow that rule.

Chapter Two

'Schooldays are amongst the unhappiest in the whole span of human existence. They are full of dull, unintelligible tasks, new and unpleasant ordinances, with brutal violations of common sense and common decency.'
Henry Louis Mencken

I often wondered how I ended up as a teacher. It may be that it was akin to some form of inbred malformation, a genetic disability or a nascent inclination. Both my parents were teachers as was my grandfather and, in those nepotistic days, my uncle and his son-in-law also taught in the same school as my father and I.

My direct experience of education was painful. I hated primary school, where in Primary 4, we had a teacher whose concept of education was to set us large tracts of 'transcription' which involved copying entire chapters of books into a jotter. This work was supervised from behind a copy of the *Daily Mirror*. A friend, Frank, once brought in a small draughts board and, securely hidden behind the broad shoulders of the boys in front, we spent most of our lengthy 'transcription' periods learning the finer points of draughts and our own form of chess. Each afternoon the requisite punishment for failure to complete the task was two slaps and the withdrawal of 'library time'. This consisted of fifteen minutes when one was allowed to pick a book from the library but since I had better books at home, it appeared preferable to take the slaps and continue to play draughts. It was determined that I was leading Frank astray and my reluctance to conform resulted in my mother and the Principal agreeing that my brother and I might be better relocated in another school.

I'm unsure if there were any problems with my brother's behaviour but I think he would be disappointed if there were not. The lucky recipient of this fraternal influx was a school about a mile or so away.

The teacher there was uninterested in 'transcription'. Looking much older than his age, he had thinning grey hair and a back that was permanently slightly bent. He smoked constantly and it was one of the few pleasant times of the day for us when he would splutter into a paroxysm of painful coughing. His nose was running permanently and a drop would form and crawl slowly downwards. Just when it seemed certain natural gravity would take over he would sniff violently and the bubble would disappear upwards. This would be followed by the withdrawal of a Vicks nebulizer and he would take gigantic snorts of the stuff. His ambition in life was to raise good Catholic, Irish-speaking little Republicans who could sing 'Eileen Aroon' in tune. We would be lined up as he twanged his tuning fork and pick the appropriate note. We would then proceed into 'Oh, Rowan Tree' or a similar dirge.

He would parade behind us and if he deduced you were out of key, your head would be cuffed. For those of us with less ability in the singing stakes it seemed sensible to merely mouth the words and look bright-eyed. This was not always a successful ploy however as he sniffed continuously behind until you were cuffed even more viciously for 'not singing'.

His particular penchant, by way of some inquisitional medical experiment, was to punish pupils by attempting to lift them off the ground using only hair locks. He was vicious and dull and I loathed him. Three of us were deemed bright enough and 'lucky' enough to have appropriate birthdays that gave us the chance to sit the Eleven-plus exam a year early. If we failed we would still be able to sit it the following year. One of us passed while another pupil, Eugene, and I failed. After upbraiding us, we were scolded for disgracing him, the school, our parents, the Bishop and the entire Catholic Irish-speaking confraternity of the Northern Hemisphere.

I was related to the then Bishop of Down and Conor as my grandmother was his sister.

The fact that an 'insignificant pup' like me was related to the great man, while he was not, seemed to cause him great angst. He would demand that I tell him the name of the Bishop's house (presumably as a test of my devotion!). It was actually called 'Lisbreen' but that was a name that, through fear and confusion, I invariably failed to remember. My forgetful omission was rewarded with another lock-pulling experiment. I would, each evening, ask my mother the correct name and repeat it to myself over and over. However the following day with his face stuck closely into mine, his rancid breath billowing the profuse grey hairs growing from his purple-veined nose, my knowledge evaporated.

I would stutter… 'Lisburn… Lurgan… Lisnaskea.'

My attempts to complete the entire Northern Ireland geographical alphabet would invariably be terminated with the inevitable cuffs and a question to anyone listening.

'Can you believe that? My God! You don't even know the name of his house… and you related to him! You're an ungrateful pup.'

The sad truth, however, is that he was no worse than a

number of teachers at that time and might even have been better than others I was yet to meet.

Relief at getting to the grammar school a year later was ill-founded. Appropriately bounded on one side by the Crumlin Road prison, I occasionally had cause to envy the unfortunate inmates as their existence, bleak as it was, appeared preferable to mine. The school was run by a balding President and contained a number of other priests, as it was the diocesan seminary school for intending 'vocations'. The lay staff contained a number of psychotic misfits who, though small in number, ensured that, if they took a dislike to you, they would adversely colour your entire view of school life and profoundly change attitudes to authority and regimentation. One in particular I came to detest and fear in equal measure. He taught Latin and despite his size and gruff bellow, we determined that he was essentially a weak-minded psychopath whose talents would have been better served in the Third Reich pulling out fingernails. Another fellow bully who ensured that any potential love of his subject was aborted had a long, angular nose as sharp as a razor edge mounted on a head that twitched continually, like a bird on a wet lawn. The fingers were continually fretting, playing some invisible instrument but without any enjoyment or talent. His entire demeanour was akin to an epileptic sparrow.

I came to realise later that the good dedicated staff must have cringed when they witnessed the actions of some of their colleagues but were powerless to prevent their excesses. My hatred of the place may have been due in part to something in my make-up as I had and have friends who profess (to my disbelief) that they enjoyed their time there. But there were others whose lives were blighted and who recall their secondary school years with loathing and hatred.

I remember vividly a smallish, ineffectual boy of thirteen, Kieran, who was systematically, verbally and physically mistreated until the tears flowed copiously. It was harrowing to watch and after the incident, which must have lasted twenty minutes, we inwardly wished the class to continue so that we didn't have to look at or communicate with Kieran and be enforced into some sort of platitude that would only serve to highlight his embarrassment and pain. He was not the only one that suffered this brutality and I was no stranger to the same humiliation.

It was that kind of gratuitous bullying and cruelty that prompted me to parody G. K. Chesterton's poem 'The Men Who Died for England'.

> *'The men who died from hunger*
> *In that horror famine day*
> *Their grassy graves are nameless*
> *Above them as they lay.*
>
> *The men who left old Ireland*
> *For a better life afar*
> *Their graves are spread around*
> *Beneath the turning star.*
>
> *The men who taught us children*
> *And caused much pain and sweat*
> *Alas, alas I tell you*
> *Their graves are empty yet.'*

Not a particularly sympathetic view of many of my teachers and not a view I would, in hindsight, endorse but it does reveal the contempt and hatred with which I then viewed them.

It was not uncommon for an entire class to be punished for the misbehaviour of one or two. One of the two obsequious clerks who collected the roll numbers was called George. Although only a few years older than us, he pretended a greater authority. He was welcome to the membership of that oligarchy but even as a foot soldier, he was commonly disliked by the pupils. One day, during break, someone chalked up on the blackboard 'Go home George – you're only a bottle washer.' He took umbrage at this, admittedly slanderous, slight on his duties and reported us to the President. (We were much too posh to have a Principal.) When no one admitted to the transgression or was prepared, in the best prison parlance, to 'squeal', the entire class was lined up in alphabetical order and each pupil got two cane slaps on the left hand. When this was concluded the inquest was resumed but with the same blank response. To allow him to recover his strength and energy further punishment was deferred until after lunch. We then moved to the other side of the corridor and were caned on the right hand. I said a grateful prayer to my ancestors for a surname that began with 'R' as, by the time the President got to me, his strength had obviously flagged and he had barely enough energy to do more than tingle.

★

I must have had a rebellious streak and when I was fifteen, I was an habitual 'mitcher'. With Mickey and John, life seemed to offer no better way of filling a day than spending the morning in the 'News and Cartoon Cinema' followed by an afternoon in the 'Ritz' or the 'Regent' watching Audie Murphy or Glenn Ford wiping out a band of villains. This led to a profound difference of opinion between the authorities and myself on the perceived best way to occupy my school days. An ultimatum was issued which requested a more or less continuous attendance. Unfortunately my parents endorsed this entreaty and I reluctantly decided to obey. I kept to the agreement until, one afternoon, Mickey and I decided to leave school before the last period and go to the shop for a smoke. The period we missed was held once every month and was taken by an elderly man who, dressed in the habit of the Third Order of St Francis, exhorted us to eschew the ways of the flesh and follow a just and righteous path. Our righteous path had taken us over the back wall to the shop. We knew the roll was never taken for that period. Unfortunately we were spotted by another teacher and reported back to the office. When we returned to school later to collect our bikes we were met with a chorus of 'You're dead! Harvey came in and took the roll.'

This spelt serious trouble. There appeared to be only one solution. Admit my failings and weakness, throw myself on their mercy, beg forgiveness and accept my punishment like a man. As a new generation of miscreants are wont to say, 'Yeah, right!'

The other more acceptable alternative was to lie. At home, I confided to my mother that I had not been present for the last class. I explained that I had been suffering from a serious bout of diarrhoea and had spent the time in the toilet.

'Just tell them that,' she advised.

'I can't. You know, I'll be teased and made fun of,' I protested. 'But, if you write a note saying that you know that I was absent and that you, being fully aware of the circumstances, fully understand and support my decision not to attend. In the circumstances, I had your full permission to be absent.'

My poor old mum duly wrote the dictated letter and I headed to school the next day in a happier frame of mind.

Notes, etc. were handed into the office, which was manned by the anaemic-looking George, who was to the Dean what Captain Darling was to General Melchett. He took the envelope, opened it, read it and looking at me, as if confronting some type of quantum physics conundrum, stuttered, 'But, there's no reason here.'

I was beginning to realise the power of the letter.

'I'm sorry, it's personal. I can't tell you!' I answered politely and apologetically.

He stood there baffled, mouth hanging limply open gawping like a celestial-eyed goldfish. At that very moment the door opened and in walked the Dean of Discipline. He was a huge man but had a reputation for fairness and was popular. The obsequious clerk's eyes glittered in triumph.

'I think there's something here you should see, Father.'

The Dean read the letter and then re-read it. He too was puzzled.

'What's all this about, Robert?' he boomed.

I shrugged my shoulders and sighed wistfully, as if nothing would have given me greater pleasure than to have bared my soul to him, but a greater, unsaid duty hung heavily on my shoulders.

'I'm sorry, Father, it's a personal matter.'

His mouth opened momentarily and then closed slowly like a disappointed Labrador. His confusion slowly changed from bafflement to one of concern. Tucking the letter into his cassock he glanced at George, standing with a face like a tortured toad.

'It's all right, I'll deal with this.'

He took me outside the office. He was trying to look warm and friendly – an appearance at odds with his practiced role of grand inquisitor.

'Surely you can at least give me some idea of what the problem is, Robert?'

I shrugged resignedly. 'I'm sorry, Father, it's just something that I'm going to have to deal with myself.'

I was an amalgam of Marlon Brando, Robert Mitchum and James Stewart.

It was unfair that circumstances prevented me from unburdening myself to this kindly confidant... but... (I didn't quite say *there are just some things that a man's got to do*). I allowed my voice to trail off dejectedly. Inside I was bouncing with triumph while outwardly suffering the most potentially painful trauma a young man could.

He leant a comforting, unpractised hand on my shoulder. 'You know, Robert, Father Wilson is the school chaplain. If you could bring yourself to talk to him I think you might find he would be able to help.'

I was Alan Ladd in *Shane*... a man with a hidden past and a present problem. It's surprising looking back that I didn't lapse into a Western drawl.

'No, thanks Father but it's definitely something only I can sort out.'

God! I was even starting to feel sorry for myself. He stood there, towering over me. Despite his size and position he was like a lost child, baffled and weak. I walked slowly away, my head bowed... to bravely face this torment on my own. I had screwed the system. They were powerless. I almost limped away from them down the corridor sighing heavily. 'Billy Liar'... eat your heart out! During the following weeks I was rarely asked a question in class and one or two of the staff showed an unlikely and unspoken sympathy. That one act of victory against the system was one of the very few I enjoyed.

After that President retired he was succeeded by a more humane, but equally strict, Commandant. Gifted with a sense of humour he made my last two years if not enjoyable, at least tolerable. A new library/study hall was opened and a degree of independence was allowed as we sat our 'Advanced level' examinations. This independence only went so far, of course. Some periodicals and magazines were now placed in the library. Included in these was *National Geographic* and this was extremely popular with all of us showing, as it did, the naked breasts of exotic jungle women. Becoming aware of the reason for this newly found thirst for knowledge it was not long before an edict was enforced that 'Only Geography students may borrow copies of *National Geographic.*'

A few years later a friend of mine who was studying for the 'Priesthood' in the wing of the college was stopped by the President and asked what had happened to me.

David replied that I was at university studying English.

'Really?' the President replied, 'I always thought he would go far.'

After a few seconds he added, 'Totally in the wrong direction, of course.'

★

My sole ambition at university was to get a degree and get away as soon as possible. When my primary degree was completed I was at a loss about what to do next. If truth be told, the main reason I did a post-graduate certificate in education was that it delayed any serious decision on my future. Educational grants were reasonable in those days. Even when I qualified my thoughts always turned to joining the navy and becoming the captain of a fast patrol boat like President Kennedy or going to drama school and becoming the new Brando. That summer I worked as a gardener in a London park before joining the London School of Painters and Decorators where we blithely lied about our extensive painting experience back home. Kieran and I started work in the Home Office in Whitehall at 7.30 am and were sacked promptly at 4.30 pm. With the help of the local library's *Roget's Thesaurus* and the *Oxford Dictionary* and rejecting any word with less than three syllables, we penned an extremely articulate protest to the Head Office protesting about our 'unfair' dismissal and we were rewarded with a small cheque and an invitation to re-enlist. This doubtless created a slightly unrealistic judgement on the educational qualifications necessary to qualify as an Irish painter. However, by that time I had been lucky to gain employment in Charrington's Brewery on the Mile End Road. The job involved cleaning large beer tanks, sampling a lot of the products and generally wreaking considerable damage on my health. In fairness the last two activities were not recognised parts of the job description. I also managed to poison myself and seriously burn my hand. I had already undergone a medical after assuring the personnel department I wanted to devote the rest of my life to bettering the products and profits of Mr Charrington. It wasn't surprising when the firm's doctor told me scathingly, 'There are hundreds of people who have been working here for years and I don't know them. You've been here for five weeks and already I've dealt with you three times. So when is your next visit planned for?'

Apart from one incident when I was introduced to one of the infamous Kray twins by my workmate it was a boring and soul-destroying occupation. So, when my father phoned me to say that there was a job in his school I reluctantly agreed to do it for a year. This was many years before fair employment and niceties like applications, interviews, school governors, etc. and I, like many others, was appointed to teaching with nothing more than the endorsement of someone in authority. It was to be a stopgap measure. I did not see myself as one of the bullying psychopaths, often moronic, invariably insensitive, vicious thugs and ne'er-do-wells that seemed to populate the schools I had attended. Their actions ensured that the greater number of good teachers was forgotten. Whatever the teaching profession was, it was not one I was greatly enthused about.

Chapter Three

'Life is what happens to you while you're busy making other plans.'
                                                    John Lennon

Within the space of six months I decided to stay with teaching, at least for a while. My one resolve was never to treat any child the way I had been treated. That's not to say I didn't make mistakes and my reactions to some things don't reflect much glory on me but I hope that I never made any child's school life miserable. I suppose the complete contrast between the smug regimentation, the ironed shirts, school badges and the tree-lined avenue of the college I attended and the barely contained anarchy of St Cuthbert's helped me to view the entire process of education differently.

The rules of the school were simple. The nature of many of the pupils led to a feeling that if you got through the day without blood being spilt, it was a fairly good day. There was no overall discipline. Teachers lived very much within their class. They evolved, if not an ethos, a modus operandi that suited them. Some were successful but there were also others who had little relationship with their pupils and appeared to have little desire or ability to build one. The lack of direction and ambition permeated the school despite the fact that within certain classrooms, excellent things were happening. Some staff had not yet given up.

Literacy, or more correctly the lack of it, was supposedly our main concern. It was before the knowledge of dyslexia and other learning difficulties and many just thought a lot of the boys would never read because they were too unintelligent.

The Department of Education had an annual census which pigeonholed each pupil into categories such as disruptive, illiterate, ESN (educationally sub-normal) and most gratuitously offensive and totally inaccurate 'ineducable'.

Over the years I came to distrust intelligence scores and the interpretation of that nebulous substance 'intelligence'. In the dark days of the Troubles when sectarian assassinations were not uncommon, one of the staff was in the habit of walking home through a Loyalist area in the very early hours of the morning where Catholics (and some that were thought to be) were brutally killed. The fact that the percentage of inhabitants involved was tiny had to be balanced with the fact that at one or two o'clock in the morning, a blood-crazed minority were out and about looking for victims. One of our teachers was a Catholic and he regularly passed through a totally Loyalist enclave walking towards a Catholic area, yet he never considered himself in danger. His argument was that since he would never hurt anyone, he himself would never be harmed. This imagined generous reciprocity flew in the face of logic and experience. He was an 'intelligent' teacher. If one had asked any pupil in the school to carry out the same journey they would, undoubtedly and rightly, have questioned your sanity; 'Are you completely insane?'

★

The school occupied the site of two large semi-detached houses, which despite corridors between them, failed to give any sense of unity. In essence it still remained two conjoined large semi-detached houses. Boys' toilets had been added along with a gym with showers, a canteen and a woodwork room. In later years a metalwork room was added. The exterior resembled a silver birch in that despite, or perhaps because of, the local education board's maintenance workers' somewhat infrequent visits, it invariably had large sections of peeling paint for most of the time. This was a constant invitation during lunch break for pupils to see who could peel off the longest intact strip.

There was also a fair-sized football pitch with a superb view over Belfast Lough. Inside the main building gym-vests, shorts, etc. were kept in cages. The aroma served as a fitting hors d'oeuvre as one crossed to the toilets, which were totally inadequate. Despite the efforts of the cleaners the smell of urine mixed with stale smoke permeated the entire gym area and it was a brave or foolish teacher who tried to extract a pupil from the 'bogs'. Like many other denominational schools placed in 'dodgy' areas, weekends and holidays resulted in many broken windows, break-ins and general vandalism. We had a large state school nearby. In Northern Ireland at that time state schools were largely Protestant, though there was nothing to stop Catholics attending. It was a single sex school and when our boys left the school to board buses for home, staff had to be continually vigilant for trouble as the two sides met. Eventually it was agreed by the two school authorities that the end of day times were staggered.

The grounds included a large gardening section, the preserve of Paddy Tomelty. He tried valiantly and with a fair amount of success to impart an interest and love of gardening. Shortly after I started he was successful in having a large greenhouse built. The problem was that as the school and grounds were empty during July and August the garden was easy prey for all sorts of pests, the most damaging of which were a neighbourhood gang that would regularly trash everything that stood or grew. Nevertheless a number of pupils gained great enjoyment from his horticultural endeavours and would often return home with flowers or vegetables. Paddy was immensely likeable but was the bane of the cleaners. The idea of removing mud-encased wellies before he and his charges entered the main school appeared to Paddy an unusually eccentric concept. More than one staff meeting contained a plea from the Principal for 'teachers to ensure that pupils removed their gardening boots before entering the main school'. The plural of 'teacher' was frequently employed in order to avoid giving offence in any situation. Paddy lived just outside Belfast and had access to a plentiful supply of horse manure, which he distributed liberally around the school garden. One of nature's free spirits, he also was less than fastidious about the boundaries of his gardening pursuits. He and his pupils trudged the offending substance throughout the school daily.

It appeared to some that it was equally divided between the rhubarb and the corridors. Paddy was an annual visitor to Spain and loved everything Spanish. He studied the language assiduously and I did often wonder if the Spanish for stairs and rhubarb were similar enough to be confused. When he eventually retired, I penned an ode to Señor Paddy which contained the lines:

> *'He's gone now, that old Señor Paddy*
> *He's gone now the man with no cares.*
> *There's no more soft padding of wellies*
> *And there's no more horseshit on the stairs!'*

★

I was on a journey. I had no lofty vocation. I just wanted to enjoy my job and have a good effect on the pupils. Gradually over those first months I knew I was winning over all the boys, with the exception of Jimbo. He was only eleven years of age but he had an inner strength that lay within the heavy rolls of larded fat. He was capable of contorting his face into the most angelic countenance like a St Paul's choirboy or suddenly becoming a homicidal maniac, laughing and screaming as he attacked someone. No transgression was necessary for the assault as the attacks were sudden, unexpected and random. It wasn't, I hope, any dislike of me but an ingrained habit of behaviour that caused problems. Jimbo, having decided his work was over for the day, would roll out of his desk and, screaming and laughing alternatively, would then proceed to kick out savagely at anyone who came near him. I had been warned about him before I even started. I'd been told that whenever he had one of these 'fits' I should bring him to the Principal's office.

This blithe advice cheerfully ignored the fact that Jimbo was at least eight stone, the consistency of whale blubber and the Principal's office was up two flights of steps. After a couple of occasions when Jimbo descended into one of his regular departures from reality, I eventually decided to carry out the threat of bringing him to the Principal... bad mistake!

Determinately, I grabbed him and struggling to hold him, started the long ascent. Every step of the way he laughed uproariously and inflated his body so that my grip kept sliding. I knew how Sisyphus felt when his efforts to push the boulder uphill failed. The sweat ran down my face and every muscle screamed with the effort but I eventually passed base camp and began the final ascent. As he grew heavier and more indeterminate of size, his maniacal laughter became more frenetic. He was bloody well giggling. Eventually I half hauled, half pushed him into the Principal's office where he quite suddenly dramatically straightened, stood still and silent. The Principal, the demure white-haired sage, was confronted by a calm, quiet pupil in reasonably good health and a sweating, dishevelled, panting halfwit.

'This boy is out of control!'

I knew, as I said it, how ridiculous it sounded. To a casual observer if anyone was out of control, it was me.

'What's all this about, James?' enquired this sage... the honest searcher for truth.

James, an affronted angel, spread his hands trying to help, completely bewildered, but failing to suggest any reason for the antics of his half-crazed teacher.

'I don't know, Sir,' this paragon of reasonableness replied sincerely.

His chubby face, transformed from Fagin to Oliver Twist, a picture of innocence and bewilderment... pale and freckled, an innocent accused... the Dreyfus of North Belfast.

'Are you going to behave, now?' the Principal asked.

'Of course, Sir.' His look suggested hurt that anyone could think he could do anything else.

'Good boy... was there anything else, Mr Rooney?'

James had played me like a hooked fish.

Later that lunchtime another teacher, Mr Mac, had an altercation with Jimbo in the dining centre.

While he had probably forgotten about it, Jimbo had not. Part of Mr Mac's duties was to carefully tot up the number of pupils attending and make an estimate of the number of bottles of free milk that were delivered each day. It was as if the entire future of dairy farming in Northern Ireland was at risk, so assiduously did he ledger the information. He would then, very meticulously, enter this tally in a small notebook that he placed carefully in the top bottle on the left hand corner of the topmost empty crate. He was not overly pleased when, looking through his window towards the playground, he saw Jimbo remove the book, look up to the same window and, slowly laughing, carefully tear out a page and begin chewing it. The rest of the book he held up and bit by bit pulled the sheets apart and let them confetti the yard. Mr Mac was singularly unimpressed and so startled by the effrontery of Jim's actions that he was reduced to stuttering incoherence. After he regained some composure he proceeded to chase him, unsuccessfully, around the school grounds.

Jimbo was becoming the brake on class progress and I found myself scrutinising the buses as they arrived each morning to ascertain if he was present. Without discussing the proposed action with anyone, I decided to visit his house one night. The door was opened by James himself who, for the first time ever, looked distinctly concerned. I shook hands with his parents and finding them exceptionally sensible and caring, told them something of James' proclivities. The father was an impressive man with an intelligent open face. He listened with calm attention and concern. His wife, unsure and nervous, smoothed her hair, quickly made tea and produced a packet of rich digestives. James stood fidgeting nervously, looking alternatively at his parents and me.

The reception was so gracious that I found myself backtracking on the litany of transgressions and assuring them that Jim was normally a very good pupil. (Normally he was as well-behaved as a tiger with an arrow in its ass.) The father faced James and asked him about his misbehaviours without raising his voice; 'Is this true?'

James nodded his head in assent. His mother appeared with another cup of tea and I apologised for having to visit. They, in turn, apologised for James and it ended up with warm handshakes all-round and I made sure James was included.

I was slightly worried that the calm waters would erupt as soon as I left and I did not want James to suffer physically...

well not much! But the father reassured me and his last words were 'Don't worry, Mr Rooney, it won't happen again.'

It never did.

The only other pupil I remember causing me concern was Dermot. He was a tallish boy with two large protruding teeth, which earned him the nickname of 'Chip' (after chipmunk).

Presumably, he had a more or less full set of teeth somewhere in the cavern beyond but they were never visible. He had dirty fair hair over a pale freckled face and long ungainly arms. It took some weeks before I got him to talk as he sat at his desk silently, removed from the hubbub of the rest of the class. Just how 'dirty' was his dirty fair hair was revealed one morning as I sat beside him and saw his hair moving slightly – like a badly fitted wig. His hair was forested with an entire colony of head lice. I don't mean the one or two travellers that are familiar to every teacher and parent but a virtual colony. Like medieval explorers or *Star Trek* commanders their mission was to seek out new virgin territories where they would transfer their attentions and nits to the rest of us. Knowing something of his family background I knew a letter home appealing for help in exterminating the guests would be ineffectual. After consultation with others, he was sent to the local clinic to be treated. Within days he would be re-infected. This meant that Dermot was often taught at long distance. It was sad but close contact invariably resulted in my fine-tooth combing every day after school. Such was his generosity that Dermot extended his pastures to other guests, including the ubiquitous flea. The only sure way to get rid of a flea involves stripping off and shaking one's clothes over a water-filled bath. They are then paralysed and can then be dealt with in the most vindictively satisfying way possible. While reading with Dermot one day a flea hopped off his clothes onto the book. He rapidly, with a speed born of experience, licked his fingers and squashed it with his nail. A red blood mark was all that remained. It was only then that I really noticed his nails. They were at least three-quarters of an inch long with a permanent black crescent under each one. My attempts to persuade Dermot of the benefits of a cleaner body fell on deaf ears and the district nurse told me that anything she did would be quickly undone by the mother. In the rash foolishness of inexperience I suggested that he might be better off in a foster home.

★

Years later I realised the folly of my suggestion. I had another boy in my class who lived in very poor circumstances. After a number of interventions Sean's parents were sent to prison for three months 'for neglect' and he was placed in a care home. He was a bright boy who progressed rapidly through the reading schemes. I once took a number of boys home after a football match and returned Sean to his care home. His case worker showed me his room which was bright and clean with a little work desk and posters on the walls. I was impressed and thought of the contrast between that and his home conditions. Some weeks later, when the class was going to Portaferry for a week's holiday I learnt that Sean had been returned home. As his parents had failed to respond to letters concerning the trip I sought out his house one glorious May Saturday afternoon to seek their written permission and assure them that a charity, St Vincent de Paul, would make up any financial shortfall. The house lay in a warren of streets between the Falls and Shankill roads. At a gable house I enquired where they lived and was directed to the first house on the other side of the street. The next house was beside a derelict boarded-up shop and I was somewhat alarmed when I called there to be told, once again, that it was next door. The derelict shop was indeed the home I was looking for.

After knocking, the door was opened by the mother. She was pleasant looking and polite. The only light inside appeared to be from a small black and white television glaring out of the gloom like a malevolent eye. There was a smell that was a mélange of damp and dirt. I was secretly glad not to be invited in. They briefly signed the consent form and I, just as briefly, left. I had never imagined such real poverty. I wondered what life must have been like for Sean leaving the clean, fresh, well-fed, comfortable care home to live in that stinking hovel?

Well actually, as I discovered later, he not only preferred it but had absconded back to his home a number of times. There was no substitute for the warmth of the family, even one that was mismanaged and inadequately provided for. Many years later when we discovered the terrible abuse that occurred in some of those children's homes, I wonder even more. Too many teachers come from middle-class families where there is little appreciation of how difficult life can be for their more unfortunate neighbours. A combination of ignorance and snobbery provides a lack of insight and respect. It was not uncommon in a staffroom to hear comments such as: 'their parents just don't care' or 'they shouldn't be allowed to have children'. Luckily the proponents of such philosophies are outnumbered by more enlightened colleagues.

In the years that followed I often wondered about the 'social responsibility' of a certain family who temporarily fostered a number of children. Their combined income accruing from their charges was twice what was being brought into my house each month despite both my wife and I teaching. I had to call at their house a number of times and they invariably, after delivering their charges to school, returned to spend the morning in bed before heading out shopping out in their massive Land Rover. Their lives appeared to lack any of the normal pressures of home or school.

★

As the weeks passed I became more confident and more adventurous. The frustrated actor in me was blooming. If I didn't know something I made it up. During one lesson I inaccurately but enjoyably described the condition of leprosy. There were enough boys in the class to enjoy my vivid performance as much as I did as I described and acted out a leper 'disco' where each gyration resulted in the loss of another limb. I described the reaction of finding one's nose in your hankie after a particularly violent sneeze. (Propriety stopped me, just in time, from describing the reaction of finding your willy in your hand after a pee!) My performance proved a little too vivid as one boy quietly fainted in his chair. This caused me to abort my performance in mid-stream. Reining myself in, I told them about the famous leper priest, whose name had escaped me. I baptised him Fr 'Vincent' and told how he had devoted his life to lepers in a colony in Hawaii and how he, too, had died from this terrible disease.

The following day Frank, whose mother was a teacher, arrived in with a smug rebuke to inform me that the real name of the priest was Fr Damien of Molokai.

'Of course,' I agreed, 'Fr Vincent Damien of Molokai.'

As the conversation resumed later, Fr Vincent Damien eventually was reincarnated without my additional title.

Any new task presented a challenge for both me and the class. One day I decided to try an art lesson that involved colouring in a sheet with different coloured crayons and then etching out a picture to reveal a multi-coloured scene. This would indeed be messy.

'I was going to do a thing in art today that has only ever been done a couple of times in Methodist College and once at Queen's University but when I told some of the teachers in the staffroom about it they said I was mad. Because it involves crayons and scrapping they said it would end up so messy that the cleaners would go on strike and the room would have to be completely repainted and all the desks would be ruined from all the muck. So we'll just have an ordinary painting class.'

There were immediate howls of protest. Insistent voices claimed that they would leave the room spotless. I appeared to give the proposal further consideration but shook my head ruefully.

'No! It's too risky. I could be fired if this went wrong.'

More loud entreaties followed, begging the chance to prove everyone wrong. Very, very reluctantly I agreed and told them in detail what was required. I presented the picture of a man who had just made a serious misjudgement.

It hardly needs mentioning but suffice it to say that when that very successful lesson was finished, the room was a good deal cleaner than it had been for many years. Desks and floors were examined by pupils with the meticulousness of a health inspector. I praised the class exuberantly and boasted of their abilities. Of course the final accolade (totally pre-arranged) was when another teacher entered and displayed aggrieved shock and complained that his classroom hadn't been cleaned like that. He insisted that we must have brought in special cleaners and asked what that had cost. The collective pride was sighed around the room.

The school contained pupils from early primary age to secondary level (and beyond). Even in the secondary end, the classes were based on a primary model and were attached to one teacher for the greater part of the day. At secondary level the class was split into smaller groups and taken by specialists for woodwork and metalwork and later PE. The class teachers had a more difficult job. (Well… I would say that, wouldn't I?)

Having said that, a good teacher is a good teacher and I have known some specialist teachers who easily outshone some of those based with one class. Some of them were among the best teachers I've ever met. Ability, dedication and success were certainly not confined to class teachers. There were, however, some specialists that appeared to believe that discipline was the remit and responsibility of the class teacher. We once had a temporary PE teacher who thought that she could only 'pick the nice children'. Unfortunately she said this to a colleague whose temper could be volcanic and he quickly disabused her of this notion. It certainly ensured that she was much more in fear of the teacher than she was of any of his charges.

The range of personalities and abilities within each class was eclectic. There were some pupils whose abilities suggested they should have been placed in 'normal school', coteried with others who had considerable intellectual problems. I tried to tailor the work on an individual basis but it was not always possible and at times when we discussed things in an open forum, one had to be conscious that some points would have to be explained at two or even three levels. When George one day complained that a boy in his street 'had called my ma a dirty H', there was a collective aggrievedness. Bernard caused more confusion when he pointed out that the word started with a 'W'.

There was a lot of humour and comedy in the ordinary interactions. I had a very pleasant boy called Ciaran who suffered badly from epilepsy. He would tell me about his 'turns'. When queuing for dinner one day Willy (not the brightest shilling in the bag) asked him what exactly a 'turn' was. I could see Ciaran evaluating both the desirability of imparting the details and Willy's doubtful comprehensive powers of understanding dizziness, sickness, collapse and medication. He looked at me and half smiling, replied, 'You know… a turn!'

He then proceeded to turn round 360 degrees. Willy accepted this without blinking.

Ciaran was disinterested in soccer and became a real nuisance in matches when, unaware of his surroundings, he would wander offside. As physical retribution was being threatened by his team-mates, I brought him to the centre circle and told him that it was critical to the success of his team that he stay there.

'Any ball that comes near you, kick it that way.' I pointed. I had to laugh when, ten minutes later, I saw him trace the outline in a constant walk singing 'All my Life's a Circle'.

The biggest contribution to having good discipline depended on the amount of effort, novelty and enthusiasm one could bring to the job. Provided one had good discipline and was well organised, you lived in a cocoon away from mainstream interference. This was encouraged by those in authority who steadfastly refused for many years to have a phone in the building. I was happy in what I did. I was more or less a free agent and, unlike teachers in other schools, we were not obliged to follow any syllabus other than a vague reading programme. The nearest I got to examination pressure was when a fourteen-year-old pupil whom I had praised for his work implored me, 'Sir, what about letting me have a crack at the Eleven-plus?'

While other teachers in other schools complained of long hours and nights spent in lesson preparation we, more or less, closed up shop at 3.15 pm and re-opened at 9.15 the following morning. The rest of my time was my own which, like most young men, I used diligently, purposefully and selflessly! A number of people would say that because of the difficult nature of many of the pupils we deserved that and comments such as 'I don't know how you do it,' and 'I wouldn't have your job for twice the salary,' maintained our delusion.

Nevertheless the job could be difficult and for some impossible. On a number of occasions I came across teachers in the staffroom upset or weeping and swearing they would never enter their classroom again. But, if you were eccentric enough to cope and crazy enough to enjoy it, then it could even be rewarding. I also discovered early that every school staff I saw or heard about had at least one 'old bitch' who exuded negativity. I also discovered that often they were neither old nor female.

Many a teacher who would have and often did become an excellent teacher in 'mainstream' education left the school with relief. I doubt if the few eccentrics like us could have coped with that normalcy. The upside was, of course, that if you did have discipline and were an aspiring actor and saw the boys as personalities and characters then the job could not only be rewarding and satisfying but also, believe it or not, good fun… well… at least for most of the time. Anyway, as I thought to myself, it's only for a while!

The years between 1965 and 1969 were very happy ones. I was serving my apprenticeship and becoming increasingly confident and competent in the school. I had money in my pocket and was fit and healthy. In my naivety, I thought teaching must be one of the easiest jobs around. When I heard my friends talking about their jobs in banks, the civil service, in medicine or in law I was convinced that many teachers in education were underworked and overpaid. I caused a lot of consternation when I was incautious enough to voice that opinion in front of other teachers from other schools who laboured long and hard with examinations looming.

Chapter Four

'He didn't tell me how to live; he lived, and let me watch him do it.'
Clarence Budington Kelland

During those first three years I learnt more about teaching from other teachers than I ever did from college. The greatest example to emulate was my father. He had a wonderful rapport with children, particularly the more difficult adolescent ones. His enthusiasm was infectious. Having acted in the Group Theatre at one time, I often felt that he never really stopped acting. I appeared to have inherited this.

I remember one incident where I saw him in conversation with the Principal when a pupil walked proudly past with an obviously new pair of football boots. He stopped and asked to see them. He examined them in detail, smelt them, tested the laces, and studied every stud with gasps of admiration. He passed them to the Principal to second his opinion. No expensive piece of jewellery could have been examined more meticulously. He then enquired the price and, on being told, expressed shock and disbelief that such an excellent pair of boots could have been bought so cheaply. The boy positively strutted down the corridor and my father returned to the more mundane matters of the day. I asked him about the incident later and he had almost forgotten it. He had merely seen an opportunity to lift a child's spirit and had taken it. I asked him what sort of a boy he was.

'Oh! He's not in my class. I don't really know him.'

He taught the oldest boys. There were quite a few of them who were studiously avoided by the rest of the staff, yet I saw them follow him around like pet Labradors.

He was oblivious to his own eccentricities, which caused angst to some of the other staff. Not everyone enjoyed the weekly spectacle of the Vice-Principal clad only in a 'simmit', an old pair of 'bags' and a disgustingly stained pair of 'gutties'. (i.e. vest, trousers and trainers) running out of the school with a motley gang of 'young hooligans' on their weekly training run… and this amongst the respectable burghers of North Belfast.

He was a man of contrasts and contradictions. He was not always a regular churchgoer but he was a student and collector of everything Cardinal Newman wrote and was forever writing letters to newspapers defending the Church's teachings. The enthusiastic devotee of literature and fussy grammarian was capable of quite rude practical jokes. I remember him writing to a friend asking for a book to be returned and noting, *'Unless the book is left behind the Catholic Truth Society stall in Clonard monastery with an envelope containing five pounds the photos I took at the last staff party will be circulated to your Principal, your wife and your parish priest. And then you will be in a f------ mess!'*

This from a man who detested cursing!

Many years after he died I learned how, when he was a teacher in Holy Cross, he brought the wrath of the Principal and a threatened 'sacking' down on his head with one of his madcap acts. The Bishop had been invited to the school one evening and with the respect given in those times to the hierarchy, the parish hall was packed with parents. The

Principal had closeted himself with the Bishop, the parish priest and other important personages entertaining them to 'supper' in the parochial house. The mutual admiration continued apace while, on the stage, the teachers sat in a semi-circle behind the thick stage curtains. By the time the proposed meeting was to take place the audience was getting excited. As the delay reached twenty minutes, that excitement had turned to restlessness.

When forty minutes past the appointed start had arrived, feet were being shuffled and the former respectful silence had been dissipated by coughing and mutterings. Chairs were being scraped along the floor. A thick pall of Woodbine haze was rising to the roof. The impatient buzz subsided as bit by bit, the audience noticed they were being treated to the spectacle of a bare foot poking out between the middle of the stage curtains. As the guffaws grew louder the foot became a naked leg and it waved to some unheard music. The hall erupted as the naked leg became a naked thigh and the performance continued for a number of minutes before concluding just prior to the arrival of the luminaries.

The Bishop must have been pleasantly surprised at the good-natured audience that received him that night. The following day, on discovering the impromptu floor show the Principal, however, failed to see any humour in the situation and berated the staff.

'If I knew the identity of the culprit who brought shame on us last night I would have no hesitation in recommending his sacking. It is despicable that I have been met with a wall of silence. I have my suspicions but unfortunately I have, as yet, no proof.'

The story was told to me by one of his teaching colleagues who also acted as 'lookout' on the night concerned. It was, he added, not the only harebrained action of my dad's but he refused to elaborate on anything else.

The years failed to quench the desire to amuse and shock. He had a terse relationship with another teacher, Mr Dan McFarlane, whose family lived quite close to us. Even as children we could sense the active dislike that bubbled underneath the outwardly polite exchange of conversation. He was a tall man with a monk's tonsorial garland of straggly, orange hair and a wheezing, inquisitive speech.

Although he never referred to him directly, when my dad spoke of 'pompous, obsequious gombeen men who possess a great ambition matched only with a prodigious inability', I knew the objects of his scorn included Mr Dan McFarlane.

Once on holiday in Ballycastle when my father was talking to the elder sister of a friend of mine his adversary approached them, his face open and his eyes beady with curiosity.

'Well, John,' he began, his eyes ping-ponging between the forty-five-year-old pedagogue and his good-looking, teenage female companion, 'And how are you?'

'Grand thanks, Dan, and yourself?'

The verbal fencing continued a while until Daddy satisfied Mr McFarlane's curiosity.

'Oh! I'm sorry. I haven't introduced you. I don't think I should give you her correct name: you know what some people are like... let's just call her Imelda. She's my mistress! Imelda, this is Dan McFarlane.'

Daddy looked at him conspiratorially but there was such an absence of friendship and banter between them that Dan was momentarily taken aback and embarrassed.

Years later when we had a boat in Carrickfergus, Mr McFarlane appeared unexpectedly. He now had a greyish-orange beard, which began at a wrinkled neck and wandered aimlessly around his face. We were moored alongside the wall. The tide was out and he was standing on the harbour lip looking down at us. You could almost hear his brain frantically trying to establish the value of the boat and the source of his rival's imagined wealth. After the initial pleasantries his none-too-subtle interrogation began. He quickly established the number of berths, the size of the engine, how fast it went, past destinations, etc. before moving inexorably to the only questions he was interested in having answered.

'I was thinking of getting a boat myself, John. What sort of money would they cost?'

My father appeared to give the question serious consideration.

'Well, Dan, it's a bit like asking how long is a bit of string. One could get a small boat for a hundred pounds or go the whole way up to tens of thousands.'

McFarlane was totally frustrated but with a furrowed brow of concentration and great interest continued, 'Well, you know… something like this one.'

He pointed at ours.

'Oh, a boat like this!' beamed my father, glad and eager to be able to help. 'I suppose if you were lucky, maybe five hundred or so but more likely up to eight or nine.'

At a time when a teacher's monthly salary amounted to somewhere around £150, this shocking information threatened to provoke a heart attack in McFarlane. His brain was trying vainly to connect our boat to current wages. Rooney must have won the pools. He wasn't to know that the boat had actually cost £200 and my father had, at that time, only a half share in it.

Still shaking in disbelief and jealousy, McFarlane continued, 'Really? And are they expensive to run?'

Daddy was really enjoying himself now. His brow furrowed as he sadly acknowledged, 'Yes, that can be a bit of a problem but, I suppose, it's not too bad. We would use about two gallons of petrol an hour.'

The by now incredulous inquisitor wasn't to know that our battered Kelvin Ricardo engine was only primed on petrol and after an initial couple of minutes motored along happily on TVO (tractor vaporising oil – a cheap mixture of paraffin oil, etc.). One gallon of the stuff cost two shillings and sixpence, (equating at that time to twelve and one-half pence) and that kept us cruising for an hour. McFarlane looked depressed and desolate.

As he turned to leave, Daddy thrust the knife in further, 'I'd ask you on board, Dan, but we had a bit of a problem with the fridge and the place is in a bit of a mess.'

The fact that, at that time, only millionaire yachts had fridges was a fact also unknown by McFarlane. As our visitor left, trudging desultorily back down the wall my father looked at me and gave a broad wink.

He loved boats and we had a succession of them over the years. The coat he wore when boating was torn and stained with paint, held together by fish scales, dried blood, oil and paraffin. When he would forget and hang it in the staffroom, it would be the subject of acrimonious debate.

He was a man of contradictions. An ardent Republican, Daddy had little time for the Gaelic Athletic Association which he wrongly considered narrow and sectarian. An avid supporter of Glasgow Celtic, he was a lover of hockey and rugby as well. No lover of royalty, he wrote a letter to the local paper complaining about the nature of a report noting the near-fatal choking of the Queen Mother on a fish bone. It was, he maintained, vicious and unworthy to take any pleasure from the trauma experienced by an elderly lady who, through no fault of her own, had been born into royalty. At home he would play the piano and repeated sections of nocturnes by George Field and Chopin would indicate he was in pensive mood. The more strident and louder sections of Liszt indicated a different mood where it was better to hold fire on any request about borrowing the car. This 'classical scholar' also arrived home in 1956 with a new '78' of Bill Haley singing

'Rock Around the Clock'. In between recordings from John McCormack and Kathleen Ferrier, we would be treated to 'Cigarettes and Whisky and Wild, Wild Women'!

After a succession of motorbikes, he first got a car in the late fifties. Every weekend we would take my grandmother and the family out 'for a run'. This invariably meant the seaside. Of course, initially this was such a rare treat that we all went swimming. The fact that the trip could take place in the middle of November was a minor consideration. We were at the seaside so you went for 'a dip'. After the swim, the Primus would be produced and after the obligatory 'pricking' it would flare into action. Sausages, with the mandatory coating of carbon, would be produced and we would huddle for shelter, shivering out of the wind. Every year he would take us to Dublin for the rugby internationals and after the match we would picnic on scalding tea and burnt sausages in the frozen wastes of the Phoenix Park while everyone else would dine in comfort in Bewley's or the Gresham Hotel. A day out without a Primus was simply not an option.

He and the Primus enjoyed a peculiar relationship. The latter was obviously in awe of him. While it was mollycoddled inside a biscuit tin with a slat cut for the pump and received a respect due to its aged contribution, it took it some time to get used to the undignified way in which my dad lit it. The original collar containing the wick which was to be soaked in methylated spirits was dispensed with. A more direct and brutal methodology was employed whereby my father would pump paraffin all over the stove and using matches and little bits of paper, set the entire thing ablaze. At exactly the right moment, from an experience gained by years of mutual respect, he would pump it a few times and it would whistle into a bluish green flame. They both understood that this abuse was only to be tolerated from him. Any meddler attempting to imitate the process was doomed to failure.

One September day, after school, we took a new teacher, Gerry, out on the boat for a spot of mackerel fishing. The water was oily smooth and the fish were cooperative. Having caught two dozen or so we returned on a lovely evening to the harbour and tied up at our swing mooring. As I filleted the fish, the Primus in its biscuit tin was placed solemnly on top of the engine box. My father, as usual, sprayed the lot with paraffin and succeeded in quickly setting it alight. With an athletic bound, our new shipmate leapt up, grabbed the tin and flung it over the side. The initial hiss was followed by an oily stain on the surface as it bubbled its way under. Gerry looked round proudly anticipating looks of congratulation. If he had expected gratitude and praise, he was sadly disappointed as he saw the consternation and bafflement of his fellow crew members.

'It… it would have exploded,' he stammered.

In response to our raised eyes of disapproval he weakly stammered, 'We had Primuses at home and we never lit them like that.'

'Not at all,' spat Dad emphatically. 'This is a marine Primus!' he grinned. 'Have you got your togs, Bobby?'

I dived down about ten feet and rescued the stove. Back in the hands of the master it quietly forgot the indignity and flamed into action almost immediately.

His childlike enjoyment of little adventures was infectious and he treated his pupils in exactly the same way. He encouraged them not to run away from challenges and they loved him. Years later I came across an article from a past pupil of Holy Cross, where my father taught for years, which read;

> *'After two years it was up to the "Top School" as we called it on the Crumlin Road and my great fortune to have John Rooney as our form teacher, and the "Forum" cinema close by to escape to the wild west and from Belfast.*

> *Two years ago, I got to ride horseback across Montana – known as the "Big Sky Country" in the United States and you just have to imagine what a thrill that was. I doffed my Stetson to Mr Rooney, I can tell you, because it was he who gave me the gift of and love of literature and planted the idea firmly in my head, that if I wanted to do something then I could: he unlocked the door and handed me the key.'*

I could think of no greater tribute to his contribution to someone's education than that.

*

But life is as unpredictable as a river in flood. One minute you're floating along nicely and then you are buffeted and smashed by floods and your craft comes close to sinking.

I was twenty-five, just married to a beautiful girl with the world and all its potential before us. We came back from honeymoon in August 1969. That date is notorious in Northern Ireland: surprisingly enough, unconnected to our nuptial event! The festering sickness that was politics burst open into what became thirty years of hatred, conflict, mayhem, violence and murder. All the hurt, real and imagined, refused to be buried once again. The State had primarily existed for the majority and was the seed of its own destruction. I had joined in Civil Rights marches with people of every religious persuasion and none and felt that change was coming. The brutality perpetrated by the State provoked a ruthless and terrible violence that fed an increasing sectarianism and hatred.

It was maybe time to think about going somewhere else. I wasn't keen to live in a society where the first thought on meeting someone was to wonder what his religion and his politics were. Other friends had emigrated and there were lots of opportunities to get away, even for a few years.

My mum was involved in golf and bridge and for the first time in her life had a little money from her return to teaching. I remember thinking about how happy my father was. He and I now owned a boat based in Carrickfergus and it had become the main focus of his leisure hours. He had given me ownership of half the boat the evening before my twenty-first birthday and an hour later asked me for £16, my share of payment for engine repairs!

Although they had no legal ownership, the boat was shared with three other locals with whom my dad had established a great friendship. In those times the friendship was unusual in that they were all Protestants. One afternoon after school we went down to check the boat and found the three others hotly debating a problem that had arisen. Billy had bored a hole in the mast while Davy had bought the bolt. In our absence Victor was supervising. The argument was conducted with great humour and much laughter as they decided if the hole was too small or the bolt was too big. To the entire world it was like a nautical episode of *Last of the Summer Wine*. I mused how lucky my dad was to have years of good health and vitality before him leading to a surely enjoyable retirement – just like Toad 'messing about in boats'.

How rapidly things change. Within six months Billy was blind, Darren was dead and my father was permanently paralysed from the neck down.

In January 1970 he was returning from babysitting for my sister and her husband. It was early in the morning on the motorway when a drunken driver hit him from behind and spun his car off the road. For a number of days he fought to stay alive with all the strength and determination that so characterised him. He survived but was paralysed from the neck down with only a very limited arm movement. It became obvious that he would require support from all of us for the remainder of his life. To that end, later that year, my two sisters and I bought houses close to where he and my mother had found a bungalow.

Our own lives mirrored the ever uncertain political situation. A lot of what had passed for normal had suddenly been thrown into turmoil. The only certitude was that things would never be the same again. I was inwardly resentful to follow a path that was no longer my choice, even if it was only the possibilities that had been removed. I might well have stayed exactly where I was but there was no longer a decision to be explored. I felt trapped and imprisoned. It was intensified as the Troubles escalated and we saw friends leave for a better life elsewhere. However there was little time to brood and there was much to be happy about; a satisfying job, a new house, a beautiful wife and the birth of the first of our three girls.

Many years later a quotation from Paulo Coelho's book on control and choice, *The Devil and Miss Prym,* struck me very forcibly:

> *'When we least expect it, life sets us a challenge to test our courage and willingness to change; at such a moment there is no point in pretending that nothing has happened or in saying that we are not yet ready. The challenge will not wait. Life does not look back. A week is more than enough time for us to decide whether or not to accept our destiny.'*

In the years after his accident we came to realise what a truly remarkable man he was. Before his paralysis he had been full of life and vigour. He never smoked and his relationship with alcohol was brief and infrequent. Once a year at the staff party he would have two pints and be totally convinced that he was drunk. He would giggle, flirt, ramble and eventually argue theology with any willing adversary. He was exceptionally fit and active. As more than one of his friends commented, he had lived his life so fully it was as if there lurked within some portent of the tragedy that was to befall him. His paralysis meant that he had very limited use of his hands. He could eventually, with the aid of Velcro strapping, hold a special cup and with an attached spoon, feed himself. He had been a very good artist and, now on a good day, he would paint watercolours in a completely new style. Without the accuracy of control, his style became fluid and detail was lost in the vibrancy of his colours.

Even on those days when he was in obvious pain and distress, he never showed any bitterness or self-pity. He was prone to spasms that would jerk his body like a twisted puppet. Bladder and urine problems were a continual bugbear and we became used to giving him bladder washes. Incontinence caused him increasing problems and washing machines had a limited life in our house. Despite this, his sense of humour remained intact, as did his interest in the world around him. He would forever be writing letters to the local newspapers bemoaning increasing secularism, defending Republicanism and commenting on the political situation. My sister and I would decipher the scrawling letters and I would type them out, trying to moderate his verbosity. Although he spent most of the rest of his life at home, his health would occasionally deteriorate necessitating hospitalisation for periods. The sister in charge of the orthopaedic ward would delight in his stay as she said, 'He was the best counsellor any of the other patients could have.'

He would organise draughts and chess tournaments and with a mischievous sense of humour would enliven and energise the rest of the ward. He and another patient once convinced a fellow patient that a new machine had been invented which would enable him to perform his conjugal duties!

On one occasion the ward sister asked him to help a young

man of seventeen, Drew, who had been partially paralysed when a car he had been in crashed. He had withdrawn into a shell and lay crying for long periods. With another patient, Eric, Daddy organised a draughts tournament with an ostentatious trophy for the winner. He cajoled Drew, who eventually evinced some interest. He became reasonably good and entered the tournament. As he had done in school, Daddy engineered the proceedings so that the outcome was rigged. The final was played on a Saturday afternoon with a packed audience of patients and visitors. He ended up in the final with Drew. After Drew won the first of the three, Daddy won the second. A tense, long struggle in the final game saw Drew triumphant. I watched and saw an acting performance from my father that should have won an Oscar. He feigned annoyance and regret, reliving his 'stupid move' but heartily congratulated Drew. To the generous applause of all watching, Drew carried the trophy back to his room. Later, when the patients were back in their beds, Drew's mother approached my father and thanked him for 'losing to Drew'.

Daddy again feigned ignorance insisting he had been beaten 'fair and square' but she wasn't fooled and just smiled gratefully. Drew improved quickly thereafter and was eventually able to become mobile with the aid of crutches, which, four months after he was discharged enabled him to get into another fast car which crashed. He and the driver were both killed.

A number of the patients played cards and persuaded one of the ward orderlies, Frank, to go to the bookmaker's shop each day with bets. This went well for a time until one of the security guards reported Frank for parking his car near to the unit. He was supposed to park some distance away. After a reprimand, Frank was unable to continue his second occupation as a bookie's runner. Not unnaturally this soured the relationship between the gamblers and the guard. Each morning the guard had to sign in, which involved him passing the window of the ward. They were large windows that started a couple of feet from the ground so there was no way he could pass unnoticed. Each morning as he was spotted in the distance, all the patients, gamblers or not, feigned sleep until he was just at the window. At a given signal they would all cry out in unison.

'Yah... Squealer!... Squealer!'

This guardian of the hospital, this protective employee, would then raise himself indignantly to his full five-foot height, place his hands on the window and hiss back, 'Yah... Cripples!... Cripples!'

Instead of offence, this would provoke almost hysterical laughter amongst the patients.

It could never mask the horrific injuries and pain they suffered, but that sense of the ridiculous kept a sense of normality. The unconscious humour of the Troubles was never far away. When another patient, Kenneth, was keen to learn chess he felt, accurately, that my father did not really embrace his company. This was due to his association with a vicious Loyalist paramilitary group.

'You know, John, I get the feeling that you don't like me because of my background. You know I was in the UVF not the UDA.'

My dad demurred, 'Well, to tell you the truth, I don't really see much of a difference.'

'What?' exploded Kenneth. 'No difference? Didn't they fucking shoot me and paralyse me?'

Despite the fact that the ward contained a member of the UVF, another from the UDA, a policeman, a young joy-rider and a member of the Official IRA there was a genuine appreciation and respect which often grew into friendship. Lying in the dark, silent and alone, realising the awful truth of what future life held quickly put into perspective the causes others were killing and dying for. In daytime, however, the same intelligent knowledge that Daddy used in his teaching made him aware of what was needed; that caring attitude without the mawkish pity was as equally beneficial and rewarding in the ward as it had been in the classroom.

★

With the increasing violence, relationships between people of perceived different religions became increasingly bitter and vicious. Riots were commonplace. The buses bringing the pupils to school were frequently delayed and sometimes forced to return to base because of shootings, explosions, bomb scares and riots. In one incident one of our school buses was attacked and a petrol bomb hurled in. I and another teacher, Brian, from a nearby state (Protestant) school in Mount Vernon, had a weekly night class for ex-pupils of both schools which had to be abandoned because of the danger they faced travelling at night across a war-torn city. Hindsight tends to gloss over just how vicious that conflict was. There were entire areas of Northern Ireland that were relatively unaffected but life in parts of Belfast was an apparently never-ending nightmare. Anyone in Belfast or Derry that didn't know at least one or two people who had been killed was indeed a fortunate rarity.

Most of the pupils in the school came from either North or West Belfast. The total number of civilian deaths in the Troubles up to the year 2000 was 2,037. When one discovers that from that total, 832 occurred in either North or West Belfast it's easy to understand why so many of our boys were deeply affected. There were very few that escaped the horror. Schools played an heroic part in trying to maintain a semblance of normality. Sectarianism and blind hatred were never far away however. As the centre of the city became a 'no go' area at night, pubs, clubs and restaurants began closing at six. During the day every store and shop had security guards searching everyone who entered. Fire bombs planted in department stores and shops could be easily smuggled in and were set to ignite hours later. Nightly television and radio would appeal to key holders in a specified area to return to their premises as fires or explosions had occurred nearby. Few families in West or North Belfast escaped being related to or knowing well some victim who had been killed. A young man who lived directly opposite us left his house one night to go to a party and was never again seen alive. To most he was just another unfortunate victim of a crazed Loyalist murder gang but it was harrowing to see, at first hand, the suffering and breakdown of his immediate family in the years that followed. Not one of his remaining family was ever able to truly live with what happened.

A friend of ours, Gerry, was a busman who once, after a late shift, was persuaded to go for a drink in a club. As often happens, one drink was followed by another until it was early in the morning before he decided to head home. He was drinking with a Protestant workmate who lived in a solidly Loyalist area and he thought it safe enough to take that route as a shortcut home. After having an early breakfast in his friend's house, he decided the streets would be empty and he could safely pass through the short distance towards home. He had been walking about ten minutes when he was stopped by three men who began questioning him. Who was he and where was he going? He noticed with alarm that one of the group was carrying a gun. Sobriety hit him like a cold breeze as he lied about both his identity and destination. They searched him but found nothing incriminating. Claiming to be a Protestant, he was repeatedly challenged.

'He's a liar,' maintained the most aggressive of the three.

'He's a Fenian, let's take him to the waste ground.'

Considering that the speaker was the one who was armed, Gerry was terrified. He maintained that he had been visiting a friend's house and that he could vouch for him.

'Take us to the house then, and prove it.'

As Gerry attempted to do this he suffered the most frightening experience and terror as he became confused about the actual street and number of his friend's house. As he stumbled almost in blind panic he heard the persistent jabbering of the armed thug.

'This is a waste of time. Can't you see he's bluffing? Let's do him in the waste ground.'

Whatever god Gerry was imploring must have responded for almost suddenly he recognised the street and finally the house. Knocking on the door, it was eventually opened by his friend.

'Do you know this guy? Is he one of us?'

It seemed like an eternity and looking at his friend he felt like Jesus with St Peter. Was he going to be denied?

Eventually the answer came, 'Yeah, he's a mate… he's sound… he's one of us.'

They left and Gerry went back into his friend's house. After a panic-ridden period they rang for a taxi and he left the area safely.

This happened in the area where a young Protestant woman who was suspected of being a Catholic was tortured, murdered and stuffed into a household rubbish bin by a crowd that included some women. One can only imagine Gerry's anguish. He was off work with post-traumatic stress for months and it's doubtful if he ever really recovered. There must still be nights where in a fitful nightmare he hears the whining plea, 'Can't you see he's bluffing? Let's do him in the waste ground.'

The ironic thing is that had they conducted a more thorough search of his pockets, they would have discovered that Gerry was a voluntary helper in a local youth group and was carrying a card that identified him, in Irish, as a leader in his local Catholic scout troop.

Gerry's story was not unusual and a lot of people in Belfast in those days had flirtations with death, missing being blown apart by minutes or escaping murder by a lucky chance. In addition, of course, there were the 3,600 plus who weren't so lucky. The vileness and bigotry that provoked these murders existed on both sides, although there was a resistance on many of our parts to accept that. There was a viciousness and premeditation by groups like the 'Shankill Road Butchers' that was hard to comprehend; a hatred and blind brutality that seemed beyond humanity: a deeper level of depravity. And when atrocities like Enniskillen happened there were some who, while saying it shouldn't have happened, failed to condemn it. It was always easier on our consciences to 'blame the other side'. Everyone was affected by the Troubles – if not directly then at close quarters. A lot of our pupils who came from working-class ghettos experienced a side of life unknown to a lot of their teachers.

And yet, even in the midst of all that horror and madness, there were occasional glimpses of the humour (albeit often unconscious) that characterised the Belfast approach to life.

One story I found particularly hilarious had its history in the hatred that grew up between the locals and the British army. One night, a highly inebriated citizen found himself supporting a wall at the bottom of the Whiterock Road. He was having the greatest difficulty in maintaining either direction or distance. As he tried to rediscover the basic skills involved in walking, an army 'duck' patrol passed by. Observing his condition they merely sniffed and walked past. The 'tail-end Charlie' who normally walked backwards narrowly avoided bumping into him. Regarding him with some venom our erstwhile Republican shouted at him, 'Fuck your English Queen.'

With a degree of boredom the soldier replied, 'Doesn't bother me, mate. We're the Welsh Guards.'

Digesting this unexpected failure to rise to the insult, our confused guzzler eventually staggered after the disappearing squaddie. Straightening himself as best he could, he wobbled uncertainly and bellowed, 'So… fuck Harry Secombe!'

The saddest aspect was that strong friendships which had existed before the conflict often weakened and disappeared. My father had a very good friend, Jimmy, who came from Carrickfergus. He and Daddy had often fished and boated together and he risked his safety to visit him after his accident. There were not many Protestants who ventured into Andersonstown in those troubled days and his loyal friendship was appreciated. Some months later when we had taken a house in Ballycastle for a few weeks, my father sent him a postcard. About a fortnight later the postcard was returned with a scribbled comment from Jimmy, 'Surprised at you John!'

To our horror we saw that my four-year-old niece who had been 'honoured' to stick on the stamps had placed the Queen's head upside-down. This was apparently deliberately done by some Republicans to show their antipathy towards the English monarchy. My father was deeply upset and decided that the best course was to write to Jimmy as if nothing had happened but note in the letter that he hoped he had received the postcard from Ballycastle, as he had given it to his grandchild to stick on the stamp and post it. It failed to do the trick and we never heard from Jimmy again.

★

Most of the strategies that contributed to any success I had in relationships with pupils were copied from my father. He was idolised by them. He had a temper and was not afraid of 'clipping them around the ear' but he was always insistent that any arguments were finished before the end of the school day. There was one boy in my class who caused me all sorts of problems. He was a devious bully and I could see little that was meritorious in anything about him. He forced a coolness and aloofness in me and when I saw him getting off the bus, my heart would sink. He was one of the few clouds in the fourth year of my teaching. I tried different approaches but there remained a tension between us. It was with tremendous exultation that I heard the Head tell me he was the next pupil to move up to my father's class. On the way home I began to tell my father about some of the more undesirable aspects of my bugbear, whom I was keen to see challenged and defeated. As I began the register of contemptible characteristics he abruptly told me to say no more. He didn't want to hear or know anything about him.

'I want to judge and treat him as I find him, not as you found him. If you tell me all his faults I'll go looking for them. Lads change as they move through the school and sometimes the different personalities will cause them to react differently.'

It was with jealousy and not a little chagrin that, in the months that followed, I would see my nemesis trot beside my dad like an obedient, loyal spaniel.

On the Saturday morning after his accident, two boys that he was due to take to a school football match called at the house. On hearing about the accident, and realising that he was possibly only moments away from death, they both cried bitterly. One of them had a look of desolation and despair that was harrowing. In the emotion of the moment it was only later did I realise that he was the same boy whom I had been so keen to offload on my father two years before.

Chapter Five

'Success is a journey, not a destination.'
Ralph Arbitelle

My father had taken the most senior class of sixteen-year-olds. I was flattered but somewhat daunted when, after my dad's accident, the Head asked me if I would like to inherit the position. I was very assured and happy with twelve-and thirteen-year-olds but it was a daunting move up to the 'top class' where at least half of them were physically bigger than I was. It was comparable to being asked to sleep with an aged princess… a great honour but not necessarily something one would want to do! Obviously with only 140 or so pupils in the entire school I knew some of them already. There were a couple of boys I was particularly wary about. To say they lacked any charm whatsoever might appear harsh, but suffice it to say it was obvious that a career for them in the diplomatic service seemed unlikely. Some of the other teachers avoided them like the plague. They looked and sounded rough and undisciplined. There were infrequent attenders and a number of serious behaviour problems. There was no uniform and no discernible school ethos. Discipline was what happened inside closed doors where if some good teachers progressed, other pupils and poor teachers suffered and screamed inwardly.

Any teacher will confirm that there is no more ruthless or unforgiving adversary than a class who know the teacher has little control. That applied to a grammar school as much as anywhere else. The big difference was that in St Cuthbert's the level of disruptiveness and bullying of teachers was considerably more intense. The more aware 'hard men' probably felt the unspoken wariness, even fear of some of the staff. The school's reputation outside was that it was a 'sin bin'.

If one taught in another school and had a continuous problem with a pupil, and pushed hard enough, he could probably be unloaded to us. An educational psychologist if pestered, ad nauseam, could eventually be persuaded that a pupil with significant 'behavioural problems' might, despite his reasonable abilities, be better placed in a school ostensibly catering for pupils with learning difficulties. In many cases the argument was valid. A boy who could not settle in a class of thirty with rotating teachers every forty minutes might well behave differently in a smaller group with a more constant relationship with one particular teacher. The learning difficulty could be interpreted as social as well as (or instead of) academic but the impact on the school's reputation was considerable. Most people both outside and inside the system considered the school a 'sink school'. This was a grave unfairness to the majority of pupils who attended the school because of genuine learning difficulties.

One of my new charges was a sullen looking boy who had a perpetual sneer flitting maliciously round his lips while another had only one thing in his favour... he rarely attended. There was the usual assortment of varying abilities, uncertain moods and tempers. It was with some trepidation that I began the September term. The one thing in my favour was that I was (in the absence of any contradictory paternity test) my father's son. Although I had witnessed it from outside, I didn't fully appreciate how much loved he was by his pupils. That gained me some kudos, which I unashamedly used.

Nevertheless the first time I entered the room I had a mixture of anxiety and trepidation that only teachers feel when they first face a class. I was told by a six-foot tall footballer who had played semi-professional football and was a fine amateur boxer that when he first faced a class of thirty eight-year-olds, he thought his heart was about to burst with sheer terror. (In truth it was another part of his anatomy that he thought was going to explode!)

My equanimity wasn't particularly helped by a number of staff whispering that 'Eamonn McArdle is back' in the same tones that peasant goat herders on the steppes of Russia whispered to each other that 'Ghengis Khan is coming'. Eamonn's reputation preceded him. A number of staff were sure that he had been formally expelled after a serious physical altercation with a former teacher, but in the absence of any directive from a higher source he had returned after the summer and sat on a desk with a belligerent sneer when I came in.

'Good morning boys,' I quavered. 'Right, let's get settled. Sit down and we'll get started with the roll.'

The rest of the boys, albeit in a desultory snail-like fashion, took their seats but Eamonn remained perched on the desk, with his mouth forming a smirk of hostility approaching contempt. I feigned not to notice the challenge and scribbled a note to another teacher. It merely said, 'Read earnestly, look serious and thank Eamonn profusely.'

'I need someone sensible... Eamonn, could you bring this over to Mr Matthews?'

He briefly appeared to consider the proposition but he had been sugared with the unusual epithet of 'sensible' so he went. By the time he returned, the rest of the class were getting organised and sorting out their books, etc. I approached him and whispered conspiratorially, *'Good man...* [lowering my voice even more]... *let's keep this between ourselves... not a word to anyone.'*

As he was perfectly entitled to do, Eamonn looked puzzled but was aware that some great mission had been entrusted to him and he had carried it out faultlessly. He joined in with the others.

The age range was elastic and the group appeared to be only loosely constructed on ability, size and temperament. At one time I had a thirteen-year-old who was in the last year class simply because his older brother was in it and he refused to go to school without being beside his sibling. The older brother, like some others in the class, had no more special needs than I had and was one of the most mature, sensitive and intelligent boys I had ever met. In theory there was supposed to be a limit of fourteen in the younger classes with sixteen in the top ones. In later years I did have twenty-four for a short period on my roll. The principal would tell me that the educational psychologist had a boy who was being expelled from somewhere else and would I take him for his last year. (I was assured that if he gave me trouble he would immediately be expelled.) I never quite decided if the management's desire to help these poor unfortunates was dictated by that caring professional humanity so embraced by all teachers or a consideration that the more pupils on roll, the higher the school's grade and the greater their salaries. What an unworthy suspicion!

That year was a learning curve where I became increasingly at ease with the pupils. The range of abilities seemed even greater than before and there was a widening chasm between the maturities displayed. The more mature boys were indistinguishable from many of their counterparts in 'normal' schools while there were some at the other end whose maturity and ability levels were well below their chronological age. The challenge was to keep them all occupied and progressing. Very many years later, the individual programme was introduced by the government as a formalised 'Individual Educational Programme'. In truth, many in special education were already doing just that but without all the paperwork. I was convinced that every pupil could progress. That progression might be faltering and attritional, but I was determined that the day was structured and the work was purposeful. Even with our best efforts I was aware that some of our pupils were, for whatever reason, going to leave school largely illiterate. A number of pupils felt deeply anxious about their lack of literacy skills and it was something we often talked about in class. We talked about the difficulty and the embarrassment and how they should balance that with the many positives they had. It was my job to convince them that their inability to read did not mean they were useless or incapable of finding and holding down a job.

There were 'coping strategies'. I continually told them about famous people who had difficulties with reading. The actual term 'dyslexia' wasn't in common currency until the mid-1980s. I could see that the fact that Mohamed Ali, Walt Disney, Albert Einstein, Richard Branson, Henry Winkler (the Fonz), Jackie Stewart etc. all had some difficulty in reading made an impression on them and hopefully gave them a different appreciation of their difficulties. Filling in forms was a particularly feared activity. We would urge that, if they felt embarrassed about admitting any inability, they could apologise and, saying they had an urgent appointment, take the form and bring it back later. They could also claim 'I'm sorry but I haven't got my glasses with me but if you fill it in with my answers I think I'll be able to sign it.' In later years when dyslexia became better known and almost worn by some with an air of distinctive importance, I tried to get them to have the confidence to say 'I'm sorry, I'm dyslexic, you'll have to help me.'

However, I doubt if I was ever really successful in this ploy.

It was hard not to have the greatest sympathy for a boy who tried ferociously to learn how to read without any success. I regret I wasn't a better teacher of literacy. My wife was very successful dealing with the same type of pupil but even with her help and advice, I have to admit it was an area where I often failed. There have been great advances in the recognition and treatment of literacy problems over the years but despite my best efforts there were always some who failed to progress in literacy. What I could do was try and instill other qualities. The importance of reliability, time-keeping, honesty, 'stick-ability', effort and humour was continuously emphasised. These were the qualities that made up 'maturity'. I imagine that I used the word 'maturity' much more than any other. Because of the nature of the school there were few outside pressures to progress. I felt strongly there had to be a purpose; an attainable, worthy and desirable objective, particularly in those cases when a boy was fifteen or sixteen and was still illiterate. Had I concentrated on literacy to the exclusion of other things, I felt I may only have compounded the sense of failure. We tried to develop a curriculum that was broad and encompassed a number of areas that exam pressures would have prevented in 'normal' school'.

I developed a series of worksheets covering not only English and Maths but also History, Geography, RE, etc. As the school year progressed I covered two sides of the large mobile with pink manila sheets, which were neatly ruled and contained all the scores against the pupils' names. The scores ranged from A+ to E. Practically every morning was devoted to 'tests'. Pupils worked at their own rate and some took several days to complete what others had finished in half an hour. Attendance and behaviour were also marked. The beauty of the system was that no matter how big a mess one made of a particular test there was always the option of doing it again, after tutoring from the teacher. It was important not to overdo the process and suffer the 'death by a thousand worksheets' syndrome but the test sheets had the advantage of starting afresh each time and not continuing in an exercise book that was splattered with corrections.

Each pupil was marked not on a score, but on how hard or diligently he performed. The class had no difficulty understanding that one pupil might get an A for work that was much less correct than someone else who only got a B. I remember Tommy once being aggrieved that while he had only got two answers wrong, he got a B while another pupil with lots wrong got an A+. As he leant on my desk, I feigned disbelief as I asked, 'You're not going to tell me honestly that you think he's as good as you are in Maths? You shouldn't have got those two wrong. You were careless. He wasn't and he tried his guts out.'

Tommy stood up and appeared to consider the proposition. 'Fair enough!' he concluded.

Successfully completed worksheets were punched and stored in important-looking individual files, which were carried with a sense of pride.

When I completed a bronze medallion life-saving course I used to gather the boys around and put them through the same course. This broadened out into a basic first-aid course. Their efforts also merited a score. A number of them were very aware and angry at their lack of literacy and I felt it important that they gain other skills that their counterparts in other schools possibly didn't have.

'Have you ever thought that one day you might arrive home from school and find your mother lying on the floor after a heart attack; or be in a situation where your brother or sister started to choke on a piece of food? What would you do? Stand there and watch them die?'

I would relate true stories of people who had suffered brain damage because a number of others in their company didn't have the knowledge to do anything. My wife once used the Heimlich manoeuvre in her classroom when a child of fourteen started to turn blue while choking on a sweet. She grabbed him from behind and after pushing up from the stomach, the sweet flew out like a bullet. Years later I performed the same procedure on a lady choking at a wedding. The difference was that I got a reward of a dozen bottles of wine! Teaching doesn't pay!

'If you know what to do you can save a life. Now that's a lot more valuable than being able to read or multiply fractions.'

I was once able to borrow the mannequin 'Resusci-Anne' along with an instructor from the Royal Society of Lifesaving and we had a lesson on the correct techniques. It was very successful apart from the evident disappointment for some of the boys that Anne was a creature of plastic and rubber rather than the real thing.

Another subject that was enjoyed was Geometric Drawing. Simple lines joining to different coordinates created very complicated patterns, which were proudly displayed on the walls. Some of the boys who had literacy problems were good at Maths and it was important that they were pushed to more demanding tasks and problems than some of the others. This is where the individual worksheets came into their own and it was possible for one boy to be working at a quite complicated mathematical problem while the boy at the adjoining desk was having a torrid time with number bonds up to twenty. Both were 'doing sums', but while one was working with very basic computation some others were creating five square 'magic boxes'.

★

For a number of years my class was almost an adjunct to the main school. Located as it was in a mobile behind the main school we developed an independent ethos. With our own toilet, we only went to the main building for dinner and specialist subjects. With the main school containing some classes of primary children, it gave the older boys a sense of independence and aloofness.

In the mid-70s another teacher, Jim, was moved up with the second oldest class into another mobile beside me. This was an arrangement that suited us perfectly. Despite the satisfaction of being apart from the rest and having the freedom to do my own thing there was, at times, a sense of isolation and loneliness. Without any deliberation or intention we became increasingly removed in philosophy and ethos from the main school. It certainly would have been extremely difficult for us to operate within the vicinity of primary-age and other younger pupils with the freedom that we allowed. For example, before we became fully aware of the lethal potential of cigarettes, the boys were allowed to smoke inside the toilet, and being teenagers they were often rowdy and loud. We made allowances for high spirits and increasing levels of testosterone but knew that we had complete control when necessary. We became a bit of a mystery to younger pupils who would see this strange world as somewhere one 'graduated' to when you were older.

A lot of the senior boys would only come to school if they both enjoyed it and saw a point to it. Realistically, no one in the Educational Welfare Office or anywhere else was going to break sweat if a boy with less than a year to leaving school refused to attend. A couple of warnings might be issued but that would be the extent of the sanctions employed. The total number of absences was calculated each month in the 'dinner-books' and it became a matter of pride that we were consistently in the top three of lowest absentees. The lack of any legal sanction to ensure attendance gave us, the teachers, a fair degree of freedom.

It was possible, for example, to suggest to someone who was being particularly obstreperous that, 'Maybe you should take a day off and think things over,' with there being no suggestion of a suspension! As long as things ticked over smoothly we could be left to our own devices.

Chapter Six

'A friend is someone who understands your past, believes in your future, and accepts you today just the way you are.'
                                                                Unknown

My fellow teacher, Jim, was a fascinating character and a man with whom I bonded very quickly. He had come into teaching by the scenic route and had a whole wealth of experience of the 'real world' before entering the profession. He also had a multitude of stories and episodes which he enjoyed relating. After a short time working in a chemist's, he became involved in the burgeoning cinema business and over the years became manager of one of the biggest cinemas in Belfast. He introduced the late-night Northern Ireland film premier, which became an established celebrity event attended by some of the major British film stars. After an acrimonious fall-out with his English superiors, he progressed to owning and managing a cinema in one of the border towns. However, the introduction of the Selective Employment Tax and the increasing availability and popularity of television forced him to give up. He entered a Manchester teacher training college as a mature student and came to us as a newly qualified teacher in the late 1960s. He was married with a large family and I'm sure things were tough financially for many years.

Every employment he had before teaching provided a long catalogue of anecdotes that were fascinating and revealing. He would regale me with stories about randy assistant managers: usherettes who were in the habit of canvassing for a business unrelated to their job descriptions (during the war, one of them, he assured me, had more sailors under her than Mountbatten): chefs who tried to poison certain politicians when they attended premiers: the outlandish sexual peccadilloes of some of his famous guests and some of his many fall-outs with authority figures. He liked a captive audience and ensured their attention by grabbing them firmly by the elbow, only releasing them when the tale was concluded. He too enjoyed teaching and we shared the same quirky humour. He had a lively intelligence and was talented at both drama and art where he built up quite a stock of materials from different sources. He almost always wore a suit with a waistcoat, which brought a certain old world charm to the classroom. This was enhanced when in an effort to cut down on his cigarettes, he started to bring in snuff and sniff it regularly. Of course all the boys wanted to try it as well and Jim showed them the proper way. He maintained it was harmless compared to cigarettes. For someone who was so fastidious about his appearance, he appeared oblivious to the fact that for a part of the school day he looked to have had some form of brown nasal infection that threatened to devour his top lip. Stocky and short, he moved purposely. His full head of hair was coiffured regularly and his eyes were animated and mischievous. We got on very well and shared a similar approach to teaching.

He was much more confident than I was in dealing with other adults and was able to motivate and enthuse others. He became involved in the community, helping to set up neighbourhood housing schemes. Living on the edge of a borderline area that frequently had riots at night, with others he established contacts with community leaders on the Loyalist side and they worked together to try and lessen the interface rioting. This involved growing contact with the army and the police and had to be done carefully. Others were shot dead for similar contacts.

Often, after school, we would go for a pint and the conversation was easy and enjoyable. Over the years Jim's health deteriorated and he appeared to lose some of his energy. He became reanimated when we brought the classes together for special events. I suppose some of the pressure was taken off him and we worked well together.

★

Initially we decided to amalgamate every morning for RE. Jim was very religious but he was wise enough to approach things in a non-judgemental way. Our joint morning Religion Education session could cover any subject or topic. We began by saying our morning prayers but after that the topics were wide and varied. While the imparting of 'Catholic values' was on the curriculum we took it, additionally, as the opportunity for everyone to relate to each other. After our morning prayers, it became increasingly informal and eventually it was as another teacher chidingly suggested 'akin to a meeting of Alcoholic Anonymous with the rules omitted'. A visitor to the class would have seen two teachers at a desk surrounded by a haphazard collection of boys, some with their coats still on leaning on that desk; others lounging lazily or tilting chairs to the limits of gravity; the fog rising from the damp clothes; the air thick with tobacco smells. Hopefully if they studied the scene a little further they would have realised that the main purpose was to engage the boys in discussion. There were few subjects 'off-limits' and discussions would have ranged from bullying to masturbation, from death to joy-riding, from honesty to abortion. Often Jim and I would agree beforehand to take different sides. We would discuss topics like abortion, hell, grace, capital punishment, etc.

We would argue and encourage the boys to think about things in a more open way. It was also important for them to realise that you could disagree with someone without getting involved physically or letting that disagreement affect your friendship. I, for example, would argue against capital punishment while Jim would, equally enthusiastically, adopt a 'hanging's too good for them' stance. Masturbation was the one topic where everyone suddenly became alert. A lot of boys worried about it; it was a constant source of angst. Some of them were naively innocent while others said little. It was at a time when sex education was avoided and it was still some time before the Church educational authorities offered any sort of realistic programme. Television programmes were heavily censored and it was frightening to realise how naive and innocent some of the boys were. We had to be careful about what we said. The proper terms for genitalia caused some differences. I favoured the term 'penis' but Jim substituted his own invention 'jollywasher' and testicles became 'little corduroy bags'. I laughed when a lot of the boys adopted this terminology and would tell me in all seriousness that someone in a football match had been kicked in the 'cords' and his 'jollywasher' had turned blue! Our school manager then was a priest who was very supportive of what we tried to do although I don't think he was entirely informed of everything we tried.

There was a relationship between us that meant that we were able to, very quickly, pick up the nuances and intentions behind the other's words. We each knew if we were expected to agree or argue. So, if I commented on how poor United had been the night before, he would, to the delight of the other supporters, launch into praise and a lament about how they were robbed. We both enjoyed drama and were quick to fall into a role. On more serious topics we were more thoughtful and invited and encouraged contributions. The class could become quite animated when we feigned disagreement with the sole purpose of instilling the notion that it was acceptable to argue and still remain friends.

★

A lot of the boys came from poor backgrounds and it was clear that a lot of their clothes had seen better days. In those days there was no school uniform and dress was optional. With Jim and I both having access to old clothes from family and friends, we tried to pass off some of the better stuff to deserving pupils. Initially it proved not only difficult but almost impossible. Pride was not restricted to those who could afford it. Even when I tried to do it sensitively and covertly, I was rebuffed. However, Jim and I hit on a Baldric-type 'cunning plan'. He would arrive in with a large bundle of clothes, all washed and carefully ironed with the apparent intention of giving them to me and my (imaginary) nephews. We would spread them around a couple of large desks. I would try on a jacket and prance up and down the room admiring it: 'That will do me very nicely,' or 'This will do my [fictional] nephew, Paddy.' I would sometimes try on something which was obviously too small and in a dejected bout of disappointment suggest that it would fit better on Sammy. (Well, if I could wear second-hand then so could he.) The stigma of charitable hand-outs was removed and we ended up with quite a lot of pupils vying for cast-offs. There was no difference from what we did in our own homes with Jim's sons inheriting the 'hand-me-downs' just as my three daughters did. The uncanny thing was that the very poorest lads often refused to buy into the charade.

The awareness of their own depleted circumstances gave them a peculiar sensitivity about their situations.

*

Jim had a number of sons and he greatly enjoyed their company. He carried his knowledge and affection for teenage boys into the classroom and would often quote what they said or what they did. From watching his easy manner I noticed that he would often pretend to wrestle or shadow box with them. As he did with adults, he would also hold their arms when explaining things, usually with a pressure that increased in direct correlation with their waning interest. This 'if you don't listen I'll hold you all the tighter' ploy invariably ensured a captive audience. Initially I felt his grip was invasive and reacted uncomfortably. What changed over the years was a greater willingness to express respect or friendship by physical contact. The reaction to non-sexual contact was endemic at that time. Even within families an expression of support or affection was rarely expressed by physical contact. Jim would rest his hand on their shoulder as he worked with them and pat their backs in appreciation of their work. It wasn't in the least mawkish, insincere or sinister.

I resolved to copy that approach in my own class. I had always shaken hands in a jocular manner or offered 'high fives' when someone performed some difficult task, but this was something more than that. It was part of a contract of friendship: a levelling of equality. Built into that mutual respect was the fact that there was never any question of a reciprocity that was going to affect the teacher-pupil relationship. More importantly it became increasingly more difficult to pick a fight with someone who had shaken your hand as they said 'Good morning', joked about something and patted your back when you did something well.

My dad had a great friend who was involved in the boat with him. Darren was a man who enjoyed his drink. I hesitate to call him an alcoholic but he probably merited that epithet. He was likely to engage in ferocious argument when he had partaken of what Paisley called the 'Devil's buttermilk' but outside of that it would have been difficult to meet a more pleasant and generous being. He had thinning, wispy grey hair, which hung sadly above his ears. His face had the ruddy complexion of a man who loved the outdoors but he had the facial, tell-tale, thin purple veins which showed he also liked the indoors, particularly licensed premises. He had an unparalleled knowledge of the sea and boats and when he talked he did so with an undisputed authority. His electric-blue eyes darted and danced like damselflies as he talked and there was an intensity of truth behind them. He was the only person I ever met who created ships inside bottles. He would also amuse himself by making the most colourful butterflies out of clam shells, carving the bodies from wood and attaching the wings with glue. His hallway walls were covered in them and if you even glanced at one admiringly Darren would take it from the wall and give it to you. He admired my father who reciprocated in kind. Although they came from different backgrounds, this mutual respect and affection was obvious.

In those early days of the Troubles, young men often found themselves being dragged into the fringes of the paramilitaries. Darren's son had been charged with helping in the paramilitary robbery of a post office. One evening as Dad was working on the boat, Darren approached and asked him to do 'a very big favour'.

'I can fully understand if you don't want to but I would take it as a big favour if you would write a character reference for the son. You know what he's like. He's a good lad who just did a stupid thing. I'm worried if he gets sent to prison he'll get more involved with the shower of bastards that got him involved in the first place. But if you don't feel you can, I understand. It won't make any difference to our friendship.'

Needless to say my father agreed and a character reference was produced in court, which made Darren's son sound like the offspring of Mother Teresa and Albert Schweitzer. Apparently when the magistrate hearing the case saw the reference he queried the prosecution case, asking somewhat incredulously, 'This young man is charged with being involved with a Loyalist gang yet his character witness is a Catholic Vice-Principal from the Falls Road?'

The son was dismissed with a caution. The bond between Darren and my dad became even firmer.

A short time later Darren fell ill with pleurisy and ended up in hospital. My father would often call and visit him. He would combine this with his Wednesday-night weekly tutoring in a further education college, where he taught English. One evening he called in, en route, to find Darren very hot and uncomfortable, agitated with beads of sweat blistering his forehead, despite the doctor stating that he was responding well to the drugs.

'John, am I glad to see you,' he panted. 'Could you do me a big favour and get me some ice cream? I've been lying here dreaming about the stuff.'

Daddy said he would bring him some after his class and Darren understood. As he rushed down the stairs he thought about his friend's discomfort, balancing his needs with a belated start to a class. Changing his mind and running through the streets he reached Morelli's and bought a large tub. He was extremely fit and running back to the hospital, he breathlessly presented the ice cream to a grateful patient.

The following day after school we went down to Carrickfergus to check the boat as a high spring tide coupled with an Easterly gale was expected. As we tidied the ropes we were approached by another local boat owner, Jody.

'Sorry to hear about your mate, John.'

My father looked up. 'Who? Darren... Oh I think he'll be all right... the doctor is fairly positive and he's strong you know... only last night he...'

'Aw Christ!' interrupted Jody. 'Did you not hear?... He died in hospital this morning.'

The blood drained from my dad's face and he suddenly looked frail and aged. He struggled to speak as the tears formed and slowly rolled down his cheeks. It was the first time I'd ever seen him cry. Never before had I seen him as being vulnerable. I stood two yards from him yet was not conditioned to approach or hug or comfort him. I stood, sad and useless, and mouthed some stupid platitude. It seems strange all these years later to comprehend that.

Jim was largely responsible for changing that ingrained reluctance to the tactile expression of support and affection. Nowadays everybody appears to hug and embrace each other on an hourly basis but that was a different era. I often thought about it in class when a boy needed a reassurance which best came by a friendly arm on his shoulder. Due in no small part to the litany of horrific sexual and physical abuse nowadays, those in authority stress no teacher or adult should ever lay a hand on a pupil, even to comfort them. So for all the right reasons we have come up with some very bad and wrong decisions. Even Primary 1 teachers are told not to engage in any physical contact, even when their charges are crying. All this, when it is de riguer for teenage boys and girls to hug their friends in affection or sympathy. Watch on television the reactions as pupils commiserate or congratulate their classmates on their exam results. As the world turned, so too have our attitudes.

My affection for Jim did not blind me to his faults and I'm sure that was reciprocated. He had an explosive temper and at least twice over the years he fell out with me to the extent that all social intercourse and banter stopped; our joint classes were divorced and there was an air of tension, which was as uncomfortable for the boys as it was for us. However, after a number of days I would seek him out and ask him for a pint. We would adjourn to a quiet lounge which because of the poor bar service, we entitled the 'Marie Celeste Bar'. It wouldn't be long before normal service was resumed. I always made the first move even when I believed I was guiltless but I estimated the absence of his companionship was worth the apology. Within a day or so he would be confirming to me that he was 'a silly old bugger'. I would agree emphatically and we would laugh together. We understood what the other was trying to achieve with the boys and life in the mobiles would have been a lot lonelier without his understanding and company. Together and mostly unintentionally we set up an almost independent 'leavers' school' in the mobiles at the side of the main building.

The situation was neatly encapsulated by another teacher, John, in 1982 during the Falkland crisis with an accurate if somewhat caustic wit, when he suggested that 'The Head is organising a task force to retake the mobiles!'

Chapter Seven

'Work while you have the light. You are responsible for the talent that has been entrusted to you.'
                                                              Henri-Frederic Amiel

Those years were extremely satisfying and enjoyable. Each year I grew more confident and more ambitious for success. Oddly enough, as I got older I worked harder and harder at getting the success I craved. Doubtless there are some who will accuse me of viewing my experiences as rose-tinted and inaccurate… how I wished things had been, rather than how they were but I can honestly say that I could not have been happier teaching that bunch of boys right through the 1970s and up to 1986. There were of course bad days when I would arrive home and wonder if all the effort I had put in was worth it. But the number of days I would finish looking forward to the next morning far outnumbered them.

   I remember vividly, in the mid-70s, fishing for conger eels with a friend off the North Antrim coast. He taught in a country secondary school that had its fair share of problems, though nothing I'm sure as difficult as an inner city school in Belfast. It was the last day of July and a glorious evening. The yellow sands were bathed in the purplish haze of a summer dusk and the sea was shimmering and falling to calm. We had all our bait and gear ready and the prospect of a really exciting and enjoyable night ahead. As we walked down to the rocks he turned and said, 'God! It's terrible to think that's half the holidays gone: we've only got less than four weeks left before we go back.'

I thought about what he said. 'Do you really hate it that much?' I asked. 'Most people have two weeks for their summer holiday; that is if they're lucky enough to have work. They will talk for months beforehand about that fortnight, make plans, save money, etc. and you're bitching about only having twice that amount of time left?'

'No I don't hate it,' he replied defensively, 'but you know what I mean.'

'No! Sorry I don't. Thinking seriously about it, if I felt like that I wouldn't go back. I would try and do something else.'

'Well, you're not going to claim that you're actually looking forward to going back?' he sneered.

I didn't answer, because I suspect he wouldn't have believed me but the truth was, not only did I not mind going back, I was actually looking forward to it. It was dispiriting to realise that for him and some others there were only two good reasons for being a teacher… July and August. For me, each year would throw up a new set of challenges and they were to be embraced. Every year I endeavoured to improve the relationships and realise the potential they afforded. That might appear smug and superior but it was just what I enjoyed doing. I did it because I enjoyed it and didn't deserve praise or admiration any more than I deserve plaudits for swimming, fishing, cycling, walking mountains or any other activity that I take pleasure in.

★

I loved to see the development and changes that took place at that awkward mid-teen age. The one thing I stressed above everything else was the need for self-discipline. I was lucky that the older the pupils, the more they understood that they needed and wanted a sense of maturity. They were no longer 'boys' but 'young men'. They knew that for most of them this was going to be their last year at school. As that longed-for release came closer their uncertainty and nervousness about the future grew larger. From having their days organised and planned, they would then be making their own decisions. When someone was out of line it was usually sufficient to question if they would be able to repeat that action/attitude/response in a couple of months' time. Did they honestly think that a prospective boss would cajole and encourage them like I did?

Scarcely a day went past when I didn't emphasise the fact that what went on in school was for their benefit. On one particular occasion I was scolding a lad who was failing to start (never mind finish) his worksheet. I asked him why he was working and who he was working for. He said he was doing it for me. It was a classic opportunity for a spot of improvised drama. Feigning complete incredulity I raised my voice.

'What?… Do you honestly believe you're working for me? Don't be so daft. I've got a job. What you do in here doesn't affect my life. You might cause me a bit of "aggro" but you're not going to seriously affect my life. My God!' I declared in mock astonishment, extending my arms to indicate the two walls covered in progress scores. 'And you think that you're doing all this work – all these programmes for me?'

So great was my pretended shock and horror that I shrugged my shoulders in despair, sat down and wearily asked the class, 'God Almighty! Would someone tell Johnny who he's working for?'

To my relief there was a chorus from some of his classmates. 'Sir, he's working for himself.'

'You should be so sure that you're working for yourselves that I shouldn't even have to tell you to start your work. The only thing you should need me to do is to show you what to do next or to explain something. If I wasn't here you should be so mature that you would continue to get on with things in my absence.'

It must have been a week after that when on my way to work, my car was hijacked by the IRA. It was done very neatly and efficiently. A man stepped out quickly on to a pedestrian crossing and I was forced to brake. Almost simultaneously the front doors were wrenched open and a gun was stuck into my side.

The one that opened the door said, 'Provisional IRA. We're taking your car, get out.'

The other one climbed into the passenger seat and ordered me to drive round the corner.

'No!' his comrade insisted. 'Get out now.'

Unbelievably, an argument ensued between them as traffic started to build up behind. The conflicting demands didn't exactly fill me with confidence. I assured them they could have the car but I didn't want to be shot as the result of failing to declare myself in favour of one side of the, by now, heated debate. The issue was resolved when the obvious leader who had been the crossing pedestrian came back and demanded to know, 'What the fuck are you two eejits doing?'

He looked at me with a sort of 'It's really hard to get decent help nowadays' expression and told me to drive round the corner. He added that if I had any emotional attachment to my legs I would be advised to wait at least half an hour before reporting the car stolen. I was obviously late and in those pre-mobile phone days I was unable to ring the school. In the event I arrived in about fifty minutes after the starting time.

As I walked to my mobile, the Principal was just leaving. He looked at me in astonishment and did a double take.

'I just left some work experience sheets on your desk. The class were all working away so I thought you were in the store.'

I explained what had happened and he was amazed that the class had behaved in such a way in my absence. I was no less shocked than he was but I had a surge of pride and satisfaction when I went in to see most of the boys with their boxes out and Francie looking after the cupboards, distributing the worksheets. On another day there might well have been bedlam and I doubt if it would have happened in the afternoon when they were fully awake. But you took those little successes and kept them proudly.

★

I thought a lot about discipline. Why was there an easy-going camaraderie in some classes where others were fraught and tense? Obviously the personality of the teacher was the determining factor but there was more. Discipline can as equally apply to a cold-blooded killer as a saint. It had to involve factors like 'righteousness', 'justice', and a balance between control and freedom. Within each branch of learning, different qualities are required. A dedicated 'A' level tutor of Physics may well achieve fantastic results and the personal relationship with his pupils may be determined as 'respect'. The same dedication and resolve might in another context be met with contempt. Good order is essential not only to enable work to be done but also as training for life after school. But there also had to be a genuine affection and respect for your charges. It was important to buy into their lives, share their excitements and their boredoms; understand their frustrations and rise above their pessimism. I like to think that the greatest deterrent to misbehaviour was the withdrawal of my goodwill.

The relationship of trust and friendship was too important for serious prolonged disagreement. Of course there were problems… it was in the nature of the beast. Not many of my twenty-odd pupils were going to slavishly follow me around hanging on my every word.

Difficulties with numeracy and literacy can always be exaggerated. In these days of computers, iPads, smart phones and a number of other technological advances, many of which leave me a mere baffled onlooker, an entire world of knowledge and skills is available to everyone, irrespective of intellectual ability. It is vital to stress the importance of a curriculum that allows for technological ability. When I was teaching in the 70s and early 80s, computer skills or IT consisted of a BBC computer with idiosyncratic 'floppies', which might work some of the time. The most frequent use revolved round the tennis game where one 'pinged' a ball from side to side.

Now the ability to use technology is an essential prerequisite for all pupils but I hope the electronic boards, individual iPads and computers don't detract from the pupil/teacher relationship. I always felt there was a lot to be gained from non-academic activities both inside and outside the classroom.

Friday afternoons were designated 'free time'. We had an old snooker table and a dart-board and for the last hour, matches and competitions were organised. It was important that I entered these as well. We also had draughts and chess although I only remember a couple of pupils who could play the latter. One of them was every bit as good (or as poor) as I was. The record player would be brought out and Pierce would be our DJ for the afternoon. Once or twice a month we would organise a game of Monopoly but, because of the nature of the game and the time constraints, it was rarely concluded. There were four pupils who were particularly keen, so, providing they were on independent travel, I used to organise a game that would continue after school. After the rest of the class left and the school was only populated by the caretaker and cleaners, we would huddle round the board and determine who was going to be the next Rockefeller. I would then leave them in the centre of town and they would go home from there.

Every year there was a challenge swim of a timed one-kilometre swim by one of the big non-alcoholic beer companies. I used to take two or three boys to the swimming pool to train for this after school and then on the actual Saturday competition day, we would all enter.

'Ah!' I hear you say. 'He was nothing but a big child himself.'

Your judgement would be absolutely correct.

After my father had his accident, we bought a Ford Transit van to transport him around. It had a comfortable, heavily padded seat in the main section with a long, upholstered bench on which he could lie. That meant it could, in those pre-seatbelt times, comfortably hold three people in the front with perhaps four in the back. However I proved it was quite possible on school trips to transport eleven pupils and myself. It did involve a number of them sitting on the floor but in order to avoid serious posterior discomfort, the seating arrangements were rotated every twenty-five miles or so. The towels we would invariably take also doubled as cushions. Because of his injuries, the class got more use from the van than my father ever did. He got his enjoyment from me relating the trips and telling him how much the boys had profited from them. On occasion he would also slip me money for petrol. We would often gather up swimming gear and towels and head for the shore. The Antrim and Down coasts were nearby and we would visit Carrickfergus Castle and swim near the old harbour or further up the coast at Glenarm or Carnlough. In bad weather we would talk or read about local places and then make a visit to destinations like Antrim or Crumlin Glen. I read extracts from *My Lady of the Chimney Corner* by Alexander Irvine and then we went to Pogue's Entry in Antrim to visit the actual house. We would visit parks or just explore different places. I always found most pupils were inherently interested in wildlife. They would be startled by the electric blue of a damsel fly or the excitement of carefully parting the bushes to reveal a blackbird's nest with its greenish-blue eggs. I would point out grey wagtails (why are they yellow, Sir?) on the Six Mile Water and we would find frogspawn and tadpoles in ponds. In the river at Colin Glen we saw and tried, generally unsuccessfully, to 'tickle' little trout dancing in the tumbling water. We would see mackerel being caught on the limestone rocks on the path from Whitehead and see hen harriers and buzzards on the moors above Carnlough.

One memorable visit was to Armagh where, after a morning's unsuccessful fishing, we visited the two cathedrals in the city The hats of previous cardinals which traditionally hung in the side aisles until they decayed were a source of curiosity. I jokingly remarked that the heads that had been underneath had fallen down years ago. Only after insistent questions did I confess I had only been joking. Another June day, in Caledon, we stopped at the bridge over the Blackwater and for the first time in my life I saw a massive hatch of mayfly. They fluttered and cascaded like snowflakes in a storm, not only on the banks but over the luxuriant meadow grass that framed the river. It was a scene indelibly printed on our minds. Being from the city we had never before witnessed such a generous and superlative outpouring of nature. In the river, trout were lazily gorging themselves on this annual bonanza but we had no time or licences to fish. (In reality the absence of licences was never going to deter us.)

The waterfalls in Glenarrif were a favourite destination. Because of the ongoing Troubles, it was not uncommon for riots or bomb scares to seriously disrupt the attendance. Often, long after the official starting time, there would have been more guests at a Kamikaze reunion party than pupils who had been able to brave the latest incident. Often I would find only three or four boys who had actually made it in. Depending on circumstances this was a golden opportunity to take them out in my car. I once brought three boys (the entire class!) to a place that I knew near Cushendall. I had a small stove and sandwiches. My friend, Barry, had shown me the glen some time before and it was so entrancing that I rarely revealed it to anyone else. I didn't want its unique magic to be spoilt by others. It bisected the middle of a dull, uniform spruce forest. Quite unexpectedly one came upon a small stream, no wider than a good jump, gurgling through a little glen that had some hazels and rowans alongside. It was less than half a mile in length but what a dazzling surprise! It flowed through mossy banks and clumps of mountain holly and in one place a rocky gorge. The rocks were covered in the most incredible array of coloured mosses and lichens. The sphagnum moss with its multi-shaded greens flecked with red was saturated with water. At any moment I was sure Rupert Bear would come strolling by. I lead the boys through it and, almost imperceptibly, three tough, urban teenagers found themselves entranced children again captured in an eerie, sylvan magic. Unconsciously we whispered lest we disturb the tranquillity. We walked to the end out onto the moor and then retraced our steps. The skies darkened and although it was late April, it began to snow lightly. We 'camped' by the river and in a short time I had the kettle boiling and the tea and food were passed around. We sat, mostly silent, munching dreamily as we watched the flakes stutter through the branches and melt on the moss. This bounty of nature was free and accessible to all and no educational qualifications were necessary to enjoy or be enthralled by it.

Unfortunately our time was short and we had to return to Belfast. There was little said on the return journey. There were no great enthusiastic 'thanks'; no 'that was brilliant' gratitude. It wasn't part of their upbringing. But I knew that we had all experienced something special.

Lately I took my grandchildren to the same spot and despite a number of the trees having been cut, there still lived fairies, goblins and witches in behind the mossy banks. My earnest Conn and beautiful, wide-eyed Meabh saw them all. Before we get much older, old friends Kevin, Barry and I are determined to camp in it some night and feel the magic of it once again.

★

Judgements about the limitations of intellectual ability and life skills became problematic and confusing when one realised that the experience of some of the other staff was so limited. It amazed me when talking to some staff how little they knew or had experience of nature and, while they may have travelled to the Mediterranean on holidays, their knowledge of the natural world, places and life outside Belfast was limited to the point of narrow-mindedness.

There were a number of boys fascinated by nature. Quite a few kept pets at home. Often I learnt much that was new to me and there was a dawning realisation in the class that the teacher didn't know everything. Once Fred brought in his pigeons and showed them off proudly to the class. He started to take one out of the cage but I was concerned the frightened bird would fly blindly round the room. He assured me there was no danger and he took it out carefully and gave it to me to hold. He showed me how when you laid the pigeon on its back in your hand, it lay calm and motionless. Another pupil brought in his ferrets, which he used to hunt rabbits. He was practically illiterate and yet he gave an impromptu talk about he looked after them; how he laid his nets and how he caught and dispatched his rabbits. No Dimbleby Lecture was ever received with such rapt attention. All these served to reinforce my often-repeated mantra that we each had different gifts and talents.

Each week everyone had to write a story. I had gathered a large collection of photos, paintings, etc. which were usually as dramatic or vivid as I could find. Photos included one of a woman throwing her child from a burning building; another of a party of cyclists lying in the road after an accident; the classic shot of the young girl in Vietnam fleeing down a road with her clothes in a napalm blaze; a train on fire and another of a boy standing over a body with a gun in his hand; seagulls attacking a child who was holding an ice cream, etc. Everyone got a blank sheet for spellings and I would spell out every single word if necessary. Efforts varied from a full page to a few lines. Later everyone would read their efforts from the front of the class. Every praise and enthusiasm was laid on the reader irrespective of the literary worth. With very weak readers I would read their attempts with them almost simultaneously. I would also read mine, which had to be crafted as to be of interest to that particular audience. As an aspiring writer it was great training! Some of their stories were magical and it's a matter of deep regret that I no longer have them. Poetry was always my first love. I loved painting the story of a poem, dramatising it, explaining the words, the nuances and the meaning. One knew instinctively when the mood was right and if the correct poem was picked, there were very few who couldn't get something out of it. I was always lucky to have at least one or two boys who not only enjoyed poetry but were keen on attempting efforts of their own. One year I was lucky enough to have three very enthusiastic poets. First World War poetry prompted Gordon, one of these budding Owens to pen:

> *'The gateway was blown in.*
> *Guards and debris strewn together over the floor*
> *Through the stink of cordite and dripping blood*
> *Came the soldiers, like bees to our honey*
> *A moment before Jack lay dead*
> *His brains dripping to the floor like a left on tap.'*

The horror of war was a subject that engaged sixteen-year-olds. Not all (but quite a few!) of Gordon's efforts dealt with gore and destruction. I encouraged him to look outside this at other areas like nature, etc.

The following is an extract from his poem 'The River':

> *'But come the Winter everything changes*
> *Reeds at the bank Lilies on the water*
> *The earth has swallowed them*
> *To cough them up again in the Spring*
> *The fish move to the middle of the water and live on*
> *And the only thing to watch them*
> *Is the willowing oak tree and a deep blue sky.'*

OK! I'm not exactly sure what sort of beast a 'willowing oak tree' is but doesn't it fit in beautifully? It was efforts like these that kept me motivated. It was easier to deal with all the mundanity, all of the frustration, all the negativities arising from inability when a little gem like that came from a pupil who had been determined as having 'special educational needs'. I won't pretend that Gordon's reaction and efforts were typical but they weren't unique and every so often a boy or two would come along, contribute an unexpected gem and life would be just that bit more satisfying. I have managed to keep his book of poems and I still get a buzz out of his efforts.

I found that even small, attritional steps forward could be very rewarding. In dealing with pupils with learning difficulties

I found that the ordinary, simple milestones that happened on a daily basis in an 'ordinary' school could be a source of great satisfaction to us. There were also curious instances where a pupil would fail to grasp an idea or concept that you knew was well within his compass. One such pupil, Michael, was above average for the class in practically every area, but despite my best efforts was unable to read the time. I even borrowed material with all sorts of clocks, etc. from my wife's extensive Maths department but no matter how patiently and slowly we tried, he continued to be completely bewildered. The nuances of ancient Sanskrit could not have caused him greater difficulty. One day his father came to collect him for a dental appointment. He informed me that Michael was really stupid and that, even at fifteen, he still couldn't tell the time. He said all this before I could usher him out to the annex so the rest of the class heard his indictment.

I felt such a deep pity for Michael as he stood there, reddening, and a building contempt for and anger at his dad. His failure to master the time was compounded and reinforced on a daily basis. Later I tried to explain this to the father, as well some well-intentioned cautions about embarrassing his son in front of others, but with no success.

*

As a teacher one had to realise that sometimes getting a pupil to write their name confidently or work competently within numbers up to twenty was a hurdle that sometimes involved a serious amount of work. One had to appreciate that progress is a relative concept. It was important to avoid frustration and as Chief Dan George in *The Outlaw Josey Wales* would have it, 'endeavour to persevere'. The range of abilities was huge and that's why the individual worksheets, which could be progressed at one's own speed and competence, were so important. But it was equally important that the class was also a unit in which everyone felt a member. That unity could be achieved in storytelling, art, poetry, games, PE, religion, etc. It was difficult, although sadly not impossible, to find a pupil who did not have a degree of ability, even excellence, in some particular area.

Chapter Eight

'Personal achievement starts in the mind of the individual. Your personal achievement starts in your mind. The first step is to know exactly what your problem, goal or desire is.'
                                                        Clement Stone

The boys were aware that their friends in 'normal' schools were often doing exams and it bothered me that we couldn't offer anything similar to reward their hard work. I decided that we would design a Record of Achievement, which would only be given to pupils who had really earned it. It would not only record abilities in academic subjects but would stress the personality, abilities, honesty, endeavour, etc. Jim designed a crest and we made the certificate as important-looking as possible. I got a very helpful girl in the reproduction section of the Belfast education board to print the official-looking certificate. What today would take a matter of minutes on a laptop then took weeks to design, alter and perfect. To create an even more important appearance I typed in the comments. This was the era before computers and we contributed significantly to the rising Tippex stock success. We made a big deal about it and stressed its worth to a potential employer.

To have any real value I decided, early on, that it would not be given out as a matter of course. It had to be earned. The class had to see it as something that required a fair degree of effort. It was inevitable therefore that each year we would have a few who would not receive it. This was difficult but those who didn't earn it generally understood. We designed another certificate and made sure that they were included in the process.

An award/graduation morning was planned for the end of the summer term. It seems de rigueur now but we decided on a then innovatory move by inviting the parents up and organising tea and cake for the visitors. Eileen made sandwiches and my daughters contributed the obligatory chocolate Rice Krispie buns. The class was tidied and a makeshift altar was prepared. There was a class Mass, which was attended by the parents, a very supportive priest and the Headmaster. Jim and I wore our best suits. I brought in a small portable organ and with Jim revelling in the role of choirmaster, we belted out a couple of hymns. After many practices we were more or less in tune though the Vienna Boys' Choir were unlikely to feel threatened. I spoke about the achievements of the boys and the pride and satisfaction we had from teaching them. The Principal entered into the spirit of the event and made a short speech before awarding the certificates.

We tried to ensure that the comments and results on the certificate were honest and realistic by ensuring that any learning difficulties were mentioned but not emphasised to the detriment of other positive characteristics. It was better to paint a partial excellence than a full, but not fulsome, adequacy. The newly installed school phone number was included and any prospective employer invited to get in touch with me. I fervently hoped it would become an opportunity to persuade an employer that despite any academic shortcomings in the applicant, they would be employing a steady, reliable worker.

To have any credibility I had to be honest. If a boy wasn't suitable, I said so.

Once I was delighted to successfully persuade the manager of the local abattoir on the suitability of a past pupil. Initially he had been highly sceptical. About two years later he rang and asked to speak to me. I had immediate scenarios of knives and bloodied corpses, terrified that my ex-pupil had done something terrible but he told me that Joe was doing exceptionally well and he wanted to make him a charge-hand.

'I've another one of your boys in here looking for a start. Do you think he would be suitable?'

He named the prospective applicant. I paused.

Henry wasn't a bad fellow but he had a terrible temper and was generally short in the maturity stakes. I equivocated and hesitatingly pointed out his good points.

He interrupted me. 'You know the sort of conditions that exist here... be honest... if you were me, would you employ him?'

I had a vision of Henry standing with a slaughtering knife in his hand and a dead colleague lying on the floor. 'In your situation... not in a million years.'

He thanked me. The benefit of my honest assessment was that the following year he rang about another ex-pupil. After a glowing reference from me he was also employed.

As the years passed the job became more and more fulfilling. I was in charge of career guidance and with the help of a number of government career officers, we had a fair degree of success in placing leavers in jobs. The government's employment service included a number of visits to the major Belfast employers. Most of the bigger engineering and industrial firms were located in Loyalist areas and it was galling to walk a number of boys from Nationalist backgrounds through workshops that were draped in Union Jacks and Loyalist paramilitary banners and slogans. My pupils might have as well aspired to be candidates for the Russian space programme. I once questioned a particularly friendly manager as he was showing us around a factory that looked like a preparation hall for the Orange Twelfth.

'Do you really think one of these lads from West Belfast would feel particularly welcome here?'

He looked at me apologetically. 'Believe it or not, we only have a small number of fanatics in here but unfortunately every time we try and secularise the workshops they threaten all sorts of strikes and hassle. Nothing would give me and most of the management more pleasure than to mix up the workforce, but sadly this is the bloody Belfast we're living in.'

It was hard not to doubt his sincerity but as he shrugged his shoulders, we both knew any change was a long way off.

Nevertheless we had our successes. We encouraged the boys to take reasonable risks. I established a close rapport and indeed became lifetime friends with David the first careers officer I worked with. Opportunities were not that plentiful. A number of the bigger firms could afford to select better-qualified applicants. One way to afford our boys a better chance was to get them into job situations as 'work experience'. This involved them working one day a week in a real job placement. I was convinced that once they could demonstrate their trustworthiness, enthusiasm and dedication, any perceived worries about their lack of academic abilities would be ignored.

There were a number of problems. The first was trying to convince some pupils and their parents that they would not be shot if they moved twenty yards from their own area. The Troubles engendered this fear of other areas even if, realistically, they would have been as safe there as in their own patch. It was understandable with so much hatred and sectarianism around that this was so. Nevertheless, I remember the frustration I felt when after I had brought a pupil to a placement where he had been warmly welcomed and I knew there was a possibility of a permanent job after school, his mother insisted that he would not be safe and terminated the post. The fact that at least half the workforce came from his area and the firm was in a neutral district didn't alleviate her perceived fear. I could understand the anxiety but it made placement of pupils very difficult.

An additional problem was the 'wise uncle' syndrome. More than once after I had arranged work experience a boy would explain to me that he was telling his uncle about it and the latter implied that he was 'a mug for even thinking about it'. 'Work experience is a scam. It's just a way for the bosses to get something for nothing. You do a full day's work and they don't have to pay you anything.'

It was sometimes true that, despite my briefing outlining the purpose and requirements in the work experience scheme, there were employers who abused it. It was seen as unpaid and unskilled labour and little or no training would be given. But over the years I built up a number of dedicated employers in companies that I used continually. One was the owner of a large fruit and vegetable firm who had a real understanding of what was required. He was involved with the Boys' Brigade and being aware of the difficulties a lot of our youngsters faced, was very sympathetic. One of our placements quickly took root there. The first day he started, Packy was sent for 'two orange'. He didn't realise that what was meant was two boxes of oranges. (Why should he?) When he walked down between the vegetable racks holding a single orange in each hand, the other workers mocked him good-humouredly in the normal Belfast 'slegging' vocabulary. To his credit, Packy saw the funny side of it and despite his embarrassment laughed it off. Many another would have 'thrown up the head' and stormed out. After he left school he began work permanently and as I write, has been working there for the past thirty-five years. He was one of the many successes I used to quote to the boys in class.

★

Another success, an ex-pupil from years before I started teaching, arrived up to school one day in a new BMW. The Head introduced me and told me that John had come back looking for some basic reading books as he was, he explained, almost 'totally illiterate'. It transpired that he had an excellent, well-paid job as a sales director in a large distribution firm. He was clearly intelligent but obviously dyslexic. He explained that he bluffed his way through meetings by scribbling an illegible scrawl on a pad that he ensured was never seen by any of his colleagues.

He was married to a nurse and at home he repeated what was said, what he wanted to do and she transcribed his responses. I tried to point out that the reason he was well paid and employed was that he was able to do a difficult job very well. His lack of literacy had obviously not impinged on his success and that maybe he should confide his problem with some of his bosses. He imagined the embarrassment he thought he would face and rejected this. He was terrified of being 'found out'. It was many years before there was a universally accepted appreciation that a serious literacy problem or dyslexia could be unrelated to either intelligence or ability. In that sense things became easier through time.

★

There were a number of government training courses, most of which could be described as woeful, disgraceful, ineffectual and a sponge for the large amounts of money being thrown at low-income urban areas. The British government believed the massive political dysfunction that was Northern Ireland could be dealt with by providing meaningless courses to the rioting youths – the 1970s equivalent of the proletariat eating cake. I once had a group of fourteen pupils being shown around a 'training scheme' in West Belfast. Overseeing the scheme was a good-looking but totally inadequate female 'supervisor'. As we passed through the different sections she was subjected to the crudest sexual innuendoes by her charges. I could feel the eyes of my boys on me wondering why I wasn't saying anything, but it wasn't my place. She was embarrassed but was also powerless to do anything about it. In each section there would be a number of bored-looking teenagers lying over benches smoking. The supervisor would appear from another room and inform us that they were on a tea break. The bill for that beverage must have been considerable because over the course of the next two hours, everyone appeared to be on a tea break. Again I was aware of my boys looking at me, perhaps expecting me to bring some form of order. Then, suddenly, we were in a room where one supervisor had a group of twenty or more youngsters working assiduously at leather making. There were belts and skirts being produced at a phenomenal rate and the place was buzzing with activity. There was a radio playing music and a number of the group were singing along with the songs. I asked the supervisor how many he had in the class. His eyes twinkled as he said, 'About eight on the roll, but sure the others just wander in. I don't mind,' he added somewhat unnecessarily.

It was such a contrast to the other rooms where a few sad efforts of craft were displayed under a two – or three-year-old covering of dust. It was galling to see the evident waste of money when teachers were annually balancing their meagre requisition totals. The amount of money that was needlessly thrown at the political problem was clearly demonstrated when a friend in a government commerce department rang me and asked me did I know any local business that needed £3,000. It had to be given to the West Belfast area and it had to be given out before the weekend or it would be returned to the English Exchequer. When I answered 'No', he thought for a while and tentatively asked had I ever considered opening up a little business!

In the late 1970s we and two other 'special' schools approached the local college of further education (known then as the 'tech') with a view to allowing our pupils to take part in the job sampling courses that were offered to most secondary schools. The courses comprised bricklaying, joinery, basic electrics, plumbing and painting. The session comprised one morning or afternoon a week. We met with the Vice-Principal and one of his senior tutors. They greeted us with all the warmth and understanding that one would expect if the local National Front asked to stay in your house for the next year and would you mind supplying the drink?

Their 'No!' could not have been more emphatic.

There was no way, they protested, that their staff could be subjected to the sort of anarchy and destruction that our 'type of pupil' threatened. They had, they said, enough problems with the pupils currently attending from a number of 'normal' secondary schools.

Fortunately, some weeks after, the matter came to the attention of a sympathetic Department of Education inspector, who despite his mild exterior strongly reminded the college of their responsibilities and also, presumably, about the source of their funding. I would have loved to have been a fly on the wall. Another meeting was arranged and a somewhat chastened college leadership decided that providing one teacher from each school attended with five pupils each, they would allow us to partake of their unrivalled expertise. This was in stark contrast to other schools where entire groups of fifteen or sixteen boys attended with a single member of staff. However, it was a 'foot in the door'.

This involved restructuring our timetables back at school only as far as the time when I had been previously free to organise careers guidance was now spent at the tech. We each picked five exemplary pupils and began the course. It was obvious that initially the tutors were as nervous and uncertain as a diver being told to play with a great white and teach it the basics of chess. It was galling to realise how misinformed they and most of the outside world were about the type of pupil we had. Of course we had our difficult pupils and some of them could be seriously problematic but we were confident that our boys (or, at least, the group we had taken) were as keen, capable and disciplined as any other. We were told that the teachers usually went to the staffroom while the class was being taken but we were determined that we would remain and ensure a trouble-free period. We needn't have worried. Our boys were super. They took part in everything and worked cheerfully and competently. There was a fifteen-minute break and we allowed the boys to go to the canteen and mix with the others. I could feel the increased confidence in their swagger as they came back and their excitement that there were girls around from other schools. It was also one of the few opportunities that many of the boys from the three schools had to mix with pupils from a different religious and political background. Watching fifteen boys laying bricks was marginally more exciting than watching daisies grow so I brought my jeans and old clothes with me and took part with the rest. I learned a lot and found the different experiences new and exciting. I also learned the frustration of cleaning bricks and knocking down a wall that one had just spent the best part of two hours building. We also discovered that the behaviour of a number of the 'normal school' pupils was well below ours.

This was due, in no small part, to the fact that the greater number of teachers 'dumped' their pupils shortly after they arrived and headed for the staffroom. The following year I took the entire class and offered to be with them the entire time. This time they leapt on my offer eagerly. One of the staff confided to me that he and his colleagues had found the sessions with our boys a pleasure and their enthusiasm was in contrast to a number of other sessions. 'Never mind a special school,' he confided. 'They should be locked up in the bloody zoo.'

Together with some of their staff we devised new courses in basic household tasks, such as how to wire up a plug, change a tap washer, and rethread a copper pipe, etc. We learned how to make impressive glass etchings and I still have a glass chessboard etched with Chinese maidens in opposite corners. The Thursday afternoon tech sessions became quickly established as part of the curriculum.

Possibly of greatest benefit was the sense of normality that the boys experienced mixing with their peer group from other schools and you could almost smell the hormone level rise as they talked awkwardly to the girls. Not wishing to deplete their chances, they would assert confidently that they attended either a local secondary school or 'St Cuthbert's Academy'.

*

The confidence stakes increased hugely when on one visit, we were shown the catering department of the local technical college where aspiring Jamie Olivers were trained. Each Thursday the public, if they were members, could enjoy a superb meal for a heavily subsidised fee. I could see Joe's eyes light up at this. On the way back he and a few others asked if I could arrange a meal for them. The entreaties resumed the next morning so eventually I said I would try. I had got on well with the supervisor but when I talked to him, his enthusiasm for the proposal was less than heartfelt. He had obvious concerns. I assured him that I would only send four of the pupils and they would be individually coached and threatened. He agreed reluctantly while I thought carefully about the four potential gourmets.

'OK! It's arranged but there are a number of conditions. First it's a one-off and they'll only allow four of you. So we'll pick them by ballot.'

The ballot was rigged. There was a not inconsiderable risk in letting some of my more 'active' boys loose on this trip. Surprise! Surprise! The four lucky winners just happened to be the four most mature and sensible pupils. (Any teacher, worthy of the name, knows how to rig a ballot!)

I held them back for a minute before the class went to their craft classes. I didn't want the event to be the cause of jealousy among the others. I wanted to establish a few pointers without being over serious… it was after all supposed to be an enjoyable occasion.

'You've got to be well dressed and clean. Think of it as if you've got a really good-looking date and you want to impress. I don't want you to let me down and more importantly, I don't want you to let yourselves down.

'No picking your nose, burping, farting or otherwise acting the clown. Don't nick the cutlery or tell the chef you've eaten better jam sandwiches.

'Don't all fall in love with the same waitress. I'll get the bus tickets and you'll travel there and back on your own. Agreed? And one last thing, don't start bumming to the others that you were picked and they weren't… if you do your invite will be scrubbed.'

At the agreed date my four stars arrived in school dressed impeccably. They looked like four young men heading for their university freshers' day. Tommy and Billy had resurrected suits last seen at a family wedding while Joe and Michael sported neat jackets, shirts and ties. After congratulating them on their appearance and giving them their bus tickets, I slipped Michael some money for orange juice and they headed off for their big meal.

I was as nervous as they were. Although I knew they were sensible lads there was always the possibility of something going wrong. Throughout the lunch period I resisted the temptation to phone my friend in the college and find out how things were going. I needn't have worried.

The next day they were full of it. They had really enjoyed the meal and the whole episode had left them proud and confident. They described the meal in detail and what the waitresses were like and how they were the youngest people there. The rest of the clientele were 'auld guys and auld dames'. After school that day my friend rang me. He confirmed that they had behaved impeccably and appeared to have enjoyed the meal thoroughly. There was just a short hesitation before he added, 'They ordered a bottle of wine from one of the girls. She didn't realise they were underage. God knows they didn't look it. They had finished half of it [not much between four] before I spoke to them quietly but they said that you had agreed it would be OK. I wasn't sure but I just left it.'

'I think that's what I would have done,' I said.

I never commented on it to any of the dinner guests.

An Alphabet for the Students of St Cuthbert's

A is for ASSUMPTIONS…the mother of all cock-ups!

Jono was a bright boy who came from one of the most violent areas in the city. Although bright, he wasn't actually thirsting for knowledge but acquired it in much the same way as he got his freckles… they just happened. I remember my surprised delight when he came to me one morning before class and asked confidentially, 'Sir, can we learn Irish?'

I smiled smugly to myself. Just as I thought; provide the right sort of supportive and caring environment; show them the benefits of learning and they will come to see education as something to be embraced.

'Well, we'll certainly do our best. And don't worry, I'm sure there are one or two others who would like to learn as well. Unfortunately Jono, I only have a few basic phrases in Irish but my wife speaks it fluently. So, if you like, I'll ask her for some simple phrases like 'Good morning; how are you? What time is it? Would you like a drink? We could start off with things like that?'

He looked doubtful and slightly unsure. 'Not… really,' he hesitated.

'What sort of things, then?' I asked.

'I was thinking more of things like, "Left, Right, About Turn, Quick March, Shoulder Arms"!'

The penny dropped. 'Don't think she would know those ones, Jono.'

Poor Jono later ended up spending eight years in the Maze prison… presumably with some of his more fluent comrades.

★

In the late 1960s I and another teacher, from our equivalent state (Protestant) school, ran a night class for ex-pupils. Despite the fact that we were living in an increasingly bitter and dangerous sectarian war, the boys mixed well. We offered basketball, football, woodwork and a general 'open for anything' class. This would often consist of filling in official forms or explaining the intricacies of the social welfare system. It wasn't a sign of maturity but rather a fear of launching into a 'what aboutery' session that politics and religion were avoided. About the only time I remember religion being mentioned was during one of the latter sessions when Harry, an ex-pupil asked me to help with a form for 'the dole'.

'I thought you were working, Harry,' I said.

'Ach! I was but I lost the job.'

'What happened?'

'I hit a fella.'

'Well, that was a bit daft. Why did you do that?'

'He called me a Fenian bastard.'

'Harry,' I reproached, 'I'm surprised at you. You should realise there are better ways of dealing with problems. You should have gone and told the foreman. He's the one person that could have sorted it out.'

Harry stared at me momentarily as if I had lost the plot.

'He was the fucking foreman!' he protested.

★

Part of the curriculum at that time involved me taking my class and half of another senior class to the swimming pool. We were allocated the small pool at the city's Ormeau Baths. It became obvious fairly early on, that given I had roughly twenty to twenty-eight pupils, the facilities were too small. At that time the priorities of the attendant (it was before the days of swimming instructors) were to ensure that we exited on time, didn't make too much of a mess and behaved like well-behaved citizens should. The notion that he could actually help in instructing or supervising appeared a novel one which he never quite adopted. He was, however, keen to ensure that none of the boys drowned and to aid this, he would insist that we leave the pool at least five minutes before the allotted time. Obviously the shorter time they were in the pool the safer they would be! When I realised that this was done so that he could have an extended break I became increasingly loathe to ask the boys to leave. When he would blow his whistle I would ignore it and shout loudly to the boys that there were only a couple of minutes left. Our relationship became fractious.

I contacted the education board and spoke to the person in charge of sports provision. Explaining that the pool was too small for the size and numbers of pupils, I asked if there was any other facility available. I was delighted when he returned my call and said that there was a free period, almost twice as long, in the Falls Centre. He pointed out that unfortunately there would not be a pool attendant available and if I accepted the offer I would be responsible. I was a keen swimmer and held the bronze medallion in lifesaving so I was happy enough to agree. To some, reading this today, in our health and safety culture, the agreement appears incredible but, in my innocence or naivety, I was delighted to accept. At that time I would have taken boys to the seaside and cheerfully accompanied them into the water. I remember swimming (or in some cases running in briefly) in the last week of October and at least some of us had a customary April Fool's ducking.

My two concerns were unrelated to swimming. In the event that a pupil was behaving particularly badly, I regretfully had to deny him swimming. This was always done on the basis of: 'Paddy, we have a problem. Three times this week you've been very reluctant to do what I've asked you to do. Basically I can't trust you to do what I say. In the class if you don't do what I want, it's a pain in the butt and it might drive me mad but it's not the end of the world. But in the swimming pool if you don't do what I ask you to it might result in somebody getting into serious danger or even drowning. So, I'm sorry, big man, but you can't go… not until you show me you can do what I ask.'

Withholding swimming, football or any other activity was commonly practiced by teachers as a punishment but to me that was completely illogical. It made the activity an optional one. It also put the teacher in an awkward situation whenever a pupil didn't want to take part. One envisioned a situation where at the same time an eager pupil was told he was not going because he had misbehaved while another less enthusiastic pupil was being ordered to go because 'he had to'. I remember trying to convince another teacher that forbidding a pupil to undertake an activity he enjoyed put that activity in the 'exceptional activity' bracket. Would he, for example, deny a pupil an English or Maths class because of bad behaviour? I won't deny that there may have been a degree of cunning subterfuge in my approach.

My other concern was that the journey from the school to the new venue would necessitate crossing the 'Peaceline' – surely the biggest misnomer to come out of the Troubles? The seriousness of one or more of the pupils shouting something or giving a two-fingered salute could not be underestimated. A number of our school buses were not infrequently attacked and heavily stoned on their journey to school. I was fairly confident in my control but I was wary of the potential danger. As we crossed the solidly Loyalist Shankill Road I stood at the front of the bus, maintaining eye contact with as many of the likely suspects as possible. Any singing, gestures, obscenities, holding up oranges, Celtic shirts, etc. could have provoked a riot. Football shirts and oranges were forbidden but short of manacling hands and taping mouths there was always going to be a risk. Aside from these ongoing concerns, the swimming sessions went very well.

Apart from two boys the rest were all competent swimmers. Some of them were very good swimmers indeed. Each year there was an inter-schools swimming gala and it was a matter of great pride to win the schools' shield. The one point I emphasised each time was that on no account was anyone to pretend that he was in difficulty in the pool. I spent most of my time patrolling the sides or organising races and so on. Every so often I would dive in and place five pennies along the bottom blue line. Boys would then follow me and, without surfacing, follow the line up the pool and pick up the coins. Anyone that wished could join the game.

I was standing beside the pool when I became aware of Gerard standing beside me looking intently at the coin game. 'Can I have a go, Sir?'

I was slightly puzzled by his uncertain look. I knew him to be a strong swimmer.

'Of course you can, Gerry.'

He continued to watch and then asked me again. I repeated my permission and he took his place in the queue. The boy who picked up the coins had to replace them somewhere on the line. Gerard's turn came and he made a graceful swallow dive, surfaced and immediately began thrashing his hands and spluttering. I was angry, surprised and disappointed that someone who was normally such a good pupil would break one of the cardinal rules.

'Gerry! Out right now!... Out of the pool...You were warned about messing about like that. Get out and get dressed,' I shouted.

Gerry continued to thrash and I quickly realised this wasn't a performance but a genuine problem. I quickly reached the long safety pole to him, which he promptly grabbed and I brought him to the bank. We helped him out and he looked both shocked and embarrassed. I got some towels and as he dried himself off, I reassured him. I was puzzled.

'What happened, Gerry, did you swallow water?'

'No!... I guess I panicked.'

It was a surprisingly mature assessment.

'But you're a terrific swimmer,' I protested.

'Yeah!' he acknowledged.

'And I remember we taught you how to dive.'

'Yes,' he conceded. 'But I've never done that before.'

'Done what?'

'Dived into the water and started swimming.'

It transpired that Gerry indeed was both a competent diver and a competent swimmer but he had never actually dived into deep water and started swimming. His entries before had involved a dive into the shallow end, standing to establish the depth and then swimming. His aquatic accomplishments had all been achieved but as Eric Morecombe might have said, 'Not necessarily in the right order!' However, after a few basic lessons, he graduated to submariner number one.

★

One ex-pupil, Peter, who became a paramedic, told me about one great assumption he made and lived to regret. I've heard a similar story from others but he was adamant it happened to him. He and his colleague had to transport an elderly lady to hospital for out-patient therapy. On entering her house, after the customary chat she pointed to a large jar of peanuts.

'If you like peanuts, son,' she offered, 'help yourself.'

This he duly did and then drove the lady to hospital. Some hours later they were detailed to make the return journey. Arriving home, expressing her gratitude she told them to take away the entire jar of nuts.

'Don't you like nuts?' enquired Peter.

'Ach son!' she answered, opening wide a cavernous mouth 'Sure I have no teeth. I just suck the chocolate off!'

Peter has never eaten nuts since.

B is for the BULLY

The Principal sought me out one afternoon after school. He asked if I would consider taking a pupil called Harry into the class. He was only fourteen but was very big for his age and was constantly in trouble. He was bullying a lot of the other boys in the class and had already been suspended a number of times. His reputation had preceded him and the entire school knew him as a serious and, let's be honest, hateful nuisance. He rejoiced in his nickname of 'Rocky' but because of his size and reputation, he rarely got any takers and missed the chance to emulate his hero. The boss thought that placing him in with my bigger boys might settle him.

It was a long shot. I wasn't keen on the idea for a number of reasons. I thought that in a perverse way his move might be seen as a reward and it meant that he would be with me for nearly two and a half years. We were both assured that if he didn't settle down, he would be expelled from the school and given home tuition. I knew he had been fostered and I knew his parents slightly as they lived near me. Additionally, I was probably vain enough to view him as a challenge so reluctantly

I agreed. I also, at that time, had probably the most mature and supportive class I'd ever had. He was to start with me the following Monday.

The next day the rumour mill had been fully cranked and was operational.

'Is it true, Sir, is Rocky McKerney coming into this class?'

The tone of the queries indicated incredulity, some fear and a general agreement that a tea and buns welcome wasn't on the cards. Normally I would not have commented on any prospective arrival but two or three of the smaller boys were clearly worried. At the end of our morning RE lesson I gathered them around the desk.

'Listen and listen carefully. What's happening is Harry McKerney is coming here to see how he gets on. We'll treat him just the same as everyone else. Maybe he's got problems like the rest of us. At any rate just remember we're all different. I didn't exactly like the idea of some of you balloons coming in here and you turned out all right. So, we agree, OK? He comes in here the same as everyone else.'

Monday came and Harry presented himself at the front door of the mobile. I tried to warm to him but I was less than effusive. Shaking hands I gave him the usual spiel about how the class worked: what was acceptable and what wasn't and how this could well be his last chance. I told him I knew his reputation was that he was prone to getting into fights but that was something I wouldn't stand for. In truth it was unlikely to be a problem as there were already a number of 'hard men' in the class. As a boy I had been bullied in primary school by another pupil and in secondary school I, and many others, were bullied by staff. I made no distinction in the distaste I felt for either. Years later we were told that bullying involved two victims. Educational psychologists told us that compassion, understanding and help had to be doled out in equal measure to the bully and the bullied. I accept that there can be a number of factors but I never could embrace that philosophy or the general thesis that man was the sole product of external influences. I still believe in free will and taking responsibility for one's actions. I actively disliked bullies. As Inspector Barlow, a detective on the old television programme *Z Cars* said years ago, 'There was no psychology when I was growing up!'

I briefly introduced him to the class and showed him our method of working. I got him sorted with his programme and was not altogether surprised to discover he had an agile intelligence and was well above average ability for the class. At break time I explained our tea routine and told him to bring in his own teacup or mug the following day. Francie gave him a cup of tea and a biscuit and he sat quietly drinking, cautiously evaluating the actions of the others. It was noticeable that no one went near him so I approached him and told him that I knew he was a smoker and if he wanted a smoke, he would have to use the toilet before our break was over.

For three days he worked diligently and his confidence and cockiness grew. I treated him very correctly and I could see his confusion when I would laugh and joke with some of the others but still kept him at a distance. I needed him to realise that to become fully accepted he had, along with everyone else, to prove himself. Nevertheless I was well satisfied with the progress so far. My smugness was instantly shattered on the Wednesday afternoon.

As he was too young to travel with tokens, Harry travelled on one of the school buses. Each bus was under the initial supervision of a teacher whose job was to settle them into their seats and before leaving, ensure that at least the first hundred yards would be reasonably civilised. After that it was up to the bus supervisor. Harry was on my bus and as I came down I saw him sitting with his feet up on the seat opposite. I didn't make a hanging offence out of it but merely said, 'Right Harry, take your feet off the seat… people have to sit on that.'

I sensed a hardness in his look and moved on down the bus, not wanting him to be seen to submit too readily. However, coming back up it was obvious a challenge was coming.

'Come on, Harry. Stop messing and get your feet down.'

'Why?' he asked belligerently.

I hardened my voice. 'I've given you a reason but the main one is because I told you to.'

He sat in a sullen silence with the feet still across.

I leant down. I was giving him every chance to save face in front of an ever quietening audience. I whispered to him, 'Harry this is going to end up in trouble if you don't do what I'm telling you.'

He looked up at me and with a cold sneer said, 'Sure, you can do fuck all.'

There was a collective gasp from the rest of the pupils and the escort. I was furious but took a second to formulate a response. 'I'll show you what I can do,' I said with emphasis. 'Don't you come into school until next Monday and, when you do, bring your father.'

The Principal travelled home on the school bus and as I was getting off, he was coming on.

'Terry, I'm sorry but Harry's only after telling me to "F off". I know I really don't have the authority but I'd rather he wasn't picked up again until Monday and then only when his father comes with him.'

'That's fine. I'll keep an eye on him on the way home.'

As I walked back to the mobile I bristled with anger.

The following morning I was amazed to see him arrive in as usual. He was quiet and unsure. He followed me at a distance back to the mobile. I stopped and waited for him to catch up.

'I don't know where you think you're going, Harry, but you're certainly not coming in here. You may go and sit in the office.'

He turned and walked away.

I discovered that, unfortunately, the Principal hadn't been on the bus that morning.

We were at our 'round the desk religion' session the following day when there was a knock at the mobile door. Francie opened it and said, 'Rocky McKerney says he wants to talk to you, Sir.'

'His name's Harry, not Rocky,' I said and went out to find a contrite-looking Harry.

'Mr Gordon said I have to apologise and say that I'm going to behave myself.'

'Tell you what, Harry, you go and tell the Principal that it's not up to him. I told you Monday – and Monday with your father!'

At break-time I went over to the office and confronted the boss.

'Terry, there's no way I can ever get his respect if I'm seen to change my mind.'

I explained again the situation and my feelings.

'That's fine,' he tried to mollify me. 'I didn't realise it was that serious!'

Harry's father, Harry and myself had a long talk the following Monday and the necessary actions and behaviour were promised. It took the best part of the next three months for Harry to become a real part of the class. I couldn't have effected the change without the behaviour and support of the rest of the class. The biggest persuader for Harry was pupil power. There was more kudos and satisfaction from being accepted and even admired than by being ostracised.

I had him in my class for the next year and a half until I was made Principal. It was June when the appointment was made.

Some of the boys who were returning in September were concerned when they knew I would no longer be teaching them. It seemed a long time from the incident where he told me to 'fuck off' when Harry stopped me at the end of the day and asked, 'Does that mean you won't be teaching us next year?' I noticed with some disbelief that his eyes were filling up.

'Well, not all the time, but I'll still be around. I mean I'll see you every day. I'll even try to take some classes every day. Sure if I didn't see your ugly mug every day I'd think I'd died and gone to heaven.'

He didn't smile. 'It won't be the same.' He walked away and didn't look back.

C is for CUNNING

While on paper many of our pupils were considered intellectually weak, there were many instances where they displayed an ability to think outside the box.

Years later, as Principal, I was walking out with the senior boys at lunchtime to have our daily diet of handball when we stopped to examine a new, very flashy red sports car. It had been just bought by one of the female staff. With me was Henry, a pleasant enough pupil but with a penchant for finding himself in stolen cars.

'That one will stump boys like you,' I joked. 'It's loaded with all sorts of safety... electronic keys, anti-theft locks, all sorts of alarms.'

'Naw!' he scorned. 'They're dead easy. What you do is climb onto the roof and jump down hard on the bonnet. That automatically inflates the airbags and the doors open immediately. You just get in and cut away the airbags with a knife, hot wire it and drive off.'

I never actually put this to the test but it struck me as being entirely feasible.

'You know, if you used your brains honestly, you'd probably finish up a millionaire rather than ending up in casualty with your knees in plaster or worse, being in a car that kills someone.'

'Oh I don't do that anymore,' he protested. 'I'm just saying that's what the "hoods" do.'

★

Another teacher reported on another slice of cunning when she was chatting to a pupil who had just returned from a holiday in New York. She was surprised, as she knew the family to be less than well off.

'We got a cheap flight,' he continued. 'We stayed in a big hotel at a very cheap price.'

She continued her probing. 'Was the food not very expensive in the hotel?'

'Well, what you do, Miss, is you watch for someone who is leaving their room… someone with a coat on, which shows they're going out. Then you ring room service and order a meal and give them that room number. You tell them that you'll be having a shower and to just knock the door and leave it outside. As soon as it's delivered you pick it up and bring it back to your room. When you're finished you just leave the tray outside someone else's door!'

★

An ex-pupil who used to visit us regularly was working in a factory in Belfast that produced car parts and did minor repairs. We were delighted at his success and it was great to see his pride in his job and his wages. On one visit he told us sadly that the factory was going to close and all the workers were being laid off. I was surprised as well as saddened, as it was commonly believed that the factory was thriving.

'That's a shock, John,' I commiserated. 'You'll certainly miss the job – not to mention the wages.'

'Yeah!' he agreed sadly. 'And the perks.'

'What perks?' I queried.

'Well, every week we put away so many tools, bits of socket sets, spanners and so on. Every month we would have gathered a full set of tools, which we would sell. You would get about £80 or so, more if you were lucky. We shared that out.'

He quickly detected my disapproval.

'Everybody did it,' he protested.

'Don't you realise John, that what you've done is steal yourself out of a job?'

'Well, it wasn't only me,' he claimed defensively. 'We all did it.'

The candour with which information like that was shared showed that somewhere between home, school and work the notion of honesty had been misplaced. It was difficult not to have sympathy for him. A young man at the beginning of his working life would have found himself ostracised, or worse, had he refused to participate in the illegal 'fringe benefits'. Another ex-pupil allowed himself to be talked into hiding an expensive crate of fruit. His more practiced Fagins ensured that when he was caught, little risk attached to them.

★

It was important to develop a trust between us. Often I would give someone the keys to my car and tell them to fetch something. I used to keep the tea money in a tin in my desk and it was never locked. Often I would hear boys asking for change for their tea and I would send them to the desk without any supervision. My jacket with loose change in the pocket would hang over my chair. Often I would buy a packet of sweets and give them to the first table, telling them to take one and 'pass them on'.

I remember one occasion when Francie, with a white, alarmed face, reported that the money had been stolen from the tea-money tin. The class immediately fell silent and I could feel their eyes boring into me. I went to my jacket and got my car keys.

'Harry, do me a favour and go to the car. There's some change in the little recess beside the gear stick. I think there might be about a pound there. Bring it round.'

When the break was over I asked Francie and Joe to try and work out how much was stolen.

Part of the success of our morning tea routine was that each week, pupils were rotated to count up the takings and enter them in the 'Tea Ledger'. They estimated about £2.

Counting the money Harry brought from the car and adding some from my jacket, I made a show of giving it to Francie to replenish the missing money.

'It's my fault,' I sighed. 'I should have kept a closer eye on it but I thought I could trust everybody. It looks like I was wrong. I just hope that whoever did it is sorry that he did it and that he decides never to steal again. At the end of the day we have to be honest with each other and that means not cheating or stealing. I have to trust you in the same way as the boss has to trust me. Christmas is coming up. There are some lovely new books in the store, packets of lovely coloured markers, gummed paper, paint sets, etc. No one would know if I decided to bring some of that stuff home for my children for Christmas. It would save me a few quid but who would I be stealing from? The Education and Library Board? The Principal? The people like your mums and dads that pay their taxes?

'Well yes, yes, from all of them. But more than any of them I would be stealing from you, and if you respect people you don't treat them like that.'

Every time an opportunity occurred to instil a sense of self-worth and self-respect I grabbed it and played it out. As the class went back to work, Jim leant over and said, 'Here endeth the lesson. You reminded me there of one of those old-time religion preachers… you know – the type you always try and avoid!'

D is for DISCIPLINE

Over the years I thought more about discipline than any other area of education. Any teacher visiting a class will, almost immediately, be aware of the quality of the relationship between teacher and pupil. It requires little skill to determine if that relationship is healthy, productive and respectful.

The success of any class ultimately depends on discipline. I came to realise that the most effective form was one that was agreed and enforced by the pupils. You set the rules and if you knew your job the rules were just and, equally important, feasible. Within the class one had all sorts of abilities, levels of understanding, maturity and intelligence. It wasn't a 'one-set-fits-all' scenario but because you were trusted and respected and just as importantly liked, things would work smoothly. A more mature pupil would come to realise that the gifts that he had could allow him a tolerance of other lesser abilities and more difficult personalities.

Genuine discipline and order is dependent on mutual respect. The class had to buy into it. The more potentially difficult and fractious the personalities within the class, the more critical this is. Fear of sanctions or pressures generated by examinations wasn't a factor.

It's important to distinguish between control and discipline. A group or individual is only controlled when it reacts within the guidelines laid down by another. Control often means that once the presence of the overseer is removed, the control vanishes. Paul Newman's chain gang in *Cool Hand Luke* could be said to be under control but I don't think the appellation of 'disciplined' applied. It struck me often that to be successful with the variety of pupils we had, there had to be a genuine reciprocal regard for each other. If you were able to achieve that mutual friendship and affection then the greatest weapon one had in maintaining discipline was the withdrawal of that easy friendship. There were times when a pupil would annoy me so much that I would drop the humour and banter and resort to a very correct, formal approach. It was much more effective than shouting or screaming.

If the class had bought into the ethos, the greater controller of behaviour was the boys themselves. They had to believe that I was totally on their side and anyone that threatened that productive coexistence was an annoyance to them as much as it was to me. If a number of boys were unsettled in class when they were supposed to be actively engaged in something I would pick on the worst offender and ask him to be quiet.

'Listen Harry, you're keeping Paddy and the rest back from their work. If you want to waste your time and mine then put your head down and go to sleep, but don't keep anybody else back.'

It mattered little if 'Paddy and the rest' were as disengaged as Harry. It was always 'You are disturbing the rest': never 'You're keeping me back!' Within seconds the others, (who may have been doing as little as my selected culprit) would nod their heads wisely in agreement, view the victim with annoyance and go at their tasks with a will.

Older pupils are adept at distinguishing generosity from bribery. They would enthusiastically accept all the bribes but that guaranteed nothing. I remember one teacher complaining bitterly that he had brought in buns that his wife had cooked and after they had been distributed there was a near riot in his class. He only lasted a short time in the school. The teacher's 'If you do what I tell you then you'll get a treat' can quickly become the class's 'If we don't get a treat then watch out!'

I learnt that in any confrontation with a pupil, it was important to remove the audience factor. Any satisfactory result depended upon avoiding putting a pupil in a situation where he felt obliged to defend his actions loudly: avoiding a loss of face, a firm but quiet admonition was enough to pour oil on the water. But there would always be the occasion when this wasn't going to work. Then it was a matter of temporary exclusion.

'Jimmy, you've been acting the clown long enough and now you're really starting to become a pain in the rear. Look, before both of us get too worked up about it why don't you go outside the room and take a breather until we've both calmed down?'

It was always understood that this 'invitation' was more of an order than a request but the decision to return was always his. When he did he would whisper an apology and normal service would be resumed. I always feigned great interest in some task when such a miscreant would re-enter so that the matter didn't require an abject surrender. My father once described the exasperatingly inquisitional manner of another teacher as the Yeames 'When did you last see your father?' syndrome.

As I understand it, this temporary exclusion is now forbidden. In those days of our splendid isolation it was a valuable ploy. I was, after all, teaching boys who in a few months would be expected to cope with the discipline required by a working environment. The sooner they learnt the constrictions imposed by both work and society the better.

E is for ENVIRONMENT

I imagine that it is quite possible for learning to take place in a sterile classroom. However I could never understand why it should have to. In my opinion, classroom walls had another purpose other than defining the limits of the room or holding up the ceiling. They were there to be covered with examples of pupils' work; photographs, graphs, pictures, thoughts, ideas, cartoons, etc. I had little respect for teachers who, on being told that an inspection was imminent, became engrossed in covering what had been previously bare walls. It said little for their appreciation of what teaching is supposed to be about, but a lot about their laziness and hypocrisy. To me blank walls in a classroom indicated a total lack of commitment and a disinterest in the education process. I wonder do they display their own child's work at home? Are their fridges, walls and cupboards totally in pristine shop condition? To me the classroom environment had to proclaim 'interesting', even 'odd' and 'quirky'. I've seen some excellent examples of this with other teachers where, for example, there was a fascinating display of the contents of an owl's pellets and another, in a different school where a full skeleton was on display. The teacher had a brother, a doctor, and had borrowed the visual aid for a couple of weeks. I had two fish tanks, one for display and the other for breeding. (That's sex education taken care of!) It had a poem above it:

> *'Cats have kittens, dogs have puppies*
> *But guppies just have little guppies.'*

The room was also large enough to allow a number of plants, some of which were winter refugees from my garden. We also took a number of cuttings and planted seeds that, if and when they developed, the boys took home.

As the oldest class, we were involved in the mini-enterprise scheme operated by the local education board. For a couple of months every year the class made candles and plaster of Paris models that were painted and then varnished. It was time-consuming so a couple of different boys each morning would work at it. Every May we would sell them off to staff and pupils and the proceeds would go to increase our resources.

The entire wall was devoted to the ongoing tests and scores, which led to the Record of Achievement. Any boy could see immediately how he was doing and knew where to get the sheets that he had not completed. It meant that for a considerable length of the school day, everyone was working independently and the sheet was marked on their ability. We also had a large map of Ireland where boys would bring in postcards from home and we would stick them near to the card location. One year we had an enthusiastic girl who was a student in the art college doing teaching practice with us. In the absence of available wall space involving other projects, we decided to cover the ceiling with a representation of the sky at night. This involved splattering large black sheets of manila with white paint but there were a number of boys who actually found constellations in an encyclopaedia and copied them accurately. However, their haphazard positioning would have caused great angst for Patrick Moore.

Each of the different areas of class routine involved rotating the responsibility for maintaining them in some sort of order. Duties included: filing and distributing the test sheets, responsibility for the cupboard keys, feeding the fish, maintaining the toilets, watering the plants, organising the games, buying the biscuits, looking after the tea money, washing the cups, etc. All were designed to give joint ownership of the class ethos. The only task not rotated was Francie's ritual tea making. We all realised that he had an exemplary talent in this respect.

Slogans such as 'Welcome to Class H' and 'Today is the first day of the rest of your life' may have been clichéd but they helped to develop a genuine pride in 'our classroom'. Just occasionally this sense of ownership became excessively protected – particularly so in the case of Kieran. He was a small, undernourished boy with dirty fair hair over a dirty fair face. He spent a lot of his day looking through the window despite my exhortations and encouragement to do something. In a previous life he must have been a sailor who had been posted in the crow's nest to warn of apparent enemies. Perched on his desk he would shout out at the approach of any visitor from the main school as if they threatened our existence. He just about tolerated other pupils but he viewed the impending arrival of any adult with loathing and abuse. This was always done audibly but not loudly, almost as an aside to himself. Frequently I would have to tell him to be quiet. It worked for about a minute, when he would look up, say 'Sorry Sir!' before he continued his obscene abuse at the intruder. This would take the form of 'What the fuck does he want over here… nosey bastard… here he comes now… the big shite.' This particularly applied to the Principal who would be greeted with a litany of muttered obscenities referring to human genitalia and repeated suggestions that he was a less than clean, illegimate son of a loose woman's melt! These comments were essentially made to himself and years later, when I first heard about it, I became convinced he suffered from Tourette's syndrome. Kieran was the classic example of what D. H. Stott, the famous educationalist, described as 'the inconsequent child'. This described a child who failed to reflect on the consequences of responses resulting in impulsive and often inappropriate behaviour. On leaving on the school bus one Monday, Kieran screamed out to his then teacher, 'Fuck off! You baldy bastard.' He appeared both baffled and aggrieved when the same 'baldy bastard' met the bus the following morning intent on some form of retribution.

F is for FISHING

There was always, and still is, something about fishing that intrigues and consumes me. There's a wealth of literature on the subject and a lot of the authors ponder on the nature and cause of the addiction. It might be some deep-rooted primitive, residual gene that comes from our hunter/gatherer existence or a need to bond closely with nature. Whatever the reason, I know of few greater excitements than those instances when a float dips, or a fly line straightens. For a second or so the cause might be a catch that will live in your memory for the rest of your life. There is so much more to fishing than catching fish. To fish for a big sedge-devouring trout in a nervous dark with a million stars winking on the calm water, when the smoothness is only dimpled by a trout sucking down a fly is an experience that will live long in the memory... as was that night in the Glens when, fishing for sea trout, at two o'clock in the morning, I tripped over a sleeping sheep! It was extremely difficult to determine who was the more terrified. Those days when I trekked through the hills to arrive at a small lake with a tired, midge-blistered body only to spring into full alertness and vigour when a trout rose are episodes to be relived and enjoyed years later.

I don't expect or particularly need or want others to understand this, but I do know that if a child is introduced to the sport properly he or she will develop a passion that can enthral them for the rest of their life. Every so often a fishing trip would be arranged and with the help of Jim who agreed to take any surplus pupils, we would head off to Maghery to trot floats down the canal in the pursuit of rudd, roach, perch and gudgeon. I would also take a couple of pike rods. We would bring sandwiches and flasks or bottles of juice. It would be a real adventure, particularly when one considered that a lot of those boys had no experience of life outside the city. I would bring a selection of old rods borrowed or liberated from friends and would spend the better part of the day instructing or, more probably, disentangling lines and repairing reels. The look on a boy's face when he catches his first fish is something that burns bright in the memory.

Damian was a boy from the New Lodge area who had to be persuaded to give fishing a try. I set up the rod and, much to his disgust, nipped a few maggots onto his hook. After an unproductive twenty minutes or so he professed himself 'bored and fed up'. He wanted to go to the local shop but considering factors such as the capacity of his stomach and his ability to gather snacks out of all proportion to the actual money exchanged, I refused. After he sat sulking for a while, I again encouraged him and set up a line.

He sat desultorily with all the enthusiasm of a vegetarian at an abattoir as he watched the float slowly process down the canal. Suddenly the float dipped and Damian had hooked a large perch. It was like a last-minute death row reprieve. Shock, astonishment were followed by excitement as the line zipped from the reel. A list of somewhat less than devout invocations were screamed out. It was obviously a much bigger fish than any caught that day and very quickly the others stopped their fishing and started shouting often contradictory instructions to Damian who was now slobbering, mouth open and fingers tightly holding the rod. His face was a mixture of tense anticipation and anxiety. For the first time in his life he was experiencing the realisation that a fish of perhaps a pound and a quarter could challenge his ability. I coached him carefully and eventually, after perhaps the longest three minutes of his life, he netted the prize. We gathered round to admire it. Lying in the grass with its bright red fins and bronzed scales, an accusing eye failed to melt his heart. It was a lovely perch and Damian was determined to take it home and eat it, or at the very least display it and boast about his expertise in its capture. A fisherman had been born.

Years later as I drove to school early in the morning I would see a much older Damian waiting at a bus stop with his rods and fishing bags heading off for the day to fish at Toome. He did this every Wednesday and it was probably the biggest excitement of the week in a bleak world of bombs, bullets, unemployment and poverty. But for a few hours every Wednesday he was the master of a river, an authority and a power. He could people that world with everything he imagined and every so often, the float would dip and everything was possible.

★

Not everyone became hooked but I don't remember anyone who didn't gain a lot from being exposed to the countryside and its magic. And, of course, there was a multitude of classroom activities that could be built into the activity. I had about twenty worksheets that I concocted, all relating to fishing. Maths was covered by weights of fish, numbers of each species, averages, length and weight, distance travelled, and so on; geography by places visited, shortest routes, nearest, etc. While I knew these in-school follow-ups were useful I did have sympathy with Jimmy, when just before we left on a trip one day he asked me forlornly, 'Does this mean, when we come back, we'll have to do another bloody worksheet?'

Most of all I gained a lot from listening to the boys relating their experiences to each other and like all anglers, before and since, lying sincerely and convincingly about their exploits.

G is for GRATITUDE

Very occasionally the teachers would get gifts; normally only at Christmas but infrequently at other times. The practice has now reached absurd levels where expensive presents are almost seen as obligatory. Thankfully a number of schools have now either discouraged the practice or set sensible levels. In my early years teaching, the most one would get was a bottle of aftershave or a couple of packets of cigarettes. However two exceptions stand out.

Frank was a sixteen-year-old who had a history of petty crime. By the time he was in my class he had been in court a number of times on minor charges. Each day he would cycle to school from home. I was also a keen cyclist and I admired him and encouraged others to do the same. It was only when one of the other boys drew my attention to the fact that every so often he would arrive on a different bicycle that I learnt the true nature of his love of cycling. He would take the bus into town, steal a bicycle, keep it for a week or two and then sell it off to a dealer in Smithfield Market. It was only after his activities were noted by the local paramilitaries that he was persuaded to stop. What they threatened to do to his knees would have prevented walking, never mind cycling.

He was an affable boy who caused no bother in class. One year, a day before the class broke up for the Christmas holidays, a few of the pupils brought me in presents. Frank must have thought he too should provide one. On the last day he arrived in with an electric razor. It wasn't wrapped and one of the other boys mischievously suggested that it was so 'hot' I'd better wear gloves. I thanked him profusely but rarely with such conviction did I tell anyone 'you shouldn't have'. I examined the box after the class left and examined the new razor. Well not quite new, as there were a few hairs attached to the tiny shaving wheels.

As luck would have the EWO (Educational Welfare Officer), Desi, was in the school and I talked to him. I told him the razor was obviously 'nicked' and asked if he could call at the house and delicately explain the situation. Desi was excellent at his job and he knew the last thing I wanted was to get Frank into trouble. I knew he was looked after by his older brother and his wife and having had previous dealings with them, I knew they were understanding and sympathetic. Hopefully they would find out somehow where the razor came from and would get it back to its rightful owner. I phoned Desi the next day to see how he had got on. He was laughing and could hardly contain himself.

'I went to the house and it was answered by the brother. He invited me in and as I was mentally rehearsing my story he apologised for the untidy state of the place, telling me that his wife had given him a new razor for his birthday and he had mislaid the damn thing!'

★

I had at one time a very pleasant boy named Anthony in my class. He was a great worker and very keen on school. So keen, indeed, that at seventeen-and-a-half-years old he returned at the beginning of the school year. I had assumed that he had left and was unsure what else I could do for him. I decided to try and place him in another work experience situation. His last one had been very successful but the firm had closed. One day after school I took him to a local car accessories supplier. The owner talked to me and I explained that apart from literacy difficulties, Anthony was as reliable, hard-working and honest as anyone he could find. He then took Anthony on his own and interviewed him for a full twenty-five minutes. He returned and said, 'Anthony is over the school leaving age isn't he?' I agreed.

'In that case I'll not be offering him work experience… I'm going to take him on full-time.'

I was delighted, as was Anthony. I offered to drive him home so that he could tell his mother the good news. I knew it would be a big relief for her as her husband had recently died suddenly. I explained the situation to her and her delight was evident. As I talked I couldn't fail to notice that she was eyeing me up and down in a rather intimate and rather invasive way.

'Before you go, just wait a minute,' she said.

She disappeared only to re-emerge with a large, heavy, black overcoat.

'It was my husband's,' she explained. 'He only wore it once and it would be a pity to see it go to waste. There's just a wee bit of mud at the back where he collapsed in the street but that will brush off.'

Despite protesting about denying her this last remnant of her husband's wardrobe I was forced to try it on. He must have been a very tall man and it was with relief that it became apparent it would have fitted two of me. With gratitude and regrets that it did not fit me ('What a pity and what a good coat'), I thanked her profusely and left.

★

Sometimes gifts came in strange guises. Years before the Troubles, in the days before health and safety strangled a lot of worthwhile activities, our Mr Murphy sent two boys into town with a list of items to buy for the school garden. The list contained items as diverse as garden shears, plant pots and a soft drink for Mr Murphy's lunch. To the disbelief of the rest of the staff, he gave them a £5 note and instructions on where to buy the items. The general view of the other bemused and cynical staff members was that it was good that Paddy had no particular affection for the fiver or any of its constituent parts, as he was unlikely to see either ever again. That scenario appeared increasingly accurate as the afternoon hours bled into home time. However with ten minutes to the end of the school day, the boys arrived back with every item accounted for. Paddy's relief was somewhat tempered when in addition to the items, one of the boys handed him back the intact £5 note.

'But', stammered Paddy, 'how did you get all this stuff without paying for it?' (As can be seen, Paddy was somewhat naive in the ways of the big city.)

'Don't worry, Sir,' smirked one of the boys. 'It's coming off a broad board.'

H is for HUMOUR

Both Jim and I loved drama and we would often act out different scenarios to the amusement of all. Some of the things we did could be considered slightly insane and in the eyes of many, unprofessional. Often we would indulge in little flights of fancy that owed more to The Goons than any great educator. We shared a madcap sense of humour.

An example of this was when, once at break time, we began a discussion on the possibility of sending an Irish rocket to the moon. I had been doodling with a ballpoint and showing how when the spring was depressed and then released, the pen would jump into the air.

'Essentially all we need is a giant ballpoint pen. An extra large spring replaces the rocket and if we just scale everything up, our penship would gain orbit easily.'

'That's possible all right, but without retro rockets how could we send it into orbit? It would just keep going on and on.'

'What about putting an elephant on board?'

'Well, Professor Snodgrass, the beast would have to be in the bottom otherwise the whole thing would fall over before it was launched and, something you may have overlooked, we would need to get the elephant to get to the top to change the flight path after it leaves the Earth's atmosphere.'

'Bananas.'

'Pardon?'

'Bananas, we tie big bunches of bananas to the inside ceiling of the rocket and when the elephant gets hungry it will climb to the top, tilting the pen into orbit. After it has eaten the bananas it will be heavier and that will tilt the rocket into a descent mode… back to Earth! The entire project will take years, however.'

'To build the rocket?'

'No, that's easy enough but we will have to teach the elephant how to climb stairs!'

'No! We'll employ a circus trainer.'

'Thank God. I was worried for a minute there but you've cracked it, Professor Snodgrass.'

'No problem, it's a pleasure to work with such a genius as yourself, Professor Humdinger.'

That sort of nonsense appealed a lot to most of the class.

Although there were one or two who possibly gave the proposition serious thought. Our banal and sometimes quirky relationship continued outside of school. One summer, on our first family foreign excursion, camping in France, I sent him an elaborate package that contained two corks. He had been complaining of diarrhoea before the school broke up. Later he professed himself mildly amused when he opened the package and found two wine corks and a note explaining the efficacy of the enclosed Dr Humdinger's Patent Diarrhoea Plugs!

★

One of the most pleasing aspects of teaching the older boys was that there was a better understanding and appreciation of the sort of idiosyncratic humour I enjoyed. I was a good mimic and would adopt a different persona at times throughout the day. These flights from reality were, of necessity, brief. One of the characters I adopted was a German officer and in what I fondly imagined to be a German officer's clipped speech, I would stiffly limp (an old war wound… don't ask) about the classroom as the boys worked. If someone had stopped working I would locate the glass lens from my drawer and feigning a monocle, clip my heels together and stand in front of them.

'Agh so! You do not vont to vinish yur vurk, eh? Is not enough that I, Baron Von Kipperhoven, can no longer shoot down ze Englanders because of my vounds but now I hav to look after you svinehunds vile you do zis stupid zings. So! You do not vish to vork?' (I would limp away slowly, considering the problem before returning.)

'Vell, I vill give you a very gud reason for ze vork. If you do not do it I vill have all your fingernails pulled out with a pair of hot pliers.'

Often this would be done just before break so that serious work could continue thereafter! Often the 'performances' would be done to amuse Jim as much as the pupils and he would join in enthusiastically. Another favourite would be John Arlott, the cricket commentator, and as break time approached I would deliver my observations on the classroom activity.

'Good morning, ladies and gentlemen, boys and girls, and welcome to the shed behind the Oval. In the distance I can see that famous fast bowler Tommy "Killer" Henshaw limber up for the tea break. Francie's out of his seat and moving steadily towards the kettle. He's moving with all the sinewy strength of a coiled tea bag. Eddie's out of his seat now and lurching towards the biscuits. Yes I think he's going for the Jaffa Cakes…' etc.

I hesitate to relate the following.

One morning when, having been delayed in the office, I had arrived slightly late Jim began to scold me, asking, 'What time do you think this is? I've had to teach this lot on my own.'

As the class laughed, we engaged in hurling insults at each other and I feigned annoyance.

'That's it! I can't take any more of this. Every day you moan, moan, moan. I've had enough. I'm going to drown myself in the fish tank. Mickey, take the lid off.'

After Mickey somewhat uncertainly removed the lid I climbed onto the desk beside the tank and very slowly and deliberately took off my shoes and socks. As Jim's insults continued I then removed my shirt and vest while the class howled with laughter.

'Go ahead,' said Jim. 'We don't care.'

After more instructions Mickey did indeed remove the lid. This time he looked nervous and anxious. 'Don't do it, Sir,' he pleaded. I dipped my toe in.

'I think I'll wait until it warms up,' I said and redressed.

I remember one or two of the boys with tears of laughter rolling down their cheeks but I dread to think what would have happened had an inspector suddenly appeared to see a teacher standing on a desk dressed only in trousers and threatening to jump into a fish tank! Tommy observed the performance with just a hint of a smile before turning to the class and asking, 'And they think that we're the ones that need help?'

Of course it was done primarily to amuse myself and any others that enjoyed it but it also involved pride that I could act the clown at a minute's notice and still have control a moment later. I was having fun and there was nothing in the rules that said we couldn't enjoy ourselves. These flights from reason often sustained us and hopefully, entertained the class.

After such madcap episodes I just had to say, 'OK that's the craic over for now. Let's get on with our work.'

And they did. I realised that only when you had total

confidence in your relationship could you indulge in antics like that.

*

One of the more onerous duties was lunchtime supervision in the dining centre. The 'outside play' aspect of it was not a problem but trying to establish some semblance of order with fifty-odd pupils in the dining centre was more difficult. The most effective method was to stand with my hand outstretched to begin our 'Grace before Meals' and wait for silence. The dining hall seemed to magnify every noise and even a slight cough appeared to resonate and reverberate from the insipid green walls. One of the biggest problems was the dinner ladies themselves who were under enormous pressure to complete all the sittings within the time allotted. Often we all would wait silently until the banging of saucepans and the splashing of water ceased. On one occasion when total silence had been established, a barely audible drumming started. I looked vainly for the culprit as the tempo became louder and more insistent. I was shocked. I couldn't imagine who had the audacity to openly 'face me down'. Centring in on the tattoo I discovered Danny, one of the most pleasant and amenable boys, clenching his knife and drumming violently on the table. It was with some concern (and some relief) that I saw he was having an epileptic seizure.

On a different occasion another pupil, Paul, began a fight with a fellow diner as they sat at a table in the school canteen. Not to put too fine a point on it Paul was a regular pain in the neck. His fits of temper and violence were all too frequent and I was never totally convinced that he was out of control. I shouted angrily at him and moved towards him to separate him from his fellow combatant. He jumped up and grabbing a dinner knife, screamed some obscenity at me.

I knew that all I had to do was to tell him to put down the

knife and come outside so that we could sort out the problem. He would probably eventually have agreed. But as he screamed and became more abusive, a little bit of the mischievous devil actor entered my soul.

I threw my arms back and crouched in true James Bond style. 'Get back, everybody… he's got a knife!'

There was an immediate reaction as boys scattered out of reach. Paul was dumbfounded. He looked puzzled and confused, standing there with a pathetic bent knife clasped in his hand.

A dinner lady shouted excitedly, 'Jesus Christ! Mr Rooney, be careful.'

Another shouted for one of the boys to run and get the Principal.

By this stage I had got to Paul and grabbing his hand tightly, wrestled him to the floor making sure all the time that he still held the knife.

'Drop the knife Paul,' I commanded in my best Sean Connery impression. 'Drop the knife.'

The fact that Paul was unable to drop the knife as I had my hand clasped firmly round it and the somewhat obvious absurdity that one of our dinner knives could barely make an impression on a slab of butter were lost in the melee. Eventually (employing all my best imaginary kung fu and karate skills) I removed the knife and, safe now from a tragic stabbing, released Paul who sat despondently sobbing on the floor. It was really unfair of me and I apologised afterwards but every so often, a teacher does something they later come to regret.

★

A lot of the unconscious humour in classes is generated by the pupils. Every teacher has his own memories of the schoolboy howlers.

My daughter was teaching a Primary 3 class when they were asked to draw something from the 'Hail Mary'. Among the expected 'Angel Gabriels' and 'Holy Marys', she was intrigued to see what looked like a hooded member of the Klu Klux Klan surrounded by water. It took some time for her to realise that 'blessed art thou amongst women' had been interpreted as 'blessed art thou – a monk swimming'. I know that a play later surfaced with that title but I wouldn't be at all surprised if that incident begat it. Another daughter told me how her four-year-old son told her that he 'hated' a fellow pupil in his P1 class, Mickey Granley.

She immediately did what all good mothers do and told him that he shouldn't hate anyone. She probed why he didn't like him and was told that, 'He is disgusting and he eats nuts.'

She protested, 'But that's silly, sure I eat nuts.'

'No!' he continued, raising his voice in emphasis. 'He eats nuts.'

Further questioning established that what he was actually saying was, 'No! He eats snots.'

★

Jamesy was a bright boy who was keen to progress. He had an open, alert face and rarely missed school. More than once he would have to be told to stop working as we were going to PE or woodwork.

Invariably he would plead, 'Sir, I just want to finish this page.'

Just as invariably I would insist that he could finish it later.

One day he was working on an English task that required him to place the titles of different books into a number of categories.

Henry the Eighth would be placed under History while *Top*

Goals for United would be placed under Sport. As usual Jamesy worked efficiently and I marked them shortly after he had finished. I was surprised at one of his answers, as under Sport he had listed *Travelling in Tibet*.

'How come, Jamesy?… Travelling… Tibet? Don't you think that might be placed somewhere else?'

He suddenly flushed with embarrassment. 'Oh!… I thought it meant going into the bookies to place a bet!'

This was a popular exercise and I enjoyed making up titles that would amuse and sometimes tease different pupils. Tommy was a very keen Manchester United supporter so on a worksheet that I gave him I had titles such as, *Liverpool – The Greatest Team Ever*. Anything in this vein would always be unlisted and Tommy would hand it up with a smirk, 'Couldn't read those ones.' He reciprocated brilliantly, one day, when he handed a sheet back and under *Arsenal – Great Wins Over United* he had boldly spelt 'Fiction'.

Of course it was easy for children to pick up a word or a phrase and misuse it with humorous results, as when a twelve-year-old girl explained to my wife that she wasn't able to come to school because her mother was in hospital having an 'ex-directory'. My daughter told me how her eight-year-old son explained to her that a boy in his class, Harry, didn't have to do Maths because 'He's got hamburgers'. It was only after some thought and further questioning that she realised what her son had overheard between two teachers was a diagnosis of 'Asperger's'.

In Religion one day, Jim asked what makes a good Christian.

After the usual suggestions, George volunteered, 'Going to holy places like Lourdes.'

Jim agreed and talked briefly about Lourdes. 'Are there any other places?' he asked. Another boy helpfully proposed Fatima. Jim then talked about Fatima.

'Anywhere else?' he probed. 'What about Knock?' (another Catholic shrine in Co. Mayo.)

George thought for a moment. 'That's right,' he assented. 'You shouldn't knock anything either.'

One of the best true stories was told to me by an elderly female teacher. As a young probationer she was given a position in her local country primary school. She took the first class, known then as junior infants. She quickly realised that she needed a stock of emergency pants as a number of her charges would occasionally have 'accidents'. When this would happen, she would give the child an emergency pair which she expected to receive back the next day, cleaned and washed. After one such transaction, a little girl forgot to return the pants and was mildly scolded. As she travelled to school the following morning the young recipient of the borrowed pants climbed onto the crowded bus with her father. One can imagine the teacher's embarrassment when the child, in a large voice, announced to the entire busload, 'Don't worry Miss, my daddy's got your knickers in his pocket.'

Humour was an essential part of the school day and there would be an easy, unhurtful banter at times. There was a confidence within the class knowing where the lines were drawn. It was probably the greatest barometer of control when you could allow and even encourage high spirits and raucous laughter but quickly establish control by clapping your hands and saying, 'OK, that's it… we had better get back to work!'

I is for INDEPENDENCE

I was very aware that although many were outwardly tough and confident, a great number of our pupils were ill-equipped to cope with life after school. Often in June with school leaving on the close horizon a number of pupils who had previously been keen to leave asked to stay on. On some occasions I agreed and arranged with the Principal that they be allowed to do so. I did have to be convinced, however, that there was a better reason than merely deferring the evil day. At one time I had six boys over leaving age in the class.

The introduction of bus tokens was an initiative that had been introduced by the education board and the Principal and had an enormous benefit for the older boys. Normally they travelled to and from school on education board buses. These were 'policed' by bus escorts who generally, with the odd exception, understandably kept their heads down and saw their function as reporting misdemeanours to the teachers the following morning. The trips home were often fraught with trouble. In addition to the fights and squabbles that would break out, there was the additional problem of sectarian attack as these 'Catholic' buses passed through 'Protestant' areas. On one occasion, one of our buses was petrol bombed and some pupils injured.

With the introduction of tokens senior, more reliable, boys were able to travel independently to and from school. This greatly enhanced their self-esteem. There was a real stigma attached to travelling in a 'special' bus. Even in Catholic areas, they were sometimes seen as distinct enough to be stoned! A number of boys often got on and off the bus some distance from their homes to avoid being labelled as 'special'. Travelling independently they could claim to be attending any of the bigger secondary schools near where we were located. An important but unintended benefit of the bus tokens was that if a boy was prepared to walk, he saved one space on his token and could then sell his virginal ticket at a slightly reduced rate.

Because the mobiles were so far from the main building, either Jim or I would have to brave the elements to get a cup of tea at the eleven o'clock break. The problem was solved when we brought in an electric kettle and a teapot and made tea in the classroom while the boys had their daily free one-third pint of milk. Thatcher's abolition of free milk did not apply to special schools. This provoked the usual disparaging comments from some of the boys about how ill divided our worlds were. Tommy would sidle up to the desk and laconically complain about the world being 'ill-divid'. They supped on cold milk while we dipped our biscuits into warming tea. The banter was good-natured but it caused us to introduce a tea break for everyone. It was long before 'economic awareness' became a cross-curricular theme and it proved valuable on a number of counts. We bought a large teapot and the boys had to bring in their own mugs. Two boys each week were responsible for washing and drying as well as ensuring there was a clean drying cloth. Our caretaker, Jimmy, kindly agreed to have them washed each week. Initially the cost for each boy was two pence per day, paid weekly. Two other boys were selected each fortnight to look after the finances and ensure that no one ran up too large a debit. The money gathered went to buy tea and biscuits, which was a job allotted to another two pupils. The choice of biscuit was theirs' alone. They were allowed out of school to go to the shop and buy whatever was required. In the spirit of equality and democracy Jim and I also contributed our tea money. After trying different candidates, Francis, one of the most pleasant boys I ever taught, was selected to make the tea, a task he carried out with precision and efficiency. His surname was McEntee and he quickly became known as Francie 'Makingtea'. He carried out his duties for two years before he left and each day at 10.45 am he would stop work and fill the kettles. It was interesting to see how the boys embraced the different tasks. No one who wanted tea was ever refused. If one didn't have the money he would be treated by one of the rest. It encouraged generosity and independence. Opinions concerning the choice of biscuits or the quality of the cleanliness of the cups were often voiced. Although generally confined to the morning, occasionally, when a mood of lethargy descended on either teacher or pupil, an impromptu tea break was deemed in order. Of course nowadays such a shared activity could not happen: health and safety would prevent any sixteen-year-old pupil from engaging in such a potentially dangerous activity as boiling a kettle and pouring out hot tea – and those cups – surely that was an open invitation for some pernicious disease to disseminate and wreck havoc and death on all?

We were so fortunate to have lived through a time where common sense preceded many of today's regulations.

Sharing an activity like tea making might seem like a minor thing, but it established another commonality between us.

J is for JOINT ENDEAVOUR

There was never going to be any equality of leadership between pupils and their teacher. The latter had all of the responsibility and the onus of progressing the former. Very early in my career, however, I discovered what many others had discovered already. One had to bring the same enthusiasm and involvement to any task if one expected a reciprocal response. When the class was set a task, I would ensure that I, too, was involved in something. More often than not, if it was practical, I would attempt the same task. In an art task I would sit, preferably at a desk, amongst the pupils and attempt, with little skill, to achieve something that looked less and less than the meanderings of a drunken spider that had been dipped in paint. An exercise in geometric design would find me involved with the same intense dedication. (This essentially involved drawing straight lines with a ruler between different coordinates.) Simple as the exercises were, they produced complicated, flattering results that were proudly displayed on the walls. It was better to wander throughout the class sitting beside and helping any pupil who was having difficulty than to sit on high at the teacher's desk. I would often feign frustration or inability when attempting some task. In games of skill like draughts or chess (for the two that could play the latter) it was a proud coup to beat the teacher. On a number of occasions, my defeats were due entirely to the skill of the opposition. With one particular draughts player, Charlie, it was considerably more difficult to win than to engineer defeat.

The PE sessions were a super opportunity to show that talents were more widely spread than in academia. In my mind I was a superb footballer but that failed to translate physically into anything more than an ill-coordinated, lunging turkey running from a Christmas butcher. I was much better at basketball and at lunchtime thoroughly enjoyed handball. But even there I was still inferior to a couple of older boys. My inadequacies in certain areas were regularly used to boost the self-esteem of others.

When we wrote our stories every week, I wrote with the rest and became fully preoccupied with trying to construct something that was appropriate in language and content. Taking part on an equal basis in activities at the technical college such as bricklaying and joinery also served to demonstrate that in other areas, one could be better than the teacher. When we made moulds or candles I painted mine with the rest.

When things went wrong, as when one or two of the boys got into trouble with other staff, I showed solidarity in disappointment and regret. If someone had got into trouble around the school it was always a case of 'We've let ourselves down'. The class was always 'us' never 'you' or 'me'. It was amazing how anyone disrupting the class or causing problems was isolated. The greatest punishment was causing a rupture in the class ethos of goodwill and camaraderie.

Accepting the very different abilities and responsibilities, the class to be successful had to act as a unit. That unity depended on assuming a joint responsibility for its failures as much as for its successes.

K is for KNOWLEDGE

If one was employed to teach Physics or Maths, it would be fairly easy to identify the main subject areas one was supposed to impart. Our problem in St Cuthbert's was that the older the pupil, the more nebulous was the interpretation of what constituted 'knowledge'.

It was easier further down the school where basic literacy and numeracy were rightly prioritised. As the pupils grew, their needs became wider and more vague. It didn't stop us trying to build on those basic skills but other aspects became increasingly important. The curriculum for the type of pupil I taught was thought of primarily in terms of personal adequacy, social competence and individual development. Pure academic attainment was always going to be subservient to that. We would habitually quote words like 'socialisation', 'maturity', 'awareness of possibilities and limitations'. We were dealing with boys, some of whom had very real educational or emotional problems, who were shortly going out into a world peopled with individuals who were going to be much less understanding and tolerant than we were. Few employers were going to spend time beseeching, humouring or encouraging a reluctant employee. An aim had to be that when a boy left school, he was as competent in basic skills as possible. More than that, we strove to make them confident and independent:

mature enough to accept challenges and brickbats and aware enough to know where to get help.

Every boy I taught was different. Sometimes one would be lucky enough to hit on a hitherto unexpected talent. I have always been attracted to cricket. Though I never had the opportunity to play, I became fascinated by the game in my early thirties. It was prompted by the 1975 Ashes series, when Australia's Lillee and Thompson arrived to challenge the English captain's boast that the Aussies would be 'humbled'. With the two fastest bowlers in the world, bowling at around one hundred miles an hour, the series was eagerly anticipated. Australia were so dominant that even my dad and I hoped England would at least make a contest of the series. That summer as we waited for the district nurse to come or sat outside with the radio perched on the table of his wheelchair, Daddy and I saw it all in our minds' eyes. It must have been the only time in our lives that we supported England in any sporting contest. Not, of course, that we wanted England to win but we grudgingly wanted them to play well. Normally we wanted humiliation and disgrace. But there was something about cricket that calmed our detestation of the normal 'jingoism' and made us semi-tolerant – even approaching impartiality.

As we listened to *Test Match Special* on BBC Radio 3, we were introduced to 'Johnners', 'Arlott', 'The Alderman', 'Blowers', 'CMJ' and 'The Boil'. The programme occasionally touched on cricket but portrayed everything that was admirable and decent in the English character. Everything was discussed: chocolate cakes; pigeons; trains and buses; how to bring up children; what was wrong and what was fair and decent; etc. For the majority of our pupils and a lot of people who had never spent any time in England, they seemed a mythical creation, difficult to reconcile with some of the bullying, foul-mouthed soldiers that were patrolling our streets. They would have found it hard to equate the essential decency of the commentators with some of the 'squaddies' who, in 1971, murdered ten innocent people in Ballymurphy and fourteen equally innocent people in Derry in 1972.

I'm sure those living outside Ireland found it equally difficult to recognise the 'Saints and Scholars' who butchered ten Protestant workers or assassinated churchgoers in Darkley. War has a habit of throwing up the worst excesses of every nation, including our own.

★

Robert was from a poor working-class background. When I decided that we would have a cricket match complete with stumps, bats and a tennis ball he was less than enthusiastic.

'It's a game for poofs!' he opined.

However, after a major bout of cajoling he deigned to partake and to everyone's astonishment (including his own) he was incredibly talented. No matter how hard the PE teacher and I threw (sorry – bowled) the ball at him he would drive it with contemptuous ease all over the pitch. If he was good at batting, he was equally adept at bowling and even his full toss was delivered with such accuracy and speed that none of us ever survived for long. As a fielder he was immense and threw himself around with a complete disregard for his well-being. Had he attended Eton or Harrow he would surely have captained the first eleven. His vocabulary might have required some engineering as one day after watching one of his batting team-mates refuse to avail of some very easy scoring opportunities he scornfully remarked, 'Another fucking maiden.'

At times like that I wondered just how far some of the boys might have gone had circumstances been different.

I was convinced that there was worthwhile knowledge in experiencing as broad a curriculum as was available. Everything from cricket to first aid to good manners; from personal dress and hygiene to how to set up a fish tank was an opportunity to learn. It was important that a teacher of adolescents, some of whom were disaffected and had limited abilities, made an effort to make himself knowledgeable about the wide range of hobbies and activities that appealed to his class. The curriculum for such a group should be thought of primarily in terms of the pupils' personal adequacy, social competence and individual development.

I'm under no illusions that I could have done more. At the time I thought that because I enjoyed it so much and had few problems, I must be doing a great job. I wonder. Did they need a knowledge that I was unable to provide? A recurring nightmare is that someday an ex-pupil will say to me, 'You really let me down.'

L is for LANGUAGE

The importance of an appropriate use of language in tone, volume and content is worthy of consideration.

Some years ago I was cycling through Rajasthan in India with a group of others. I found the Indian people incredibly warm and welcoming with one exception. Young boys in the fourteen to sixteen age group were a frequent nuisance. Generally it was no more than high spirits but there was a small element that looked on us as something to be plundered. If you were foolish enough to stop among them you would quickly be surrounded by dozens of curious boys who would examine every part of your bike. A particular source of attraction was our panniers, which they sometimes treated as Santa's goody bags. Sticky hands would surround and tug at everything that wasn't securely fastened. Some of them could undo straps quicker than a lothario could undo a bra. One of our group was an exceptional mild and pleasant teacher from an English public primary school. Once, as his belongings were being pilfered, he chastened the thieves with exhortations, delivered in a quiet, reasonable tone, to 'Stop that... you mustn't do that, you know... it's very naughty...' (delivered as he tried to retrieve his tool kit).

'If you don't hand that back I'll report you to your parents.'

This admonition failed to arouse any response other than to convince them that they had indeed found a soft target. As some of us rode back to the rescue the booming voice of one of our group, an ex-navy petty officer, was more candid in his assessment; 'Clear off you little bastards or I'll put my boot so far up your arse you'll choke on the laces!'

I'll leave it to the reader to determine which approach was more successful! It had the desired effect although our English public school teacher was as shocked and frightened as any of the kids. I'm not saying that I approved of either the tone or the content, but it was effective.

★

Too often I have heard the most inappropriate response by a teacher in a stressful situation. I've even heard teachers arguing with a pupil who is vehemently cursing at them. Very often the only avenue open to a pupil who has done something wrong is to bluster, deny and shout. When a pupil raised his voice the most effective counter I found was to try and look calm and ask him, 'Am I shouting at you?' I would persist in asking this, in an increasingly quieter voice until the invariable response came, 'No.'

'Then why are you shouting at me? We both need to calm down and think about this.'

The use of 'we both' usually gains time as the blame for the argument has now become mutual. Often I would say, 'Look we're both getting worked up about this. Why don't we both sit down and get on with what we're doing and then we'll talk about it.'

It wasn't only foul language that caused a problem.

I'm increasingly appalled at what passes for spoken English. My father had been a keen, almost fanatical grammarian. As a seven-year-old child I remember, with a friend, witnessing a man being knocked down and killed near where we lived. Bursting with shock, horror and amazement I ran home to tell my dad.

'You know what Charlie Farrell and me saw?' I gasped.

'How could *me* saw anything?' he interrupted. 'Leave out the other person. You wouldn't say "You know what me saw?" However, what did you see?'

'Nothing,' I sulked.

But those sorts of lessons stuck with me. I always swore I would not lecture my children as he lectured me but, of course, all these years later I do exactly the same. Despite our best efforts we all turn into our parents.

In class I would frequently write up the common grammatical mistakes. For some of them anything that could show ability or understanding could help in trying to get a job. If a boy could talk properly it could mitigate his literacy difficulties. Every so often I would spend a session explaining what were the more obvious howlers. Nowadays we live in a world often populated with monosyllabic, ungrammatical and frequently incoherent celebrities. In Northern Ireland we have, with a few exceptions, politicians who 'seen, have saw, have did, have came and have went'. It is now common to hear teachers with sentences such as, 'Her and Jenny were at the party with them others.'

Even those aspiring-to-be-correct newscasters are

commonly heard to bid 'Goodnight from Jenny and I.' Every time I hear that my father's ghost whispers, 'Would you say "Goodnight from I?"'

When writing this I happened to see a snippet of a programme called *Million Pound Drop*. I didn't fully understand what the programme was about but I did understand that the presenter pointed to four answers relating to a question about David Beckham. Each answer began. 'Him and Victoria…'. Obviously a complete ignorance of what constitutes basic good English was shared by the producer, the presenter, the set designer, the quiz setter, etc. Some people have a remarkable tolerance of, even a facility for, ignorance. I am reminded of one day many years ago a teacher coming into my class and telling me how he 'seen something on the television'. His ears must have surely burnt after he left when one of my 'slow learners' said, 'Sir, should Mr… not have said, "I saw"?'

I'm glad I won't be around to hear the monosyllabic grunts of future generations… 'Is it 'cause I'm a grumpy old fart?'

The blame for this massacre and murder of English is laid squarely at the door of the differing educational initiatives from each successive government. Grammar was no longer taught. When I was training to be a teacher there was a prevalent notion among some of the Inspectorate that a child's creative writing should not be corrected: 'Red pens destroy the creative flow, and "disincentivise" the child.' We were left with a generation that still has difficulty in forming a sentence as opposed to a jumble of thoughts and observations. Before I retired I heard Principals of schools speak and show the most complete ignorance of basic grammar. Having stressed what I considered to be good practice I did, nevertheless, develop a colloquial manner of speaking with my pupils. I thought it appropriate to use some of the phrases and expressions that were in their common usage. Some might disagree but I didn't find it patronising or false to use an immediacy and familiarity in speech that I wouldn't have employed in other situations. To me it was acceptable to refer to someone as 'big man' or say 'someone was 'off his rocker'.

The boys enjoyed Jim's and my inventive similes such as 'dressed like a tailor's dummy'; 'as solid as a Yorkie bar', and proficiency in the ocular department meant one had 'eyes like a shit house rat' (amended to 'bog house' for the pupils). Dishonesty meant one was 'as dodgy as a £4 note' while one's indiscretions were as subtle as 'a kick in the goolies'. Jim was proficient with rhyming slang, though whether they were traditional or inventive I was never quite sure. He would complain to me out of pupils' earshot that he had trouble with his bowels and had a severe case of the 'Eartha Kitts'.

One could balance this use of the vernacular with language that extended in the other direction. It was important that this banter was separate from the normal discourse we used. Appropriate language for a given situation was very important. The one time I would not discuss a problem any further was when a pupil cursed. Luckily enough even in the 1980s there were very few pupils who would have used that language to a teacher.

Of course it is difficult to try and blame kids for their use of the F-words when on a lot of late-night programmes, the same is used commonly. A word that once caused consternation when it was used on television back in 1965 by Ken Tynan hardly raises an eyebrow nowadays.

Many years later as Principal I used to play handball at lunchtime with the senior pupils. They would gather round the front door to walk up to the alleys when I came out of the office. One day as I walked, I was also discussing the installation of a burglar alarm system with a bright but very foul-mouthed electrician. I had whispered to him more than once to 'watch the language in front of the pupils'. He had apologised and continued to enthuse about the new system. He was quoting decibel levels when I innocently asked, 'Would that be loud enough?'

'Loud?' he protested, and to the delighted gasps of his young audience insisted, 'Loud? – It'll blow the fucking bollocks out of your ears!'

Like nearly everyone else now I've succumbed and though I use it occasionally, I deprecate the constant usage of the F-word on television. At least I know the appropriateness of its use for a particular audience but that distinction is becoming increasingly blurred. At the rate of ingression, in twenty years time the news may well begin, 'Tonight that effin bastard that rules Iran was told that Her Majesty's Government isn't going to put up with any more of his shit.'

Like every aspect of language, things are changing rapidly.

Some of those erudite inspectors and government ministers of education who encouraged the free-flowing, ungrammatical, misspelt, unpunctuated, mish-mashed compositions had little idea of the atrocities they were perpetrating on language. I remember one inspector, Mr Mc Crearey, telling me with glee how he once had a thrusting young trainee inspector 'shadowing' him as they visited a primary school in West Belfast. As he talked away to the teacher, the tyro moved through the class examining the work. He lifted a child's copy book and with a flush of excitement, showed it to his senior colleague.

The pupil had written the following in his exercise book;

'tomorrow tomorrow tomorrow
sorrow sorrow sorrow
grief grief grief'

'Can you believe the incredible honesty and emotion in that simple poem?' he gushed. 'What unbelievable pain underlies that cry for help and understanding?'

Mc Crearey examined the opus major, considered the matter and then approached the child.

Showing him the book he said, 'Tell me, son. What's this you've written?'

The boy, somewhat confused by all the attention looked at him and replied, 'Them's my spellings from last night!'

M is for MUSIC

My father played the piano quite well. While he could perform a reasonable Chopin Nocturne he was aware that such a recital might not receive critical acclaim from his class of sixteen-year-olds with the rock and roll revolution in full swing. Once a week he would gather together his and the other senior class and have a sing-song. This mainly comprised standard 'One Man Went to Mow' classics, which had the virtue of making some inroads into innumerate pupils. There was also a repertoire of Clancy Brothers favourites. With the onset of the Civil Rights marches, he progressed to Bob Dylan and Joan Baez.

His control was absolute and I once saw him in a session where a full-scale riot would have ensued had any other teacher attempted it. He had the pupils stack the desks and chairs in a barricade across the middle of the room and split the boys into two groups. Demanding and getting complete silence for the other side he would lead one section in a rousing chorus of 'We Shall Overcome'. When this was finished he would then lead the others in an equally defiant chorus of 'The Sash'. He would get as excited as the boys themselves and would address each group, encouraging them to sing more lustily.

'You are men of Ulster,' he would bellow doing his best to imitate Ian Paisley. 'Your fathers fought for this land and now this bunch of Fenians is going to try and take over this place. Arm yourselves and defend the barricades!'

Turning to the 'Civil Righters' he would exhort them to tear down the barricades.

'For six hundred years you've suffered discrimination. Now is the time to put an end to it.'

Pointing contemptuously to the assembled Loyalists he would once more lead them in a chorus of defiance; 'We Shall Overcome'.

With complete disrespect to the exercise books and sheets of paper, he ordered them to roll them up and withdraw their batons. The storming itself never actually took place. It was amazing how he established control over what was potentially a riotous denouement. When the session was over he would order the tables and chairs replaced and the class would leave in as orderly fashion as time allowed. I suspected that the main audience he was addressing in these impromptu drama classes was the other two staff members. They would be giggling more than any pupil as they understood the double entendres and nuances inserted for their benefit. This happened in the last months of 1969 when we all thought everything would soon be settled.

★

I was a much less talented pianist than my dad. As a boy I had started music lessons with an elderly lady on the Springfield Road. My mother would give me the money to pay her but I would often spend it on other entertainments, like the Broadway cinema. I did love music but practicing scales seemed far removed from any of the pop music I wanted to play. The fact that I never learnt how to read music is one of the few real regrets I have.

I did, however, have a good ear and I was able to pick out the basis of any tune fairly quickly. I took my class for Music once a week as well. 'Roddy McCorley' rubbed shoulders with 'The Auld Orange Flute' and 'Waltzing Matilda' followed 'The

Fields of Athenry'. Jim would ensconce himself at the back of the room and together we would perpetrate injustice to every song. Discordancy was subservient to enjoyment – and the sessions were hugely enjoyable. Disinterested choristers used the opportunity to nod off during the less raucous numbers. One boy John was excellent at the mouth organ and on his infrequent attendances he would accompany me with more skill and talent than I had. Because of the increasing number of bands (many of them knew only Republican tunes) we were never in short supply of drummers, so the cacophony was often loud and even on the odd occasion tuneful. The teachers in the adjoining rooms suffered the onslaught with fortitude.

Shortly after he left school our mouth-organist John was blown to pieces by a car bomb, while innocently watching an IRA funeral.

N is for NAMES (and parents)

One thing that never failed to amaze we teachers was the appellations a number of parents foisted upon their children. My wife once, encouraging a new entrant to her secondary school asked sweetly, 'And what's your name?'

'My name's Lasagne.'

Hiding her surprise she asked, 'What a lovely name, how did you get that name?'

'Miss, my daddy is a chef and that's his favourite food!'

Good job it's not Meatballs with Tripe, I thought.

The nicknames of certain pupils were extraordinarily inventive if confusing to the outsider.

A boy called Kinnaird rejoiced in the name of Budgie. The process was Kinnaird – Canary – Budgie. Another who lived at a bus terminal was called Depot, while one poor lad who suffered from alopecia was referred to as Goosey, thanks to Jim's inadvertent comment to me, after a haircut, that there was 'more hair on a baldy gooseberry'.

Unusual names can sometimes have a musicality about them. I heard on good authority of a child in England who rejoiced in the name Chlamydia but the one which gives me the greatest joy is the wonderfully entitled Pocahontas McCoubrey. That is a moniker one could be justifiably proud of. There was also the unfortunate mother whose son in my class was called Sam. She told me proudly he was a twin and his sister was called Ella. I immediately had a scene flash before me of the mother standing at her front door calling for her children, 'Come on in, Sam an' Ella … your dinner's ready.' Merlot and Chardonnay were also authenticated as Christian names of two girls… well it would have been downright silly to call boys that! Apparently, there is a mother in one of the more Republican areas of Derry who has called her children Ira and Inla (acronyms for Irish Republican Army and Irish National Liberation Army).

However, when one really thinks about it there is something innovative and refreshing about some of the more exotic names. Doubtless some 3,000 years ago Ezekiel may have turned to Ephraim on the birth of a grandchild and scolded their children with the admonition, 'You're surely not going to call the baby Peter or John?'

★

Despite some parents saddling their children with exotic if not unfortunate Christian names, the vast majority of parents did their best for their children. It is not uncommon for more educated or affluent parents to sneer from afar believing that parents with unruly, dirty, unappreciative and uncooperative children 'don't care about them'. That, of course, is a nonsense.

The number of 'uncaring' parents is very small but there are more than a few incapable or inadequate ones.

Increasingly over the course of my teaching life, the number of one-parent families rose dramatically and, as the number of children from a stable two-parent environment diminished, the number of difficult children with just a mother as the single parent increased. There were of course numerous single parents who did an excellent job bringing up their children and that was in spite of the difficulties a lot of them faced. There were, however, the rare cases where the single mother was feckless, incompetent and more suitably qualified to care for a dead goldfish than children. There were also a small number whose vocation in life appeared to be an attempt to single-handedly restore the population of Ireland to pre-famine numbers. Contraception equated with not going out on a Friday night.

One particular mother that a fellow Principal told me about had thirteen children, of whom only three shared the same father. Each year she would produce the latest from this cornucopia of couplings and present the child at the school gates. One of her offspring had a head topped with the most glorious thatch of ginger hair. Admiring the blazing mane of his new charge, he innocently commented on it.

'That's a great head of hair. Did his father have hair that colour?'

She looked at him thoughtfully and then replied, 'I don't know.' She confided, 'I never saw him with his cap off!'

Another mother with a pastime (if not a calling) that involved broadening her knowledge of 'foreign parts' brought the latest in a long line of children to school on the first day. Having previously been made aware of the intellectual shortcomings of her previous offerings, she confidently assured the Principal that, 'This one will be very smart. His father's a Norwegian sailor!'

Another pupil at the age of five was shopping 'down town'

with his mother when he was told, 'See that man standing down at that café? Run down and say hello… I think he's your father.'

O is for OPENNESS

The pupils had no real appreciation of how or where teachers lived. They were people whom you only met in school. Spotting a teacher outside of school hours was a singular triumph and retold to the class with glee. 'I saw Mr Rooney down town on Saturday.' You were like the golden eagle of the ornithological student. This ignorance and naivety existed on both sides. A lot of middle-class teachers had very little in common with and little understanding of the lives of some of our pupils. Many of us had little appreciation of just how hard and dispiriting life could be. We may have been in the middle of a ghastly and vicious cycle of murder and mayhem but few of us suffered the continual harassment by the army on one hand and paramilitaries on the other. In many Catholic working-class areas, the feeling of despondency was aptly graffitied on a cemetery wall; 'Is there life before death?'

    I remember my wife, with tears in her eyes, telling me how a girl in her school was forced by another teacher to stand out in the playground on a cold, wet November morning because she had arrived late and hadn't brought her homework. It seems hard to believe but that sort of criminal cruelty was not unusual in those days. She discovered later the child's house had been searched overnight and she had been out of her bed most of the night. Another girl was upbraided by a teacher for being late. She wasn't even given time to explain that she had to get up, dress and feed her two younger brothers before walking them to school as her mother lay in bed with the baby because they didn't have the money to buy coal. When I heard stories like that I wanted to scream out against the abuse. I had worked in one of the relief centres at the start of the Troubles when we had tried to get accommodation and supplies for people who had been burnt out of their homes. There were people who had nothing but the clothes they wore.

It seemed obvious to me that one of the things teachers should do was to demystify their existence. Some of the pupils appeared to believe that teachers were spontaneously created daily at 9 am and lasted until 3.30 pm when they defragmented into space. One of the things I did early on in my teaching was to place a small, framed photo of my wife and children on my desk. The pupils knew who they were and I often told scurrilous and completely untrue stories about them to emphasise a point. If a boy did something silly I would complain that they were just like 'my Louise'. Sometimes to show exasperation I would say, 'You and our Louise should hook up – then you could drive people mad together,' or 'You should grow up and marry our Paula, that's exactly the sort of thing she does.'

It was hard to take offence at being chastised if you were being compared to the teacher's daughter and even obliquely being invited to become a son-in-law. Conversely if you wanted to boost someone I would say, 'I should take you home and get you to show our Aoibheann how to do that.'

I really should apologise to my daughters for all the fibs and exaggerated behaviours I attributed to them… all done in the line of duty.

What was surprising was the reaction of some of the staff when they saw the photo on my desk. Some thought it was a dangerous innovation that might lead to familiarity and one teacher even suggested that if I kept it there, the boys would eventually find out who they were!

Not only were some staff unaware of how the pupils existed and how little the pupils knew about them, they wanted to keep it that way. There was of course the odd pupil who would test the familiarity by trying to call me by my first name. I would explain the situation; 'I respect you and that's why I call you by your first name, George. I might be your friend but I'm not your mate. Have I ever called you by your surname? Have I ever said, "McKenna, get on with your work"? No, never… and if I ever do… you will know you are in serious trouble. You call me "Mr Rooney" or "Sir" as a mark of respect. When you're older and uglier and we run into each other long after you've left school, you can take me for a pint and you can call me whatever you like. But right now you call me "Sir". Have you any problem with that?'

As I got older and became more confident of my ability, I also became more open.

I've already alluded to how I used my daughters to establish a commonality with someone in the class but I also talked openly, and, perhaps more openly than I should have, about other things in my life. I remember one incident when a boy called Tim was in a particularly bad mood. He was moaning and fractious, refusing to work. I always used the same stock response to anyone who didn't want to work. I tried to mollify him but he wasn't amenable to any advice.

He sat sullenly with a face like a sack of spanners. After I scolded him for his lack of effort he responded sullenly, 'Aye, it's all right for you. Our house was raided by the Brits last night and I didn't get any sleep.'

I thought about that for a minute or so.

'Really?' I responded. 'Well that's rough… and you think that gives you right to act like a dipstick… You're right though. The Brits didn't raid my house last night and I got a good night's sleep… until four o'clock this morning when my father was sick. The sweat was running down his face and he was in a lot of pain. I had to give him a bladder wash.'

(The boys all knew about my father's accident and the

resultant paralysis. As joy-riding was almost endemic in parts of Belfast at that time his story was used to warn about speed and drink, etc.)

I explained exactly what a bladder wash entailed.

'Then he went back to sleep for a full hour. Then he shouted for me because he had been very sick. I had to get my wife up and together we cleaned him up and then went back to bed until seven o'clock when he was sick again and we had to send for the doctor. Other than that I had a great night's sleep. So don't moan to me. When I walk through that door I have to give this class all the respect and work that I'm paid to do. I can't come in yapping and moaning. If you want to be treated like a man you've got to behave like one. How long do you think you'll last in a job if you act like that? You don't know what other boys around you had to put up with last night. I do and you come about fourth in the list.' (The last part was pure fiction but it concentrated a lot of minds on possible contenders.)

'OK, so you're in bad twist. That's up to you; if you want to waste your time… go right ahead. You're too big and ugly for me to get annoyed. So, if you want to put your head down and sleep that's up to you. At the end of the day you're a young man… you're old enough to be in the army and get shot for the privilege… If you'd been born a hundred years ago you would probably be married with a couple of kids… you're smart enough to know your own mind… and stupid enough to think you don't need help from anybody… I'll still get paid at the end of the month so I'll just concentrate on helping the rest of the class. But there's only one thing I won't allow you to do… and that's to interfere or keep back anyone else in the class. There's no one here who's going to suffer or lose out just because you're in stinking form.'

My rant had the desired effect. The rest of the class kept their heads down and scribbled in total silence. Tim was shaken and remained silent as I moved away to another desk.

In the afternoon he asked me who I thought would win the big European Cup match that evening. The resumption of diplomatic ties served as his apology.

★

Once, the subject of domestic violence came up and I was saying that I couldn't understand how it could come about that two people living together could get to the stage of hitting each other.

Even if they had fallen out of love, I still couldn't. George looked at me earnestly. 'Sir, do you mean to say that you never, ever smacked your wife, even a wee slap, when you had been drinking?' He wasn't being cheeky. The sad fact was that he couldn't conceive a relationship where the 'odd slap' didn't happen. I'd met both his parents and they appeared very decent, respectable people.

'If I ever laid a hand on my wife she would walk out and that would be it,' I said. 'And if any of my daughters was ever to be hit by one of their boyfriends or husbands I would expect them to do the same. I just couldn't accept it and I wouldn't expect them to either.'

George looked at me quizzically and although he wasn't about to argue the point, I could tell he didn't believe me.

Of course, today the notion that this is an acceptable or desirable degree of openness between teacher and pupil is anathema to those who keep an eye out for what constitutes political correctness. I rather liked the quote I saw on the internet which stated;

> *'Political correctness is a doctrine, fostered by a delusional, illogical minority, and rabidly promoted by an unscrupulous mainstream media, which holds forth the proposition that it is entirely possible to pick up a turd by the clean end.'*

P is for PHYSICALITY

One of the aspects I really enjoyed with the older boys was their sense of growing maturity. The sulks and squabbles of the thirteen-year-olds were replaced with less frequent but physically more dangerous ones. Some of the boys particularly were very big physically and indeed the odd one bigger than I was. When a fight did break out as they did infrequently, I had to be very careful trying to separate the combatants lest I end up being the most seriously injured party. Over the years as discipline improved and the class ethos took hold these problems largely disappeared. A number of the boys realised their similarity in size to me and I would often be asked if there was a fight between me and one of the bigger specimens who would win. Obviously, there was no way of deciding this but I thought it prudent to pretend that if it ever came to a real fight there would only be one winner. I claimed that I held all sorts of imaginary and mythical martial arts. The truth was of course that in the event of such a fracas, the pupil would always be at an advantage. No teacher, even in a rage, could possibly employ his full strength against a pupil.

I suppose, looking back, my attitude was immature and unworthy, but I was keen to show that I was able to compete with them in the gym. To this end I always played with them in sport. I was reasonably good at basketball and pathetic at football but I took part in both. It was important that I was never the captain but equally important that I was the referee! An amused spectator would have seen the referee call a foul on himself and even once send himself off.

The timetable dictated that the boys had a shower period once a week after P.E.. I tried to convince the boys that they should take a shower rather than changing directly from smelly gym gear into their everyday clothes but very few did. I would persistently tell them of the importance of cleanliness and not wearing gear that was heavily soaked in sweat. Of course, the problem was that there was only one long communal shower area and the embarrassment that a lot of them had about disrobing in front of others. Over the months I managed to persuade a few of them to use the showers but it was only when I devised a cunning Baldrick ruse that it became general. All I had to state was, 'It's obvious which boys have a girlfriend… they're the first ones into the showers,' and then stand back for the rush.

I arranged with the caretaker that towels and soap would be brought to the class along with the morning milk delivery. I also brought in some shampoo from home. Over the course of months with no sanctions other than encouragement the majority of the boys took showers after P.E.. Joe's brother was the manager of a hairdressing salon and he regularly brought in different brands of shampoo and even conditioner. It became a matter of pride to have your own gym gear including socks.

I also encouraged them if they had problems with getting their clothes cleaned at home to bring them in and one of our hygiene staff (vicariously known as 'the nit lady') would have them machine washed in school. However, pride ensured that this offer was only rarely taken up.

Once the routine of showers and dedicated gym clothing became established there was a growing sense of pride in personal appearance. The importance of this in view of impending job-seeking was heavily stressed. The only problem was that some of the boys became so fastidious that it became hard to get them to finish showering. Thereafter, when they were showered and shampooed, I turned the water cold. It then became a matter of pride and imagined machismo to see who would last the longest as they gradually turned from pink to blue.

One particular day just as we were entering the shower room, I was told that I had a phone call in the office. I gave

Tommy the keys and told him, 'Right, you're in charge. Get the showers going and give out the soap and towels.'

Unfortunately, Tommy didn't lock the door and one of the lady teachers, unaware it was in use, opened the changing room door while the boys were in different degrees of nudity.

When I came back there was an uneasy silence in the room.

'What's up?'

'Miss ***** came in and Jackie called her "an auld pervert".'

My reaction showed my displeasure. The ethos of the class was that my absences shouldn't change class discipline. I was continually hammering that message home more than anything else.

'You do not behave in a mature, sensible way because of me, but because you are mature in yourselves.'

I was silent for a while and showed my disappointment. I didn't mention the incident until we were back in the class. Over the tea break I talked to Jackie. He had been embarrassed when the teacher had entered but admitted his reaction was out of order. He was also aware that he had, to a degree, let down the class as well as me. He was quite happy to apologise to the teacher involved. I could see his moment of bravado was causing him serious loss of face.

I spoke to the teacher at lunchtime.

'I'm sorry about that incident earlier on. Jackie was showing off and I suppose he was a bit embarrassed when you walked in. In one way it was my fault because although I'd given one of them the keys, he hadn't locked the door.'

She listened stonily. I continued, 'He knows what he said was totally unacceptable and I'll send him round this afternoon to apologise.'

Maybe I was overly ambitious, but I then suggested that, after he had apologised, she could say that she was sorry for walking in on top of them.

'Me?' she queried incredulously. 'You must be joking. I would leave this school before I would apologise to a pupil.'

She stormed off stuttering at my effrontery.

She appeared incapable of understanding that good discipline does not preclude a sense of equality. If a pupil is asked to apologise when he has behaved badly, it is not inconsistent for a teacher, when he or she has made a mistake, to admit fallibility and apologise. As I walked back to the mobile I thought, 'I apologise all the time... maybe she is in the wrong profession.' She was an excellent teacher and a caring professional but her attitude and mine were a thousand miles apart. The sad thing is that there were quite a few teachers at that time that the concept of apologising to a pupil would have been anathema.

For the few years that it lasted I greatly enjoyed taking part in sport with the pupils but with the arrival of a dedicated P.E. teacher I decided reluctantly to call time on my own participation and pass it on to the professional.

Q is for QUIZZES

Every so often Jim and I would organise a class quiz. They came about after we had made a graph showing the most popular TV programmes. To our surprise, teaching as we did some pupils who had considerable learning difficulties, one of the most watched programmes was *University Challenge*. Something about the format appealed to them. Our own version was substantially less erudite. The classes would be divided into two teams, with Jim and me as team leaders. Introductions would be something along the lines of, 'Hello, I'm Henry Snodgrass, St Cuthbert's College, reading the *Beano*,' or 'I'm Hairynose Carruthers reading *Wide Range Reader Blue Book Two*.'

The questions were designed with a number of objectives. Apart from the enjoyment it was a golden opportunity to reinforce lessons that we had done in class. After a previous lesson in measurement one might ask, 'How much longer is 37 millimetres than 3½ centimetres?'

The previous week's geography might be the basis for, 'Name three counties in Ulster that start with D.'

Because the only way to answer was to hold up a hand, it was possible to play to the strengths or interests of a particular pupil, particularly if he was perceived by others as 'thick'. So a team question might be as simple as 'Where is the greyhound track in Belfast?' knowing Dinny and his dad owned and raced dogs. Even the weakest member in the class could be engineered into a correct response by asking something that he would certainly know, e.g. 'Name the number of a bus that goes down the Ormeau Road.'

Success came not only from being in the winning team but more critically in the kudos arising from answering one question correctly. The more aware pupil would know the name of the 'leader of the Unionist party; the football supporter would know the name of United's goalkeeper; the pigeon keeper would be sure to tell us what a 'tumbler' was; the gambler would inform us of the payment due on a '4 to 1' £5 winning bet while the car interests (potential and actual car thieves) could be asked to identify the make from a picture; the music fan would identify the songs and artists from the introduction. The tape recorder was also used to ask the identity of the speaker, which was often a class member who had been taped surreptitiously. Questions would be pulled from an eclectic bag of knowledge.

Jim and I would be on opposite factions. This helped to ensure that the right answer would come from the right candidate, because as team leaders we reserved the right to 'nominate'. He would set three questions for me and I would reciprocate. These were genuine questions, designed to create confusion or embarrassment rather than the elicitation of knowledge. Often we would feign ignorance of the answer to a simple question that one of the pupils would know. This allowed a pupil to show that he was better than the teacher. He would then answer triumphantly while, influenced by *Blazing Saddles* we would sit with a 'Mongo only pawn in game of life' puzzled face. Jim, who considered himself something of an authority on boxing, was less than happy that his emphatic answer 'Archie Moore' to my question, 'Who was the last man to box Rocky Marciano?' was deemed incorrect. The right answer was, of course, the undertaker!

There was always humour. The boys would enjoy the banter and enjoy the spurious questions asking, 'Who wrote St Luke's Gospel?' or 'Whose autobiography did Kevin Keegan write?'

The team members were rotated although there were, with statistical improbability, a number of draws.

R is for RESPECT

Respect should be a concomitant part of teaching. Mutual respect is often quoted as 'part of our school's policy'. Lip service is paid to it in every evaluation or report. In reality it's much more than reciprocating manners. I knew teachers who thought nothing of turning up in dirty jeans, unshaven and smelling of drink from the night before. However, come an inspection they were scrubbed clean, shaven and smelt of nothing stronger than Polo mints. I have every respect for the teacher (and I knew a few of them) who was unconscious and unconcerned about their appearance. At least during an inspection their welcome idiosyncrasies ensured they turned up in exactly the same state of disarray. There were a few teachers who were totally unsuitable for their profession. They took no joy from the humour, unconscious or otherwise, that surrounded them: they gained little or no satisfaction from the minimal but important progress that was achieved each day; they had no curiosity in what makes children what they are; no sympathy for the depressing disabilities of those with special needs; they took no pride in establishing a bond with their pupils and no regrets whenever they failed.

The staff room was at the top of the building and the staff would watch the buses arrive. If one of us had a particularly difficult *bête noire* there would a depressing sigh as you noted his presence. If the miscreant was absent, the non-attendance was the cause of an uplifted heart and a lightening of the load. However there was the odd teacher who would greet everyone disgorged from the buses with an air of similar depression. I remember being somewhat shocked as I watched a bus unload a number of boys when I remarked to a fellow onlooker about one particular pupil. He was a gift in class, eager to learn, pleasant and obedient with a good sense of humour. I happened to remark about what a pleasant boy he was. To my surprise the older sage observed him over his glasses and dismissively condemned him. 'Umph! There's not one of them doesn't have a carnaptious side to him and will give you hell at some time!' I should have asked him why he had left his last post in the Stasi prison.

S is for SEX

It won't surprise many to know that sex and all its tangled complications loomed large in the minds of our fifteen – and sixteen-year-olds. Some of them were incredibly ignorant about the facts of life while one or two others were considerably more aware. We had to be awfully careful in those days as sex education was unheard of. I felt an obligation to impart the Catholic values that I had been brought up with. I have little time for someone who elects to teach in a Catholic school but hypocritically refuses to subscribe to a Catholic ethos or worse, mocks and negates it. As I saw it, that obligation extended even to people like me who are plagued by doubts and inconsistencies. We also had a moral responsibility to teach Catholic values.

At the same time we were aware that to send a sixteen-year-old out into the world with absolutely no idea about sex and procreation was neither desirable nor healthy. Today a complete sex education course can be picked up with a night's channel flicking but in those days there was still a rigorously enforced code of propriety in television.

I had a tank of tropical fish in the classroom and there was huge excitement one lunchtime as a mother guppy started to drop her live young. This led to questions as to where they came from and what caused them. I answered the questions as honestly as I could and, somewhat nervously pointed out the male guppy's gonopodium (the male breeding organ) and where he inserted it into the female. They were full of wonder and curiosity watching the darkening belly as the young unborn grew in the mother. As livebearers, we would watch the mother expel the young, one at a time when they would drop lifelessly, then flicker and dash for cover under the nearest plants. I talked about the gestation period and compared the thirty days for guppies to the human nine months. There was no history of teaching sex education in schools and I was concerned that I would have incurred the wrath of parents, priests and Principal. I needn't have worried. The boys treated it as a personal and private knowledge they had been privileged to receive. I was lucky enough to be friendly with the local parish priest who doubled as the school's manager. Unlike some of his clerical colleagues, he had a genuine interest in the school and in conversation approved of my methods. The BBC's schools' programme on evolution also dealt in detail with mammals and explained how mammals had milk build up in the female breasts to feed their young. This, in turn, lead to human breastfeeding and its benefits for both mother and child. It also prompted a number of questions that were difficult to answer. Sometimes I just had to kick for touch and say we would deal with that later! Alan stumped me one day by asking, 'Sir! What happens to the milk in a woman's breasts if the baby dies?'

I had never thought about that. 'That's a very good question. The answer is I don't know… but I'll find out and let you know.' I asked Jim at lunchtime and relayed the answer.

My support for the radio schools' programme on evolution had a sequel when I was absent one day. An older teacher took my class and during the RE lesson began to talk about Adam and Eve. He was interrupted by one of my precocious acolytes who informed him that Adam and Eve was probably a myth and only there because people wouldn't have understood about evolution. He was appalled and the next day accused me of teaching the boys heresy. I did remind him that my view of evolution was shared by most of the Catholic theologians of the day.

★

It's difficult to appreciate how naive we were about the entire question of same-sex relationships. When we were young we all knew everything about 'queers'… everything and nothing! Of course they were around but in those days they didn't advertise their sexuality. Their activities were criminal and both State and Church combined against them. The Church's teaching on the matter basically implied they were deviant heathens. I knew a couple of 'gays' at Queen's University but they were generally considered 'weird'. I remember once how shocked I was when one of them told me that he was actively considering suicide because of his loneliness. While I was working in London my brother introduced me to a couple of lesbians who worked with him as lifeguards. It was only when I started teaching that I realised that there were boys (it was a single-sex school) who had clearly been born homosexual. They had not been corrupted by the 'dirty old men' of the downtown cinemas. They were born gay in the same way as I was born heterosexual. Up to then I hadn't really given the matter much thought but as I taught them, I came to realise that they had a difficult struggle ahead of them as they fought with a society that was content to label them 'queers'.

We had a moral duty do interpret Church teaching but we also had a duty to get our pupils to think constructively and independently. We once had a discussion about homosexuality at our 'religion' class but the boys were reticent to comment. They had already been conditioned to either ignore the matter or snigger behind closed fists. It struck me that there was just the same blind bigotry about gays as there was to others of different religions or colours. A poem I would read frequently in an attempt to get the boys to think about how they viewed others (not just gays but anyone who was different) was A. E. Housman's 'Oh Who is That Young Sinner?'

> 'Oh who is that young sinner with the handcuffs on his wrists?
> And what has he been after that they groan and shake their fists?
> And wherefore is he wearing such a conscience-stricken air?
> Oh they're taking him to prison for the colour of his hair.
> 'Tis a shame to human nature, such a head of hair as his;
> In the good old time 'twas hanging for the colour that it is;
> Though hanging isn't bad enough and flaying would be fair
> For the nameless and abominable colour of his hair.
> Oh a deal of pains he's taken and a pretty price he's paid

*To hide his poll or dye it of a mentionable shade;
But they've pulled the beggar's hat off for the world to see and stare,
And they're taking him to justice for the colour of his hair.'*

That simple poem spoke more eloquently and effectively than I ever could. It was only lately that I read it was composed by Housman at the time of the trial of Oscar Wilde.

Over the years a few of our ex-pupils 'came out' but I never felt entirely confident in talking to them about their difficulties in fitting in with society's prejudices. Proper sex education would have dispelled the myths but we only learnt about everything in piecemeal and often inaccurate slices. As a consequence children picked up some strange ideas as, for example, when an argument developed over whether John's sister was married. The discussion brought forth testaments and witnesses but the matter was only resolved when Joe adamantly but with a less than comprehensive insight of human biology pointed out, 'She couldn't be... sure she doesn't even have a baby.'

Another older boy continually plagued me by his oft-repeated question, 'Sir, can a dog have false pregnancies? I heard they can but I don't understand.'

I should, perhaps, have referred him to Benny who lived on a farm and was more knowledgeable in the procreation, false or not, of non-human species. We were once having a mime game in a class of eleven-year-olds where the boys acted out a movement that the rest of us had to guess. After the inevitable footballers, ballet dancers, bus drivers, and so on, Benny puzzled the rest of us by walking up and down the classroom with one hand clasped at head level. After a decent interval we confessed ourselves beaten.

'What was it, Benny?' I asked.

'I was leading the cow down to be bulled,' he exclaimed triumphantly.

'What does he mean, Sir?'

'Goodness, is that the time? We'll come back to that tomorrow.'

T is for THE TROUBLES

The longest time period of which I write was commonly referred to as 'The Troubles'.

I was fascinated by politics and in the 1960s joined the Civil Rights marches in Armagh, Newry, etc. It was obvious that something fairly momentous was going to happen but we had no appreciation of the sleeping tiger slowly stirring. After we were married, we returned from honeymoon to find a city in turmoil. In 1969 I, with many others, was genuinely concerned that attacks from sectarian mobs which had resulted in the burning and destruction of parts of the lower Falls was going to spread up the road. Retrospectively the idea was patently nonsense. The British army had been deployed throughout the area and the roads had all been barricaded with burnt-out cars, fallen trees and in one instance, twenty tons of grain. The fact was that a number of families on the Shankill Road probably believed the same fate was going to befall them and the 'IRA scum' (at that time the mythical creation of Paisley and other right-wing Unionists and rabble rousers) was about to fall upon and slaughter them. Nevertheless, the horror and fear engendered by the events that summer meant that numbers of men (unofficial vigilantes) gathered at night to protect their areas. We were no different. Quite what we were to do in the event of a fast car speeding and shooting machine guns was never fully decided. We could hurl stones and insults but it seemed a bit naive to imagine that this combined arsenal would be more effective than the rifles of the British army.

One night, about six of us were strategically stationed in the nearby shoemaker's shop (suitably strategic because he had a large electric kettle!) when a stranger came in. He was known to at least two of the others. He told us that he could get weapons and asked who would be prepared to take one. We talked but I declined. Without rancour he looked me straight in the eyes and said, 'I've been told that I will have guns to give to people to defend the area. If people like you that have a bit of common sense don't take them then I'll go down the line. So don't blame me if some of them end up in the hands of yobs and half-wits. They'll be given out because they'll be no bloody use lying in a cupboard.'

Years later I reflected on his words when two ex-pupil seventeen-year-old brothers were arrested, charged and jailed for being in possession of a sub-machine gun. I wouldn't have trusted those two with a plastic catapult. Every war has cannon fodder. There were other, more intelligent ones who joined and paid the ultimate price.

Sectarianism was always there. It always had been there. The State itself was artificially created to ensure Loyalist domination; bigotry and fear were the two major platforms of successive Unionist governments. I had always been brought up to respect other people's religions and Catholicism continually preached tolerance (even if it did not always respect it). My father was very Republican in attitude but was repulsed by bigotry. His paralysis and consequent removal from the immediacy and reality of what was happening in the streets meant that he still viewed everyone who took part in the IRA's campaign as another Wolfe Tone or John Mitchell. He was confused over the more blatant sectarian attacks that were perpetrated. With the increasing violence and mayhem, I was shocked and saddened to hear some of our pupils adopt the blind sectarianism and bitterness I had naively believed to be peculiarly endemic in 'the other side'. To hear the boys talk of 'orangies, snouts and blue-noses' was as depressing as it was frightening.

It forced me to rethink a lot of my own ingrained perceptions. Every week we had a history lesson and because of the increasing polarisation of a number of boys, I would endeavour to point out the great Protestant Liberal traditions evident in the early promotion of the Irish language and the Presbyterian leaders of the '98 rebellion against English rule. I told them how but for the efforts of their Protestant citizens; the Irish language would have disappeared in the North.

I would read the poem 'The Man from God Knows Where' telling of the hanging of the Presbyterian Thomas Russell. I would not claim to have been particularly successful in trying to ameliorate the distrust and hatred that some of the boys had because, as in other fields, the reasonable conversation one could have in a class was unrelated to life after school time. It was fine at 11 am to agree that there were good and fair people on all sides; that violence was inherently wrong; that we all had to take individual responsibility for our actions. But that didn't stop rioting with the 'orangies' at 11 pm. Schools on all sides tried valiantly to reduce hatreds but as the 1970s and 80s wore on in a constant, unrelenting horror-show of bombings, murders, sectarian assassinations, intimidation and unabashed naked hatred, we were doomed to failure.

As the boys got older and saw for themselves the effects of blatant sectarian killings like McGurk's Bar, the Shankill Road Butchers, etc. and started to lose neighbours, friends and relatives it was increasingly hard to preach a purely political response. The atrocities perpetrated on the 'other side' weren't a consideration to many of them. 'Bloody Sunday' in Derry tipped a lot of them into a depressingly bitter view that violence was the only way. Then, of course, inevitably some of our pupils became victims.

As events progressed and the violence became more concentrated, more and more intelligent and articulate people joined 'the struggle'. After Bloody Sunday it was said that you required an honours degree in Engineering or Political Science to join the Provisional IRA. I understood why, but I could never condone the violence that the warring factions inflicted on us all. The atrocities committed by Republicans were often forgotten as another atrocity was perpetrated by 'them' on the other side of the political divide. Without hectoring I tried to teach my pupils about better ways to achieve their aims and to convince them that behind the stories and the headlines there were real people who had real lives, cried real tears and bled real blood.

But the place being Belfast, even then there was black humour. One of Eileen's pupils told of how the family dog kept barking madly at the frequent soldier patrols. In order to get some sleep they administered Valium to the animal, which had the effect of sending it into a repeated crazy, unending race round the house. The decision thereafter was to dose it with sleeping tablets.

Some of the soldiers were young and frightened. A lot of the time they were also exhausted. One very early morning in 1971, I was stopped in County Armagh as I was going tench fishing. As requested I produced my driving licence and was asked to confirm my name and address, which I dutifully did. He perused it, yawned and returned it to me telling me to drive on. Only when I looked at it did I realise that I had handed him my wife's, which apart from having her photograph had a different name, date of birth and a different address to the ones I had given. He got the sex, photo, date of birth and address wrong… apart from that his task was carried out to perfection!

U is for UNDERSTANDING

'Mr Growthorp says you better come round to the metalwork room. Kevin McIlroy is giving trouble.'

I was supposed to be free from class doing career guidance and I was trying to work out a visit for a pupil doing work experience. In theory the specialist teachers were supposed to look after discipline in their own subject class but invariably every so often I would be summoned because one of 'my boys' had been giving trouble. So it wasn't entirely unexpected. It did surprise me, however, that Kevin was involved. He had just come to the school and seemed a nice kid with serious learning problems, a bit stubborn, but generally gave no bother.

I found the teacher and Kevin outside the metalwork door, both in an agitated state. Apparently Kevin had switched off one of the emergency switches and all the lathes, etc. had whistled to a stop. Cue teacher screaming and eventually Kevin reluctantly admitting he might have done it. The problem was that Kevin wouldn't apologise. The basis of discipline was, as I said, that any wrongdoing was exculpated with an apology. But Kevin was adamant. He was angry and sweat had formed on his forehead while his eyes were reddening and swelling. The teacher was equally adamant that he was not coming in again until he apologised. I told the teacher I'd deal with it and he left us alone outside the room.

'Calm down and tell me what happened, Kevin.'

After a pause, 'I was only messing around, Sir.'

'Good, now we're getting somewhere. What did you do?'

'I knocked against one of the switches that turns off the power.'

'So it was an accident?'

I suspected it wasn't but there didn't seem any merit going down that road.

'Yes.'

'Well accidents can happen but can you understand why Mr Growthorpe was annoyed? The power being turned off suddenly might have caused an accident.'

'I suppose so,' he agreed.

'So, what's the problem? All you've got to do is apologise and you're back in again. Everything is back to normal.'

'No way,' he replied adamantly and again became agitated.

I was bewildered. What could be the problem? It suddenly struck me.

'OK! So you won't apologise… but will you say you're sorry?'

He considered the suggestion. 'Yes, no problem.'

I never discovered what Kevin imagined apologising was. It might have involved being stripped naked, lashed to a lathe while the class took turns to carve their initials on his torso for all he knew but one thing was for sure – there was no way he was going to subject himself to it.

★

The gap that existed between what was uttered and what was understood was not just restricted to staff. Many years later I was Principal when the parents of a pupil took the school to court because the child had tripped over 'a boulder' in the school grounds. The boulder in question had peculiar physical properties in that by the time staff was notified about the incident, it had shrunk to the size of a small marble. I was extremely proud of the care and attention of the classroom assistants who were in charge at the time. Many years before, it became common practice our classroom assistants played games like skipping and hopscotch with the children at lunchtime and the suggestion that negligence was involved was inaccurate and infuriating. With free legal aid and with an eye on generous compensation the parents had nothing to lose, which resulted in my being questioned in court about the incident. The poor child who was involved was an eleven-year-old girl, Claire, who had considerable learning difficulties. Unfortunately her barrister appeared to be unaware of her difficulties when he began his questioning. Tucking his hands pompously beneath his gown in best Rumpole of the Bailey style, he looked at her earnestly and asked, 'Do you recollect the day when the incident occurred?'

Claire looked at him blankly: her face pale and nervous, eyes screwed together in puzzlement. Her counsel persisted, 'Claire, have you maintained a clear recollection of the event?'

This was altogether too much for the confused girl. Her bottom lip trembled and she slowly dissolved into a flood of tears. The judge later acquitted the school of any blame.

V is for VENGENCE

Early in the Troubles, the paramilitaries on both sides were seen by some as the defenders of their areas. In addition to keeping out 'the other side', they assumed the role of 'policing' the areas. Where the police were afraid, unable or unwilling to go, they further extended that to include the detection, judgement and punishment of those within that community who were involved in crime or 'anti-social behaviour'. It was an easy role to acquire and was broadly welcomed by the community itself. Outwardly people would condemn it as barbarous and ruthless but where people found themselves at the mercy of 'hoods, druggies and burglars' and having no recourse to a police service, they quietly nodded acquiescence, if not approval. Consequently the paramilitaries found themselves exacting vengeance on the transgressors. In many cases the police blackmailed petty criminals facing prosecution and enlisted them as informers. In communities where there was little police presence, the community often connived with paramilitaries in 'protecting the neighbourhood'.

It was inevitable, I suppose, that a number of my pupils flirted with criminal activity. A few not only flirted but went steady and eventually married into it. This was distinct from those who got involved in the ongoing political violence. The distinction in Northern Ireland resulted in the former being labelled ODCs (ordinary decent criminals) while the latter became 'freedom fighters' or 'terrorists' depending on your views (or more correctly on where you were born).

The ironic aspect was that where there was a big paramilitary presence in a district the ODCs were in more danger from the 'illegal organisations' than they were from the police. A boy for example who became a serious nuisance in his community would find himself in a dark alley where he would be shot in the kneecaps by hooded men. This happened hundreds of times. The balaclava brigade became known as 'the boys with the woolly faces'.

The power and control of the local units was such that once an 'offender' was named he was expected to present himself for punishment. This would ensure a less severe shooting than if they had to go to the trouble of seeking him out. Most victims received flesh wounds to the back of their knees with a low calibre bullet. Even in 2001, there were 190 such shootings.

One of my sixteen-year-old boys, Sammy, had been breaking into a number of houses near where he lived. Despite warnings from others in the class about the inevitable consequences, when the 'woolly faces' caught up with him, he persisted. After a visit to his house from the local 'brigade', when he was lucky enough to be out, he went on the run and slept rough for a number of nights. In the Republican areas of Belfast with the number of people who had suffered at the hands of burglars and 'hoods' it was only a matter of time before he was caught, counselled and given psychological help or, more accurately, caught, interrogated and found guilty. Before he was shot in the kneecaps the gunman who was to perform it whispered in his ear, 'When you recover you'll be putting in for a big money claim for this – we'll want half, OK?' He had little choice but to agree to partake in the proposed financial prospectus. A clear case of adding insult to injury.

Normally the patella or actual kneecap was not injured: the main harm being soft tissue damage to nerves and arteries. This often resulted in extreme pain and heavy bleeding which in a few cases caused death before medical help could be called. A study of cases in the mid-1970s showed that ten per cent of kneecappings resulted in surgical removal of the affected limb. In the 1980s and 90s it was not unusual to see a young man with crutches in the city. To some it was almost a boast to their mates, like Mafioso in *Goodfellas* they were going to be 'made'… well, if not 'made', certainly blooded. The frequency of such attacks concealed the inevitable real terror, trauma and suffering. Thousands of young men from both Republican and Loyalist areas were kneecapped. Even after the peace process was well established it still remained a common form of punishment from different paramilitary groups. As late as 2011, a botched kneecapping in North Belfast resulted in a death.

W is for The Last WORD.

In my first year of teaching, I passed a room at lunchtime where there a serious fight taking place. The combatants were about fourteen and when I came in they were rolling around the floor screaming obscenities at each other. I was amazed at their encyclopaedic vocabulary of curse words. There was a crescendo of 'F's, 'B's and 'C's before I succeeded in separating them. They stood apart continuing with the same foul abuse. Nowadays the language might not appear that shocking but back then, it would have caused a drunken sailor to row back.

With exhaustion slowly replacing the invective I asked the larger protagonist what had caused the fight. Drawing himself up in righteous indignation he explained, 'He called me a dirty P-I-G,' spelling each letter out carefully so that I would be left in no doubt as to the justifiable reason for his anger.

The other epithets caused him little, if any, concern but to be called a dirty 'P-I-G' was something that couldn't be accepted, even by the mildest of saints.

Another reason for the onset of physical engagements came when after separating another two wrestlers and being foolish enough to enquire as to the *casus belli*, I was earnestly told, 'I thought he was going to hit me so I hit him back first.'

Confrontation with a pupil in front of the rest of the class was to be avoided at all costs. There were other ways to succeed without the miscreant losing too much face. After a while, ensuring that the rest of the class was occupied it was usually enough to quietly approach and ask if we could have a word outside. It was seldom that the problem was not sorted quietly.

Away from the rest of the staring eyes and the unspoken challenge, most arguments could be settled. I always tried to ensure that after an argument had been settled, we shook hands.

Sometimes the response of a pupil caught in the act was surprising and even amusing. I was passing a corridor that only contained a locked canteen and a metalwork room. Mickey had obviously been excluded from the metalwork room and was stomping about in a rage. As he was screaming abuse and cursing loudly he decided to take out his frustration by kicking the wall. Unfortunately he missed and his foot went through a four-foot pane of plate glass. As the glass was still splintering and crashing to the ground, he looked up the corridor and saw me.

He paused for a second and then loudly screamed, 'It wasn't me... all right?'

I waited a second. 'OK, Mickey... who was it then?'

Not to be nonplussed for long, he paused until a small boy passed behind me, at least twenty yards from the incident.

'It was him,' Mickey screamed as he identified the culprit.

For the rest of my teaching career it became my favourite catchphrase. In class, if Jim or someone suggested I had done something I would squirm up my face and scream, 'It wasn't me... all right?' If someone reminded me of something that I had done, I again would respond with it. The boys found it hilarious and a number of them adopted the same battle cry.

A lot of ongoing arguments or 'lively interchanges of views' could easily be resolved by allowing the last word to go to the pupil. Some teachers, sadly, found this impossible. A preferable strategy is employed by a friend of mine, who in such moments looks straight at the child, shrugs his shoulders and stretches out his arms in hopelessness. Throwing his eyes up to heaven he sighs heavily and then walks away. It invariably ends the debate. The unsaid suggestion that there is no point in continuing such an unworthy discussion invariably works.

Sometimes, however, the last word from a pupil left me so bemused that, even had I wanted to, I couldn't find a suitable riposte.

Sammy was prone to (in educational psychological speak) *exaggerated and strenuous bouts of physical activity usually involving the perpetration of violence to those nearest...* in common parlance 'throwing a wobbler'. I was once called onto a school bus by an escort who screamed that 'Sammy has gone mad'. I told the Head that I would travel home on the bus. Sammy was indeed 'throwing a wobbler' and the only thing I could do was to grab him and hold him on the seat until he had calmed down. The physical attack stopped almost immediately but squirming beside me, he launched a tirade of epithets.

'You baldy bastard!' he screamed.

I feigned surprise. 'Baldy… what do you mean baldy? I've got more hair under my arms than you have on your head. I may be a lot of things but I'm not baldy.'

To emphasise the point I ruffled my hair vigorously.

'You're a fat fucker!' he continued, but with just a little less vigour.

'Now hold on Sammy. I mean that's just not true. Is it? Look at me. Do you honestly think I should loose weight?' I feigned to examine my stomach carefully. 'Maybe you're right… I'll have to think about it.'

The conciliatory tone of my responses was quickly defusing his temper but he wasn't about to quit yet.

'You're a big shite!' he whimpered as his tirade eviscerated.

'Now wait a minute,' I protested. 'I'm not big. I'm only five foot nine and a half. When you grow up you'll probably be bigger than I am.'

In a faraway voice I added wistfully, 'I wish I was bigger then maybe I could play basketball for Ireland.'

Sammy had now settled considerably and for the first time looked directly at me for a full five seconds. With flashing eyes under a furrowed brow he delivered his final words.

'Well… fuck you anyway!' he concluded.

★

Probably the most original riposte happened to a colleague in another school who was remonstrating with a recalcitrant fourteen-year-old girl who was being as sassy and uncooperative as only a fourteen-year-old girl can. Becoming totally exasperated, he warned her that if her behaviour didn't improve he would bring her father up to the school. She shrugged defiantly. 'I don't have a father!'

Somewhat taken aback he continued, 'Well, I'll talk to your mother then.'

She considered the threat briefly. 'I don't have a mother either,' she pouted. 'A soldier took advantage of my aunt.'

As he said, 'There's no answer to that.'

X is for eXCURSIONS

Taking pupils out on any sort of trip can be a potential threat to a teacher's happiness but the potential rewards throw that into relief.

Each year legal requirements appear to dilute the type of spontaneity and adventure that we enjoyed. Children are continually being reminded of how dangerous and bad the world is. Adults and the media have peopled the planet with murderers and paedophiles. It appears, perhaps wrongly, that a lot of parents are now too busy to involve their children in adventure.

I have the most vivid memories of sitting on the bar of my father's bike as he brought my brother and me to various 'secret places'. My brother had his own bike, a red Raleigh with three-speed Sturmey Archer gears (that was just another reason why it was impossible for us to develop brotherly love). As deep an impression as those expeditions made, they sometimes appeared shallow when compared to the deep groove in my bum caused by the bar.

We lived opposite the city cemetery and one March day, when I was very young, my father lifted me up to see a nest in a yew tree with four blue eggs in it. I felt a rush of excitement and joy. When I was older, the Falls park was my adventure playground. Every Saturday the 'gang' would meet and we would once again set out to 'dam the river'. Previous failures to achieve this had little bearing on the enthusiasm and endeavour we employed the next time. Paddling in the river, we were ignorant of the fact that it had flowed through a dye works and rejoiced when it vicariously turned red, purple and, once, an exciting vivid green. No wonder we never found any fish! The banks along the river provided a gradated range of jumps from 'dead easy' to the apocryphal stories beloved by children; 'one guy jumped this bit years ago and broke his two legs. He died of gangrene screaming in agony!'

The highest of trees were climbed in search of birds' eggs. It was accepted that you never took an egg if there were only three. When we eventually got bikes we rode to Musgrave or the Lagan and discovered newts. Seasons were important and each one had its special activity. In winter a large tarpaulin was stretched between the walls of the back houses of the entry and it became a centre of excitement. As we moved into our early teens the awakening wonderment of girls, who weren't sisters, enhanced its appeal. It leaked badly but, to us, it was the most luxurious hotel. I bought the first girl I fell in love with, Una, a small box of Jelly Babies with money purloined from my mother's purse. She devoured them all, sharing them with her giggling friend and ignored me. The fickleness of women!

Spring signalled the search for tadpoles and walks up the mountain to the 'gully' and the possibility of spotting hares. In July, my parents usually took a house in Ballycastle which was the highlight of the year. Regardless of the weather, we swam three times a day. We started saving after Easter. With Kevin, who is still one of my closest friends, and six others we formed a gang, 'The Gestapo', and came into conflict with a rival bunch of hooligans (which included my brother) known as 'The French Resistance'. Despite their name they were every bit, and a bit more, as vicious as we were. One evening they attacked us with nettles held with hankies wrapped around their hands, which we thought extremely unfair as they whipped at our bare legs.

August meant swimming at Rockport or the Falls 'Cooler', watching strange white clothed men playing cricket, and 'Bonfire night' on 15th August. Autumn was cycling to the Minnowburn after school, robbing orchards, collecting chestnuts and of course Halloween. Needless to say it wasn't as idyllic as our memories would have us believe, but it seemed a freer time with few strictures on our movements and our 'adventures' were encouraged particularly by my father. Our weekly bibles were *The Wizard*, *The Rover* and *The Hotspur*. Post-graduate students progressed to the *Eagle* where illustrations showed submarines, airliners, motorbikes, etc. with X-ray views of the interiors. Nerds could bore their friends silly by discussing the placement of the 'heads' in a fast frigate.

Nowadays the strictures imposed by media frenzy, careful parents, health and safety regulations, environmental legislation and so on have combined to ensure that we have a generation of anxious and fearful children who aren't allowed to stray or wander, who never fell into a shallow river, couldn't tell the difference between a starling and a blackbird, are forbidden to collect frogspawn, have never seen a newt or a stickleback and are only allowed to cycle on pavements or designated paths.

If one returned home at six after leaving the house after breakfast, your parents' only inquisition consisted of questions about what you had to eat and where you had been. They seemed to accept that they would probably only be told lies.

When we were older, fifteen and sixteen, the same age as many of the pupils I was later to spend years teaching, we were into all sorts of activities. I cringe when I remember some of the most downright crazy and stupid things we did. A favourite activity was jousting. Two of us would race at each other on bicycles carrying our lances (yard brushes were the favoured substitute) and attempt to knock the opponent flying. There was a large water pipe in Belvoir Park that crossed a high forty-foot drop which, after the barbed-wire end had been negotiated, one stuttered across. I remember clearly in a particularly severe winter being dared to ride my bike across the iced-up River Lagan and accepting the challenge. Once I did it there must have been about ten of us, cycling and trying wheelies. Halloween was a particularly exciting time. The father of Barry, one of my closest friends, was paid to deliver soap and other coupons to the local shops. These could be up to the value of three pence. Theoretically they were only redeemable if the purchaser actually bought the designated product but that minor retail nicety impressed neither us, nor the owners of the little 'house shop' near where we lived. Severely depleting his father's coupon stocks we exchanged them for a veritable arsenal of penny bangers. On Halloween night we would run down the back entries attempting to lob at least two 'bangers' into every back yard. We took a fiendish delight in completely ruining a fireworks display in the back garden of one of our less-favoured classmates by bombarding the event with bangers from behind his high garden fence. We entitled him 'Walter' after Denis the Menace's nemesis. Pleasant little children we were not. My legs wobble when I remember how we would sometimes stick them in our mouths pretending to smoke as we lit them!

When we were older, Barry and I would take an air rifle (illegal then, as now) and go, before dawn, to shoot rabbits. We never got anywhere near one and the only casualty was a little robin who unfortunately decided to perch above our heads while we, exhausted by our early start, slept soundly. Its blithe chirping woke Barry who, startled awake and without thought, aimed and finished the contribution that little songster was making to the dawn chorus. He was immediately contrite and so great was his remorse that even now, fifty years later, it is ridiculously easy to rile him by spreading your arms and chirping loudly before suddenly falling backwards.

Once he and I found an old canvas canoe buried beneath grass. We asked nearby and eventually found the owner who was glad to get rid of it. We spent many days on the Lagan paddling up and down. Although we could swim we also lent it to any of our friends, swimmers or not, who wished to paddle away. The idea that the canoe could capsize and the unfortunate occupant might drown never appeared to enter our heads. Two years later we decided to re-canvas it and restore it to its former glory. We saved up the requisite £4 and with the help of a willing employee of Tedfords, a large sailmaker's company, we managed to make it look reasonably professional. We soaked it in pitch and after it dried, launched it again on the river.

Unfortunately we didn't realise that over the intervening years we had become much bigger and the cockpit required a huge effort to enter. Reason, apparently absent in us before, made us realise that even a swimmer would be in serious trouble if it turned turtle. Although we intended to rebuild it at some stage, I imagine that what remains of its carcass is still where we left it.

I learnt to love fishing while still young and in the summer I would often fish off the rocks in Ballycastle. Often on my own, I was always aware of the danger of high waves. I would also spend the whole day searching the river for sea trout or salmon. No parent ever enquired about your safety or discussed potential dangers… after all, you were fourteen!

My father sometimes actively encouraged our escapades. Once, Barry and I decided that it would be fascinating to know if the coin held in your hand had ever been in your possession before. Obviously to determine this it was necessary to mark the coin in some way. My father found us in the back garden furiously attacking coins with a file with no success. Initially he chided us for being 'silly' but pondering on our ambitions he disappeared to return with his trusty Primus and a pair of pliers. He held the coin over the roaring flames until it became red-hot, when he placed it on a piece of concrete and hammered the triangular end of the file into the middle. Dousing it in water he held up a completely discoloured, heavily defaced coin of the realm that sported a triangular hole obliterating half of the Queen's head. It was singularly impressive and distinctly individual. Having made this significant contribution to the defacement of the royal mint, my father passed on his skills to his apprentices. As five different service buses stopped outside our house I would hide the marked penny between two good ones, rush on to the bus and ask the conductor to exchange it for a threepenny bit. Within a week we were in full production and our exchanges became bolder and (necessarily) quicker. I would now conceal four pennies between two good ones and seek an exchange for a sixpence. Our enterprise was curtailed when one day an inspector grabbed the coins and carefully examined them. 'What's your game?' he demanded handing me back the coins. With a rapidly reddening face I backed off examining the coins intently and, hopefully, innocently.

On summer nights we would occasionally dare ourselves to walk through the city cemetery and slip through the bent railings into the open-air swimming pool in the Falls park. An illegal midnight swim was as exciting an adventure as it was possible to have. In our late teens we became fascinated with ghosts and hauntings and would seek out reputably haunted houses. Even at university there still remained the desire to do things that would appear to others completely pointless. If Ned and I were at a loose end and had no money, we would stand at the beginning of the new motorway and thumb a lift. It was a game to see how far we would get before we had to turn for home. When a car stopped we would ask where the driver was going. Stretching credulity to breaking point the destination would invariably be the same as ours. We would set a time for turning back and hope our luck was in. This led to us being marooned for hours in places I had only heard about on the radio news. Many might consider the prospect of being stranded in Cookstown at two o'clock in the morning less than entertaining but it was preferable to sitting around doing nothing and certainly preferable to studying. I have been particularly blessed in that I have a number of friends that have stuck with me for nearly all my life. We are still lucky enough to be able to go off together and are lucky enough to still swim, cycle, walk the hills and fish the rivers.

★

This sense of escaping the humdrum normality of life, of trying to light a spark and create a memory that would distinguish that day from all the others is what motivates the enthusiastic teacher. There is no better classroom than the great outdoors and no better teacher than the experience gained in adventure. After leaving school when the years turn unforgivingly into decades, it still gives a teacher a real thrill when an ex-pupil says, 'Do you remember the day when you took us… ?'

With the older boys and the use of my dad's Transit van, we explored quite a bit of the world around us. I realised many of the pupils had very limited experiences. They knew and appreciated little outside of their own area and many of them, because of the Troubles, were naive, innocent and ignorant of anything beyond their local streets. This confinement of bodies and minds extended beyond that. When an organisation 'Children in Crossfire' arranged holidays with American families for children from troubled areas, I was often struck by how little that travel had broadened the mind. When I asked a fifteen-year-old who had just returned from five weeks with an American family in Florida what he had liked best, his eyes flickered with fondness. 'You should see the McDonald's they have out there.' I suppose I shouldn't be surprised when so many people go to a foreign country to lie on a beach, eat fish and chips and read yesterday's *Daily Mail*.

Nowadays most schools have access to their own transport yet there are still teachers who rarely, if ever, leave the classroom. Whether from laziness or ignorance they miss out on a major source of learning. There are even some who fool themselves by saying they consider 'trips' an easy way out of the class. Such crass ignorance is unforgivable. Any day out with pupils where you are often on your own with all the responsibility that you assume is one of the hardest days possible, but if you can create and share the enthusiasm it's also the most rewarding.

Y is for YOUTH

Time moves on and, eventually, every pupil had to move on. Because they were in the last class there was no promise of a continuing ethos; no comfort of familiar places or people; no tolerance of their difficulties and no excuses for their shortcomings. It was an emotional time. Often the sixteen-year-old who couldn't wait to leave school in January became the nervous, uncertain debutant in June. The reality of freedom was much more attractive in the distance. Some were keen to stay on and that was only agreed with the Principal, the parents and me if we saw value in the extension. If it was clearly just a case of last-minute nerves the request would be gently rejected. There had to be a better reason for staying on other than fearing the unknown. If a boy was starting to make significant improvement in literacy, behaviour or maturity we would agree that he could stay on for a while.

There were often times where I felt the world was going to be an incredibly daunting and frightening place for some but remaining at school wasn't going to accomplish anything either.

After our leaving ceremony I would shake hands, tell them they would be welcome to come back and see us anytime and if they had a problem we would always be there for them. Many would come back but others wouldn't. For a few of them, the 'stigma' of the 'special school' was just something to be forgotten. Through other boys who were still at school I would enquire as to how someone was getting on. Often I was delighted to hear of progress. With others it was depressing to hear how someone was 'drinking a lot' or 'didn't go out much' or was 'getting himself into trouble'.

It was hard to let some of them go. They had become very welcome personalities in our little mobile world. I hope that we were open with them, accepting their difficulties and problems and trying to mitigate them. While acknowledging their weaknesses, together, we attempted to identify their strengths; enabling them to see their value and potential; to recognise their contribution to all aspects of life as being of equal value to anyone else.

God knows, we weren't always successful but when I think on the failures I also remember the hairdresser with his own business; the successful career soldiers; the successful dealers; the tree surgeon; the painting contractor; the supermarket supervisor; the bus driver; the bouncers; the chefs, cooks and waiters; the welders; the joiners and bricklayers; the long distance lorry drivers; the gardeners and the dozens of others who work and have worked since they left school; the ones that would call at my house showing off their new (to them) cars while asking if I was still driving 'that old jalopy'.

★

One of the truly rewarding moments of a teacher's life is when an ex-pupil comes back to visit. There will always be the forlorn, bored lad who realises, too late, that school maybe did contain some of the best days of his life and he can return so regularly that he may have to be gently discouraged. The real thrill was when a lad who left some time ago returns and tells you how he's doing. Jim and I always made a big fuss over our ex-pupils.

It could be difficult when many of them were without work and often our best efforts were directed at cheering them up. We would talk to them with the class; discussing their job prospects, their past wages, their love-life, etc. Francie would stick the kettle on and we would have an impromptu tea break in his honour. It was surprising how many of them did so well. Their lack of educational abilities and qualifications didn't always hold them back. Many of them prospered. They didn't all return, of course. Some had moved away and some, sadly, didn't feel it appropriate. I deal elsewhere with the depressingly large number who had died either as victims of the Troubles, self-harm or accident. They are the ones who only visit at night when you lie in your bed.

I was still relatively young when I taught the older boys. (The older I get the more relative it becomes!) I stopped when I became Principal at the age of forty-two.

I don't know how I would have managed had I continued into the new age of 'enlightenment'. A lot of the activities, antics and behaviours that I enjoyed would be anathema today. There would be no October or March swims in the sea; there would be a greater reluctance to give independence or treat sixteen-year-olds like young adults; no trips where boys would be spread around a van like rags; no revelations of our own problems; no outrageous classroom activity. It seems health and safety were ethereal considerations when the world outside the classroom was disintegrating. The brutal atrocities that occurred on a daily basis seem further away with each passing year. The passage of time has blurred and sanitised the anger, pain, suffering and death that we lived with daily. But for a few hours each day the mobiles were our oasis where the outside barbarity could be ignored. Even when it affected us, as it did frequently, we were able to take refuge in our own little artificially sealed world.

As we get older we forget the raging energy that we had when we were young. There was a dynamic that the class possessed that impregnated the air, a sense of dangerous challenge lurking just below the surface. One had to be young not only in body, but in attitudes and interests. Your mind had to be young and open to new experience. You had to be brave enough to try new things and foolish enough to think you could accomplish them. A lot of what happened within the walls of the mobiles resulted from a form of benevolent authority combined with an acceptable touch of anarchy and a relationship that depended on trust and friendship. There were other aspects that were, I'm certain, less than that. Lost tempers, anger, frustration, etc. showed that the fallibility of humanity extended to the staff.

Z is for ZERO HOUR

My perfect job came to an end in June 1986. The Principal had reached retirement age and the position was advertised. Despite some of the very good work happening within the classes, the school's reputation as a dumping ground meant that it was failing to attract enough support. Innovative and successful initiatives such as an Infant Support Unit and short term courses were unable to stem overall falling numbers.

We already had a redundancy and the prospect of more was looming. The school building itself was openly decaying. No temporary physical makeover could conceal how totally unsuitable for purpose it had become.

I applied for the post in the conviction that when I didn't get it I would, at least, have indicated my interest in any other promotion resulting from an internal shake-up.

Like others, I thought the writing was on the wall. When the phone call was made informing me that I was the new Principal my emotions were a mixture of surprise, bewilderment and trepidation. My emotions were encapsulated by my wife, Eileen, who while congratulating me said, 'For someone whose only real ambition in life was to catch a bigger salmon, get a better bike or climb a bigger mountain it's ironic you've actually made Principal.'

As a Principal I would have to rethink a lot of things and react differently. My independence had gone. I was lucky, I suppose, to have taught when I did because that freedom to experiment, that exhilaration would be much more difficult or even impossible now. As I left school on the last day of term in June, I knew that my life was going to change and change drastically. But that, as they say, is another story!

THE UNFORGOTTEN

DAN

Dan was one of God's innocents. He had a ruddy complexion spattered with reddish freckles and a head that looked slightly larger than a body could comfortably cope with. He looked ungainly from a distance but when you got up close you realised that 'ungainly' was way down on the litany of awkwardness and the adjective to describe his drunken, crablike, sideways motion had yet to be invented. The problem with Dan was that he fondly believed he was a star footballer. If passion, endeavour and enthusiasm had been sufficient criteria he would surely have graced the great stadia of the world. However, when one participated with all the balletic grace of a wounded buffalo, passed the ball like a geriatric drunk, tackled like a dead pussycat, and kicked with the force of a leaf in the doldrums then it was a case of playing not so much like Stevie Gerrard but more like Stevie Wonder.

    He was normally a gentle soul but his flaming red hair was infrequently matched by an excitable temper. He was a big boy but his temper usually consisted of verbal disagreements, which was fortunate as his propensity as a boxer equated neatly with his footballing skills. His mother appeared to share his misconception that he was the new George Best for she was always buying him new football kits and boots. He had an endearing generosity and distributed previous year's jerseys to the rest of the class. A pleasant, generous boy, he was well liked and was well settled in class.

He found the academic side of school difficult and he had a speech problem, which didn't help. The school had access to a speech and language therapist but as the pupils got older they became too embarrassed to attend and often ended the sessions voluntarily. Dan's particular problem was the indistinct and confused initial letter sounds. This meant that 'c' and 's' often sounded like 'd' or 'th'.

This often led to confusion. I suppose it didn't help that outside of the class any boy with such a problem had 'tut tut' whispered to him occasionally. One year a new speech therapist arrived who had the looks and figure of a film star. When she appeared on the scene the entire class (and the male teachers) would start to stammer and seek individual guidance and help! It was one of the few times Dan was viewed with envy.

My father, who ran the football team, appreciating the importance of football to Dan, would always pick him on his team to play other schools. He would always come on at some stage and would be referred to as 'super sub'. If a lie is repeated often enough it can sometimes be perceived as the truth. In one match when Dan, who was looking the other way at the time, turned he was hit full-face with the ball. As the blood spurted from his squashed nose, the ball trickled past the opposition keeper who was more engrossed in the realignment of Dan's face. As he fell to the ground, my father started clapping loudly and exclaimed to all, 'My God! What reflexes! Did you see that Mr Magennis?... He didn't have the time to line it up with his head so he "faced" it into the net! The only time I ever saw that done was in a Manchester

United match where Jimmy Slutterbug scored against Wolves. Incredible… what bravery!'

Although somewhat unconvinced initially the rest of the boys, as the eulogy continued, joined in the clapping. Dan lay semi-conscious on the muddy field like some obscene gargoyle that had fallen from Notre Dame: his eyes reddened with pain, his nose resisting the gravitational configuration intended at birth, blood streaming profusely from his split lips and smiling blissfully as my father's accolades continued apace. He was carried off on what must surely have been one of the most painful and happiest days of his life. In the months that followed it would often be referred to as 'Dan's wonder goal'.

*

After my father had his accident and was paralysed, the football matches stopped for a couple of months until a new, young and enthusiastic PE teacher was appointed. He had a good rapport with the boys and, despite his inexperience, very quickly related easily to them. He realised that despite our low numbers we had a fair bit of talent in the school. He was keen to show that and started to select a team. Unfortunately, despite his shiny new boots and his pristine strip Dan was overlooked. No longer the 'outside left', he became the 'left outside'. Even his by now famous 'wonder goal' couldn't gain him a place on the team. There was a different philosophy in place. It was fair enough to argue that the school collective pride in success was more important than that of the individual but it was hard not to have sympathy with him. To say that Dan saw this as nothing short of a betrayal underestimates his chagrin. After a while he ceased pestering the PE teacher and resigned himself to uttering quiet curses every time he saw him. Trying to assuage him, I would tell him the new teacher knew he was good but he had to see the other boys play to see where he could best be placed. He was neither fooled nor mollified. One day as the PE teacher left my room after telling the class which boys were playing in the team, I saw Dan look after him balefully like a doleful basset hound and just audibly entitle him, 'dilly dunt'!

It was a matter of relief, satisfaction and a fair degree of surprise that he did well in later life. He ended up in working in a bar in Leeds and came back to see me a number of times. On one occasion he arrived back with a large bottle of whisky, which he had brought from work. 'If you like it I can get you as much as you want,' he offered warmly. Doubting that his employer shared, or appreciated his generosity I thanked him profusely but persuaded him to halt this proposed importation of goods.

PETER

One of the earliest pupils who made a big impression on me was Peter. I first taught him when he was aged twelve.

Small for his age, his quiet, shy nature meant he was either going to be a victim of bullying and abuse or completely ignored by his peers. Each day he travelled to school from a different education board area, arriving in a taxi. He never missed school and sat quietly getting on with his work. He was determined to do his best and, I suppose, could be called a model pupil. He had an open innocent look and a posse of freckles, which were corralled in triangles between his dimples, and pale blue eyes of disarming intensity. His natural shyness incongruously magnified his speech when he occasionally spoke, like someone laughing uproariously during a performance of Fauré's *Requiem*. It was obvious he enjoyed school and I would notice him quietly laughing to himself whenever I was 'acting the ejit'. When I would mimic a voice he would sit quietly tittering to himself. Over the course of the year he became increasingly bold and would even venture answers to questions.

I used to ask friends of mine to come to the class to talk to the boys. This was an attempt to lessen the awe with which a lot of them viewed different professions. Kevin was a doctor and after some coercion agreed to come and talk about his role in the hospital. He did it with some aplomb and then asked for questions. To my delight at his confidence, Peter, while glancing frequently at me, persistently grilled him about the negative effects of smoking and at what age a man who smoked could expect to die. Throughout the session he positively smirked at his own probing.

To further encourage his independence and confidence, I put him in charge of my cupboard where the books, jotters, etc. were kept. No governor of the Bank of England ever took his role more seriously and a missing pencil at the end of the day would prompt an investigation worthy of Inspector Morse. The collection and counting of items returned had to tally exactly with what had been dispensed earlier. Peter loved the authority and the responsibility fed his growing confidence.

Every year a number of the staff would take a group of boys to a holiday home near Portaferry on the South Down coast. It was very hard work but enjoyable for all that. I knew that Peter's mother was on her own and would have found it hard to get the money required, although the holiday was heavily subsidised. One Saturday afternoon I went to his local presidium of the St Vincent De Paul and arranged that they would not only pay the money, but would also organise new clothes, pocket money and anything else required. Often we would get round any potential embarrassment by rigging special ballots. We would have done this for a number of pupils who were living in very abject and dispiriting conditions. The holiday was, as usual, a great success and thoroughly enjoyed by the boys. We walked them into the town which was about four miles away and let them loose on the local shopkeepers. While we kept an eagle eye for any light fingers, the boys filled their pockets with all sorts of treats. The main topic of debate was what goodies they were going to bring home to their parents and their brothers and sisters. It was very touching to see the undoubted affection or loyalty this reflected. It was as evident in the boys from troubled backgrounds as it was from those from 'good' homes. I was to learn later just how important and preferable a bad home was to any sort of state intervention. The afternoons were usually spent on the beach or exploring the rock pools. Often we would collect 'willicks' and boil them up in the kitchen. It was a mark of manliness to be able to twist one out and down it without examining the entrails. Supplied with pins, we would have the entire area littered with empty shells before a surfeit lead to either satisfaction or sickness.

The same was true of swimming in the sea. It could be extremely cold in May or June but I would lead the way and a few of the more adventurous ones would follow. We would come out in shades of blue and purple and lie bravely to the others, 'It's cold at first but you soon warm up.' There was a non-stop game of football on the grass pitch, which might have a solitary figure playing 'against myself'. In the evenings, the game expanded to include practically everyone, including even the most elderly staff. Cricket was also popular.

Peter blossomed on the trip. He was up first every morning, his face awake and alive, anticipating the joy the day would bring. Where he had been shy and reticent he became increasingly confident and even talkative. Although he had never previously taken part in sports at school he became an enthusiastic cricketer and also played hockey. He was open to every new experience. It was like a blind person being gifted with sight. He was particularly struck by the sight of groups of oystercatchers whistling low over the water, flashing black and white wings. He asked what type of birds they were and on being told, confided quietly, 'They're really beautiful.' It was astounding how in a different environment, children changed. My father had insisted that everyone in the group should be allowed to go on the holiday, despite the objections of other staff. That included some that we knew to have the potential to be very difficult but we reluctantly agreed. However, even the truculent and difficult ones changed their behaviour. Although it was exhausting, the benefits were huge. Camaraderie was built up and relationships between staff and pupils invariably improved.

There were two large dormitories where the boys slept in bunk beds. Each night after they had gone to bed, the prayers would be said and one of us would walk up and down in the dark to ensure silence. It all seems slightly odd nowadays but it was the only way to ensure that we all got a decent night's sleep; otherwise we would have had pupils running around at three in the morning. Just occasionally a head would rise and an unfortunate would venture, 'I think he's gone now.' The teacher would then rebut this and the miscreant would be ordered out of bed to sit on a chair in the lounge as an encouragement not to repeat the offence. Normally after ten minutes or so, he would be sent back to bed. One night, I had removed a big senior called Arthur for opining that the 'teachers were all away'. I sat him outside in an old cane chair and returned to my patrol. After they had settled I headed over to the main building for a cup of tea. I completely forgot about Arthur and only remembered when I returned hours later to see a huddled-over figure curled in the chair. His pyjama bottoms had slipped slightly and I saw to my horror that his backside was perfectly crisscrossed with the marks of the cane. The entire class could have played noughts and crosses for days on the 'gridded' posterior. I woke him and as gently as his crawling, foetal gait would allow steered him back to bed like a benign keeper leading a chimp with chronic arthritis. As he crawled into bed, Peter woke and stared at me. He opened his mouth and then, observing his crippled classmate, decided silence might be a better option. I whispered, 'Goodnight Peter.'

A lot of the activities we encouraged would land us in front of a Health and Safety tribunal were they repeated today. The older, more trustworthy boys (more rigged ballots!) were allowed to walk into town to the shops, others were allowed to go down to the shore and explore the rock pools. We even arranged a midnight bonfire and a midnight swim. There was more than an element of trust and independence.

At that time the home had been given a video player, which was a novelty unknown to most of us. A number of the boys, however, showed us how to operate it and with a wet, windy night in prospect I drove a few of the group into the town to rent a video. *The Magnificent Seven* (one of my favourites) was chosen and later that night a group of us sat on an eclectic collection of sofas and chairs, distributed crisps and drinks and turned off the lights to watch Yul Bryner, Steve McQueen et al. give Eli Wallach his comeuppance. There was a shortage of seats and some of the audience watched it from the floor. I was on a sofa, squashed between a number of boys. I was suddenly shocked to find myself the recipient of a big kiss on the cheek. Peter was beside me. Completely taken aback but trying not to show it I merely said, 'For God's sake will you lot move over… you're squeezing the air out of me.'

I've thought about that incident many times since. What would have happened had I patted his arm or heaven forbid, given him a friendly hug? One can imagine the scenario with the current climate of abuse and paedophilia had I responded with any reciprocity of affection. I wrote a short story based on the episode, which essentially retold the event except, in my story the teacher did give the youngster a hug. The boy had a physically aggressive father and the teacher had become the father figure the boy sought. In an argument with his father to show him his hatred, he tells him that he had kissed the teacher and the teacher had hugged him... well... you can imagine the denouement.

The incident also demonstrated the importance that a pupil attaches to a favoured teacher and the responsibility of the teacher to the pupil. Isn't it odd that the only physical contact that was acceptable in those days was that conveyed by a cane or a strap or even a slap across the face?

Peter moved to another school about a year later and I never saw or heard of him again but I'll always remember him with a little bit of fear regarding the possible scenarios of that particular night.

PIERCE

Word arrived in the form of a panic note from the Head stating that there was an inspector in the school. That necessitated a warning that there would be no smoking until after he left... otherwise carry on as normal. (It was ironic that one of our inspectors was himself practically a chain smoker and smoked any and everywhere. Years later when I was Principal and, like most others, had given up smoking he continued to light up in the office.)

I was proud of the class, their work and the discipline and ethos that we had. I suppose I was vain enough to seek and welcome the approval of others. I could never understand the fear that a visit from the inspectors generated. Teachers went to an amazing amount of effort to camouflage their failure to have done what they should have been doing all year. Teachers who were too lazy to display their pupils' work became dedicated interior designers for the weeks preceding an inspection.

Rooms that had been antiseptically barren became interesting, colourful and exciting. Once the inspection passed, they stayed there until they were removed for cleaning and painting. Teachers who were too lazy or inadequate most of the year became dedicated pedagogues. It also helped their cause that they warned the pupils beforehand that it was they who were being inspected and if they didn't do well, they could be moved to another school. The inspectors rarely found them out. This small minority of ineffective teachers fooled them with the connivance of a Principal and a fear of the unions. The vast majority of teachers I worked with were good professionals, some of them were very, very good and a few of them were idiosyncratic enough to be vibrantly excellent.

I had more than a little respect for this particular inspector as he had been a highly regarded teacher and I had heard his praises sung by others. When he entered the classroom we chatted about the difficulties of teaching pupils with learning difficulties and behaviour problems. Quite suddenly he grabbed my arm and indicating a particular pupil whispered in disbelief, 'Good God!... Is that Pierce Macken? I taught him in Primary 5. He was the most difficult boy you could imagine. He used to throw things round the classroom and climb out the window onto a balcony. We lived in fear of him falling and we actually got the caretaker to nail the window down to prevent its opening.' I brought him to Pierce's desk and reintroduced them. I left them chatting like the best of buddies. I never saw Pierce as a behaviour problem. He would arrive each morning, cheerful and chatty, and enjoyed an increasing confidence with literacy. He was particularly sharp in Maths and often had the answer before any of his classmates. He was, in essence, the sort of pupil who gave his teacher the feel-good factor.

It was not unusual for a boy to display an entirely different behaviour in a different environment. I was often amazed when parents would describe one of my 'model pupils' as a complete headache at home. One father described his offspring as 'a nightmare at home. We can't get him to do anything. His language is foul and he treats his mother and sister appallingly. He's so bad we can't put up with it much longer. He seems intent on making all our lives a misery.' He was describing the same boy who in school was a pleasant, helpful, industrious model pupil!

Similarly, the Pierce the inspector described was the complete antithesis of the boy I knew in class where he was pleasant and obedient. Children (and adults too) react differently to the circumstances and environments in which they find themselves at any given time. They have no difficulty in determining an appropriate set of behaviours to conform to the set limits.

Pierce's major issues had been well helped by other teachers long before he got to my class and my pride in him was especially attributable to another aspect of his personality. Every so often I would play some classical music on the tape recorder while we waited for all the buses to arrive. Those early birds were treated to music I thought they would vaguely know and eventually come to explore some that they didn't. It wasn't in truth totally successful and often big Tommy would look at me disbelievingly and contemptuously enquire, 'Well what sort of crap are we going to have to listen to today?'

Others still fighting off sleep would rest their heads on the desk or gather round mine to talk about the latest shooting, bombing or football… topics that formed the greater number of subjects. Nevertheless after a while it was pleasing to hear the odd boy whistle along to some Rossini overture or Bizet's *Carmen*. Pierce loved pop music and any time we had a quiz, he was sure to know the answer. He was particularly keen on 'The Who' and 'Queen'. Every Friday afternoon, Jim and I would have free time for the last hour and a quarter. We had a small snooker table, a football game, draughts, chess and darts. There was one pupil whom I rarely ever beat in chess and another, Charlie, whom I never beat at draughts! Throughout the session Pierce was in charge of the record player. He was in heaven as he picked his favourites, brought from home. But there was a price for his happiness. In order to be allowed to play his selection there was a quid pro quo that entailed his agreement that I could play some of my mine but for no more than ten minutes. This was tolerated by the others. I tried to be slightly more adventurous and eclectic in my choice and played some blues as well as Fauré's *Sanctus*, pieces from *Rhapsody in Blue*, Beethoven's *Pastoral* and Tchaikovsky's *First Piano Concerto*. The majority of the boys looked upon this cultural gala with boredom if not distaste but Pierce became increasingly interested. He eventually persuaded me to let him take home some of my LPs. I thought there might well have been an element of showing off or pretence, but I was happy to agree.

Fast-forward fifteen years; I was sitting with a friend in a local pub when the barman brought over two pints. 'The guy at the far end sent these over to you.' I went over to thank him and after initial confusion, I recognised him as Pierce.

'Thanks for the drink, Pierce, you're very kind.'

We had a short conversation of the 'How are things with you?' variety.

'Do you know what I'm doing after I leave here?' he asked. 'I'm going home and I'm going to play Beethoven's sixth. I've got dozens of classical music records and I really love them. Thanks to you.'

I felt on top of the world for a good week after that.

FRANK

Frank was fourteen when I first got to know him. I was taking the roll of my new class on the first day of the September term. Most of the class I knew already but I did a quick head count and got seventeen. This was surprising, as I had been given a register that contained only sixteen names. I called the names and got the requisite sixteen, but a further head count again showed seventeen. With customary insight I realised that either one of the pupils had grown an extra head over the summer or we had a 'stowaway'. I eventually discovered the supernumerary to be Frank.

He was a very pleasant Down's syndrome boy who was popular with everyone in the school, but he was two years short of my class age. He had a plump round face and glasses, which he was continually misplacing.

He was invariably in good humour and took a full and active part in all activities.

'Frank O'Halloran. What are you doing here? You're not in my class… you should be in with Mr Patterson.'

'I want to stay with my friend Peter,' he pleaded. 'Please Mr Rooney.'

His appeal was so earnest and I could see the tears starting to well up so I told him I would see the boss and let him know. By the time the lunch break came, Frank was so securely installed that it would have taken a seismic shift to move him. He had befriended everyone in the class and was even helping one of the older boys with his reading. So, after clearance from above, he stayed. As everyone was at a different level and essentially working at their own pace, it didn't prove a problem except that I suspected my charms would be wearing thin on him at the end of three years.

Far from being a problem, Frank was a delight. He was an excellent reader and I would often get him to read from a story. He was extremely innocent and inoffensive but there would never be a question of him being bullied. He had an army of older befrienders. The class quickly became used to his impromptu outbursts when in the middle of everyone working he would suddenly stand up and ask, 'Mr Rooney, can I say something to the class?'

'Of course you can, Frank.'

'I just want to say I have got three girlfriends… Mrs Grant [a female teacher], my mother and Raquel Welch. That's all.' He would then sit down.

Each morning during our religion period I would ask if anyone had someone they wanted us to say a prayer for. There was the usual litany of sick relatives and friends. Frank's suggestions were not always well received. It's not difficult to imagine the response from the rest of the class coming, as most of them did, from hardline Republican districts, when Frank ventured that we should say a prayer for Princess Anne because she had fallen off her horse!

'I hope she broke her bloody neck,' was one riposte.

'That's very thoughtful Frank, we'll say a prayer for everybody that falls off their horses,' I praised.

Like a number of children with Down's syndrome, Frank was very literate although his comprehension was poor. He was a regular in his local library and would arrive in school with a motley collection of books ranging from *The Secret Sex Life of Whales* to *The Amateur Carpenter's Guide to DIY*.

★

In his second year with me, there was a tragedy in his family and his father was drowned while trying to save another son who had fallen into the sea from a pier. My colleague Jim knew the family well and was friendly with Frank's mother. She was a lovely person and was understandably depressed and bewildered at the loss of a very talented, professional husband whom she felt had so much to offer, not only to his family but also to a number of others outside the family circle. He had been involved in a number of charities. I suppose she must have wondered at the unfairness of it all and may even have wondered about the relative contributions to society that others, including Frank, could make.

At that time my wife and I were expecting our first child and as everyone does when asked what we wanted, we would reply that it didn't matter as long as he or she was fit and well. Eileen had previously had a miscarriage at six months so we were understandably nervous and concerned. One day in class Frank, as he was prone to, stood up and asked to address the class.

'I just want to thank everyone for being my friend.' He sat down.

I quietly said to Jim, 'You know all the concerns we have about the baby… well if you thought the worst thing would be that you would have a child like Frank you couldn't complain: he does nothing but bring joy to everyone.' Jim repeated my thoughts to Frank's mother some time later. Weeks passed when one day, after bringing Frank to school after a dental appointment, she thanked me for the comments. She had thought about what I had said and that had helped her to realise, in the middle of her grieving, what a gift Frank was.

Over the years we taught a number of children with Down's syndrome and they were all individuals with different manners, abilities and aspirations but they all had a very real ability to inspire admiration rather than pity, affection rather than rejection and trust rather than doubt.

GOBIEMAN

His original name was Michael but the few times that appellation was used were few and far between. Some said his adopted nickname referred to his inability to stay still, to be always involved – hence motion degenerating into 'Gobie'. His full title was, apparently, 'Gobieman' but that was generally abbreviated. It seemed unlikely that he had any Jewish blood in him and if he had, he was one of a small number of Jews Israel would be keen to disown. When the Head told me that there was a new pupil starting and gave me his name, he also muttered something about him having been on probation and having a 'bit of a reputation'. He further suggested, with no sense of irony that, 'He'll probably settle down all right.'

The immediate reaction of the boys in the class who lived in his area of Belfast was a mixture of incredulity and excitement. 'Sir, he's mental, absolutely mental,' said one. Another judged him critically as he solemnly uttered, 'His head's full of wee doors, and they're all banging.'

What was slightly more disturbing was the fact that a classroom assistant whose grandmother lived in the same street as Gobie sought me out after class to establish if it were indeed true that he was joining us. The picture she painted was somewhat disconcerting. Apparently he could be quite chatty and pleasant but was also completely fearless and oblivious to all normal standards of behaviour. She told me of a woman who lived in the street and kept chickens in her small back yard. She also kept a cockerel, which as is their nature, woke the entire street at unearthly early hours. There had been a number of complaints but the cock continued to crow. One morning the offending bird went missing but the owner eventually found it dead, neck broken and nailed to her front door… a clear case of murder most fowl! Gobie's patience with the offending bird had apparently been reached. When someone asked him what he would have done had the hen owner's Alsatian dog attacked him, he pulled a pair of pliers from his pocket and said, 'I'd have pulled out every one of his fucking teeth.' I never established if the story was true but it certainly proved he had a bit of a reputation!

Gobie was going to be an interesting challenge.

As with any new pupil aged fourteen to sixteen coming into the school and straight into my class, I talked first to the class and then to the new pupil on his own in the vestibule before he joined the class.

The spiel was always the same.

'Basically Michael, this is your last chance. You're here because, let's face it, nobody else wants you. First off! I don't care what's happened before. We've a big sign on the door that says "Today is the first day of the rest of your life".

'If you pull your weight, do what we expect – no problem – you might even enjoy it. But if you act the maggot and mess us around… you're out. We have more pupils than we're supposed to have so I only have to bring you to the boss and you're out… there's nowhere else – so bang goes any chance you have of getting a decent job and staying out of trouble. Some of the boys here have some trouble with their work but don't think we're dumb. We work hard and a lot of the guys that leave here get good jobs. We don't have a big long list of rules; you just do and act like everyone else. Don't muck people about and you'll get on fine. I see by your hands you're a smoker, which means you're a mug but if you look at my hands you'll see I'm a mug too. You only smoke in the toilets. OK? My name is Mr Rooney and your name is…?'

He looked me straight in the eyes with absolutely no trepidation as he said coolly, 'My name's Michael but people call me Gobie.'

'Why do they call you that?' I asked.

He shrugged his shoulders, indicating a complete lack of interest.

'Right, Gobie, you're very welcome.' I put out my hand and we shook.

Despite his reputation, I quickly came to like Gobie. He was a small boy for his age and looked thin and underfed, though each day he came to school with bags of crisps and chocolate bars. I suspected that somewhere between home and school some shopkeeper found his stocks illegally depleted. He had fair hair and bright little eyes that searched for devilment. He would come into school early and sit up at my desk with his arms folded and tell Jim and me about what was happening in his area… whose house was raided by the soldiers (Brits); who was up in court; what was being stolen; who the 'RA' (IRA) were looking for; who had stolen cars, etc.

If either Jim or I had done so I'm sure we could, by a couple of phone calls to the confidential telephone service, have cut the crime rate in that area by half. That is based on the assumption that what Gobie told us was true.

One day I was talking to another boy in the class from his area and I commented on how well Gobie had settled in. He looked at me and confided, 'Sir, you wouldn't believe what he's like outside.' He started to relate a litany of nefarious goings-on but I stopped him. 'Thanks but I'm not sure I really want or need to know this.'

Gobie worked well and said he was determined to get his Record of Achievement. He got on well with the rest of the boys and kept many of them supplied with sweets and cigarettes, but always at a price. He rarely gave anything away but was happy to sell them at a reduced rate. At the beginning he would come into the class and throw a couple of twenty packets of Benson and Hedges on my desk.

'Gobie, I can't take cigarettes off you. I can't take anything off you.'

'Sir, they weren't nicked. Honest to God, Sir. My aunt has a shop up the Ormeau and I go there every morning and she gives me anything I want. Honestly, Sir.'

'That may well be, but even then I can't accept things from you or anyone else. It just wouldn't be right. Why don't you share them out with the rest of the smokers?'

He did, but again at a cost. His altruism only extended to certain members of staff.

I never saw Gobie show any great emotion about anything. He was never in bad form: life seemed to flow over him like a blanket of fog. He never showed regret or anxiety. He was a survivor. One day I was sent for as he was 'messing about' in the metalwork room. When I entered he was perched precariously on top of a metal cabinet about ten feet from the ground.

How he had managed to get up there I never discovered. Like Poe's raven, he was crouched watching the world go by. He wasn't in a temper – he had just decided to view the world from a different perspective. The metalwork teacher was infuriated because he just refused to come down.

I looked up at him. 'Gobie, get down now and stop acting the idiot. Come on round with me to the class.'

He shrugged his shoulders and climbed down with an air of ennui. On the way round to the mobile I asked him, 'What was all that about?'

He sighed. 'Just.'

That was as much as I was going to get, as I realised that was the most honest answer, 'Just… because that's who I am.'

★

I remember vividly one afternoon when we had finished most of the work and were gathered round the desk having an impromptu chat about money and the value of money. I asked, 'What's the biggest amount of money you ever had in your hand or in your pockets. No spoofing – just give an honest answer.'

Numerous figures were quoted ranging from £35, proceeds from a Confirmation, to the more realistic £10, etc.

'Ask Gobie, Sir. Go on, ask him.'

'Well Moneybags, what about it? What's the biggest amount of money you've ever had?'

He looked at me and frowned slightly, his lip slightly twisted in thought. 'I'm not sure I want to tell you.'

'It's OK, we don't want to know where you got it… we'll not ask… just for the craic, how much?'

He again went into a deep, silent reverie.

The buzz of conversation had begun again before he interrupted us with, '£685.'

Looking at him I realised this was absolutely true. He wasn't exaggerating.

'That's a lot of money. It takes me two and a half months to earn that,' I responded with just a hint of bitterness.

On our way to the buses, he held back and walked along with me. 'Do you want to know where I got that money?'

'Only if you want to tell me,' I lied, bursting with curiosity.

'Well,' he explained, 'you know the railway lines? There are cables that run along the side of the tracks and a lot of them are copper and stuff. I cut them with big bolt cutters and stack them up in my backyard until I bring them round in a cart to the scrap yard.'

'Gobie! You must think I'm daft. Sure a lot of that cable would be electrified. If you cut that you'd end up in smoke.'

'Naw,' he spat, amazed at my naivety, 'my Uncle Jim works on the railway and he lets me know what sections have been cut off for repair work. He gave me this big electric box with two clips and when you go to the tracks you put the clips on to the cable. If the wee needle moves up you don't touch it but if it doesn't move you can cut away!… I want to get one of those boxes for myself,' he reflected thoughtfully. 'You see, the trouble is I have to give half of that money to my Uncle Jim.'

★

Unusually Gobie went missing one day and didn't appear for a week. His disappearance was the talk of the area. Apparently one of his ambitions was to chisel the lead from the guttering around the dome of Belfast's City Hall. When you realise that this was the height of the Troubles, that everyone was searched before they went into a shop and that even babies' prams were subject to the metal detectors carried by security staff poised at the entrance of every store, it appeared an unwise and ill-conceived ambition. But common sense and a healthy regard for one's own safety were not constituent parts of Gobie's make-up. His role was to act as lookout. So one night he and another older and more hardened criminal armed only with basic cutting tools and a few lengths of rope sneaked their way into the City Hall grounds. While Gobie kept watch, his companion managed to reach the first floor pillars. It was, at this time, that Gobie heard an alarm go off and saw a number of security police running towards the building. Showing a keen sense of survival, instead of trying to hide he sprinted towards them shouting, 'The guard says they're up on the roof… to hurry up.'

With a hurried 'Thanks son,' for the information they ran on and Gobie made good his escape.

Some days later I heard the result of this escapade from neighbours of his. Gobie's companion was on remand in jail and because he too had heard about his apprentice's entreatments to the police, he put the word out that when he was released there would be a reckoning. The fact that he was also thought to be a member of the local paramilitary unit added to a bleak inevitability.

When Gobie did eventually return to school I asked him about the truth of the story. It was all true.

'So, is this guy connected or not?' I asked.

'Yeah, but he's in prison and he'll get at least six months.'

'And what's going to happen when he gets out?'

He appeared to have resigned himself to his fate.

'I'll probably get done,' he replied philosophically.

As the end of the custodial sentence neared, Gobie appeared no more worried than he had done initially. Some of the lads suggested that he leave the country, others that they run a book on how long he could remain untouched.

When his companion, the failed chiseller of lead, was released Gobie was caught and shot in his left knee. If I had doubted the truth of everything about the episode before there was no doubting it now. After a few days I went to visit him in hospital. When I went to the designated ward I was told that he had been placed in a women's ward. Apparently they had been unable to convince him to stay in bed and eventually they lost their patience, took away his clothes and pyjamas and stuck him in with the females of the species. I'm sure the tactic was probably unprecedented and certainly illegal but it worked for a while. But after a couple of days Gobie signed himself out and took a taxi home, presumably locating his clothes before he emerged.

It was about a fortnight later that a commotion outside the mobile indicated his return to school. He was on crutches and his wounds were covered in a bandage that, once white, was now grey with grime and congealed blood. I was appalled. Once safely ensconced in class he showed me the wounds, which were gruesomely far from healing. I was so shocked that I immediately went to the office and rang his social worker. How could the health authorities have let him out – was there not even the assistance of a district nurse? He listened to my rant patiently and then asked, 'How long have you taught Gobie?'

'Nearly a year.'

'And in that time did you ever get him to do something that he didn't want to do?'

That was the end of my attempt to help someone who very clearly didn't want to be helped.

At lunchtime that day I discovered that Gobie, for the price of a cigarette, was allowing others to examine the wound and see the hole where the bullet had entered.

He left school shortly after and I missed him hugely. Life in the mobile was never dull when he was around. I liked and even admired his sangfroid in the face of adversity. I heard nothing about him until many years later when he was interviewed on the television. He was working on a building site and had witnessed the sectarian murder of one of his workmates. He spoke intelligently and lucidly and was the very essence of a useful, contributing member of society.

SEAN

My first meeting with Sean was disconcerting and continued to be so for the rest of the time he was in the class. He stood at the mobile door showing absolutely no emotion. There was no hint of either nervousness or excitement. It resembled a participation in some fatalistic timeline. He was here because he was here; it was not up to him to influence the situation. He had fairly nondescript hair over an equally nondescript face. Even now, years later, although I can remember a lot of the characters vividly I have difficulty recalling any particular feature apart from his eyes. The pupils were black and the eyes appeared dark and dull: lacking any animation, they resembled the eyes of a dead fish. They weren't angry or threatening, but set as they were in a countenance that showed little reaction to anything made me uneasy. Yeats could have written his epitaph after meeting him; *'Cast a cold eye on life, on death. Horseman, pass by!'*

He was new to the school and his lack of concern struck me forcibly. He took my outstretched welcoming hand as a matter of course and there was neither sweaty clamminess nor coldness. It was like the grip of an experienced politician. I thought that, perhaps, it was nervousness but of a type that I had never before experienced. The rest of the class regarded him with curiosity but he regarded them as the inconsequential artefacts of his new existence.

'Where would you like to sit, Sean? Most of this crowd burp and fart most of the day so it will not really make much difference.'

My weak attempt at humour fell flat. He shrugged in response as if the request was unnecessary and even superfluous.

'Wherever you want,' he replied.

I sat beside him for large parts of the morning trying to establish his ability levels in English and Maths and attempting to engage him in conversation. He answered all my enquiries politely and correctly imparted the basic information required with no verbal ornamentation. A stock response was trotted out to my questions regarding his likes and interests. Where did he live? Did he like football? Did he enjoy art? etc. all elicited the same response; 'It's all right.'

He was very different from the rest. Throughout the day and into the weeks that followed his demeanour never changed. He gave no bother. He got on with his work diligently but with no enthusiasm or satisfaction. I had no call to criticise him and any praise was received as unnecessary but part of the system. He was apparently never in a bad mood but never in a good one either. He walked straight down the middle of the behavioural path. He was almost inured to whatever happened around him. He floated along among the rest of us: a sealed bottle on a sea of humanity. The rest of the class ceased to be interested in him. Neither disliked nor bullied he was totally extraneous to life in the mobile. During our 'religion' period he proffered no comments except to agree or disagree with whichever he had decided was the appropriate response. He took part in everything with the same lack of enthusiasm. In PE he was an average performer but never got involved enough to show displeasure at defeat or triumph in victory. His work was invariably performed to the same standard, with neither excellence nor inadequacy.

When he sought my help to complete an exercise he received it with an enthusiasm shaving this side of disinterest. It was, as with everything else, something that happened daily. He neither rejected the overtures of others nor did he seek them out. George talked to him frequently and animatedly but then he talked to everyone frequently and animatedly. Just occasionally he found a topic or story that captured his imagination and while he was involved in tirelessly repeating such things, I felt I was beginning to comprehend the concept of eternity. George found rejection of his overtures very hard to take in the sense that he just didn't recognise them but continued to babble despite an obvious disinterest on the part of the listener. Sean was a desirable listener. He just sat there and continued to do whatever he was doing, occasionally nodding his head politely or whistling tunelessly. This musicality appeared to encourage George, being an unusual reaction to his verbal barrages and in sharp contrast to the usual requests to 'shut the hell up' or more earnest pleas to go and do unnatural and very painful things to himself. But apart from George (or as I privately thought of him, on account of his tenacious attachment to any listener, 'Barnacle' George) he had little interaction with anyone else.

The lack of involvement caused me a lot of thought. I had never before failed to establish some form of relationship with a pupil. Generally they were positive but there were the challenging ones where the battle lines were drawn and we would skirt up to and around but rarely through each other. I don't think he disliked me but neither did he show any enjoyment in my teaching. My humour, often madcap and frequently 'earthy' left him unmoved. He was at school because that was the system, a system beyond his power to alter so he dotted the 'i's and crossed the 't's. I realised that, with some hurt and disappointment, I was, in many ways, extraneous to his being. Because his taciturn manner frustrated me I spent a lot of time during the first three months trying to incite or provoke some sort of reaction, any reaction. Once during the Five Nations tournament when Ireland was playing well and it was getting a lot of television coverage, I had asked during a discussion if he liked rugby; he had answered 'Yes'. Compared to the usual, 'It's all right,' that was wild, unbound enthusiasm. The following week I brought in a book on Irish Rugby and a match programme of the Welsh match, which my brother-in-law had attended. He thanked me politely and looked through them. A lot of the others were envious. I told him they were his to keep and to take them home, which he dutifully did. If I had expected a Damascus Road turnaround in his attitude I was disappointed. When I asked him some weeks later what he thought of the French match, it was back to, 'It was all right.'

★

Every teacher gauges their success from the relationship with their pupils and the progress resulting from that interplay. I found myself almost wishing that he would argue or lose his sangfroid. I had to stop myself from shouting at him and losing my temper. He was frustrating me but doing it with no malicious intent. I'm unsure if after months of trying to crack the shell and failing to find a degree of normalcy, I gave up on him. I continued to treat him as best as I was able but I lost the confidence that I could do anything about his Hardy-like fatalism.

His family had moved to Ballyclare away from a troubled Belfast area. I never met them and Sean never spoke about them. I would often wonder had some trauma affected him? Was there some deep, hidden secret? Had something emasculated the normal fire and passion of youth? I never found out. He never missed a day during the seven months he was with us.

On the Friday before he left I again shook his hand and wished him well. His handshake was still antiseptic. He listened to my lies about how it had been a pleasure to have had him in the class and my thanks for his contribution. He accepted it all but no tear welled in his eyes: no final longing look, nothing! He walked away as robotically as he had arrived to continue his ordained destiny with fate, unencumbered with emotions and unexcited by potential.

About two or three weeks later, Francie was cleaning out the cupboards when he found something in a plastic bag that had been tucked neatly in behind some exercise books. He opened it and brought it up to me. It contained the rugby book and the international programme.

TOMMY

Tommy was a big guy. I never understood the rationale for his placement in a special school. Like a number of other pupils, he could have easily coped with a 'normal school' but he was quite happy to be there and resisted any suggestions that he should transfer. He had a well-developed sense of humour and he liked school and enjoyed learning. He was physically superbly built and an extremely talented athlete. He excelled at football and I was convinced had he not been what Jim called a 'lazy big bugger', he could even have had a professional career. He was an intensely likeable lad with a quiet maturity that lay behind inscrutable slate grey eyes. Even at fourteen he had the chiselled jaw of a confident twenty-year-old and an incipient jet-black moustache to complement a thatch of equally black hair. By the time he was sixteen, he had such a luxuriant upper lip that I decided to shave off my own inferior excuse as I suffered badly in comparison. Although my hair was jet black, the pathetic hairs in my beard were grey flecked with ginger. It only served to convince some that my hair must be dyed! He was confident and would query some of my actions but always in an adopted inoffensive and comic assertiveness. In addition to being so much more physically mature, he loved 'adult' talk and would often confide things to me when he got the chance.

I remember when there was a particularly bad week in the Troubles, the numbers attending dropped to a trickle and I was left with seven pupils. As a change to the routine I took them to the local Waterworks and hired four rowing boats. (Health and Safety where were you?) I ended up in the boat with Tommy. He was unusually quiet.

'You look like a man with problems, Tommy.'

He looked at me earnestly. 'I've got trouble with the girlfriend.'

Oh no! I thought to myself, images of pregnant schoolgirls, etc.

'I think she's two-timing me,' he continued.

Greatly relieved I entered a thoroughly adolescent conversation, which touched on the fickleness of women, the necessity of proof, the envy of friends, God and the universe, etc. As we brought the boat to the slip he got out, offered his hand, and said, 'Thanks, Sir… It did me good to talk about that.'

I felt a real pride in his confidence.

Tommy's talent at football prompted me to arrange a trial with a local league team some miles from his home. I arranged to meet him in the city centre one evening and take him to the training ground. I was convinced I'd found the new Pelé. I was terribly disappointed but not totally surprised when he failed to appear. Inside the mature-looking teenager was all the terror of failure and self-doubt. He told me later that he had missed the bus but I think we both knew the real reason.

★

Fortunately, given his physical ability, Tommy was an affable, easy-going, good-humoured boy who enjoyed school and rarely missed attending. At fifteen he was a good six-feet tall with the physique of a light heavyweight boxer. There was no one else in the class who would have been foolish enough to fight him or to quote Piggy – 'Have a fair dig!'

Well, at least nobody in their right mind. Unfortunately Sammy didn't always fit into that category. He was a good foot shorter than Tommy and two years younger. He was an epileptic and in those days it seemed extremely difficult for the doctors to hit on the correct cocktails that would keep his problems in check. One week he would be docile and sleepy and the next agitated, talking to himself and generally at war with the world around him, strutting aggressively and cursing loudly. Most people knew to stay clear of him in that condition.

The outside door was locked each lunchtime and I was usually the first down to open it at half-past one. The boys would gather outside, waiting for me to open the door. As I came down the corridor I could see Tommy leaning laconically against the door looking at me and, as usual, 'bantering' me… something to the effect that we staff had all the comforts while they were left to freeze like stones and starve in the cold. Suddenly Sammy appeared beside him, lifted his fist, cursed and hit Tommy as violently as he could across the face.

I dropped the keys. 'Oh my God,' I had visions of attending Sammy in a hospital bed. Tommy was momentarily nonplussed and then bewildered as he struggled to come to terms with the fact that he had been assaulted. I could see the rage slowly rise in his face as the rest of the queue of boys watched expectantly. Meanwhile Sammy was still cursing Tommy and looking around for another victim. As I struggled to open the door with an uncooperative key I shouted, 'Don't! Don't hit him Tommy, please don't hit him.'

He looked at me and then turned to Sammy.

'Do you not realise I could tear your bloody head off, wee lad,' he yelled so loudly that even Sammy quietened, if only momentarily. Obviously Sammy didn't appreciate his good fortune as he continued to upbraid him until after a quiet moment, he lay on the ground and fell asleep.

'Brilliant! Well done, big man,' I said with heartfelt relief.

That afternoon in the quiet of the classroom, the incident came to be the focus of a conversation. Another pupil, Peter, had become disillusioned with his inability to read and was asking me why was he stupid.

'You're not. I don't know why you can't read but I can tell you you're not stupid. There are film stars that can't read. They learn their lines from tapes. There are millionaires who for some reason can't read. They can't half count, though. Jackie Stewart, the world champion racing driver couldn't read. You may be dyslexic, you may have some other problem but it's not because you're stupid. We all have different things that we are good at and some things we're pretty useless at. Why that is, I don't know. You are very good at art and you're brilliant at making people laugh. There's Seamus beside you… everybody likes him. There are millions of people who can read who don't have a friend in the world. Look around you. God makes us all differently. I can't beat Charlie at draughts but I'm a better swimmer than him, but I'm not as good a swimmer as Dermot. Packy looks after his parents who are both deaf and dumb. He can use sign language perfectly. I wish I had his skill, never mind his love for his mum and dad.

'I know what to do when I'm playing football but I can't

do it. You've seen me playing football… I'm a tube. I look at Tommy and I think – God I'd love to be able to play like that – even for one match. But I can't. Talking about Tommy, you all saw what happened at lunchtime. Most people as big and as strong as Tommy is would have clobbered Sammy and sent him into the middle of next week, but he didn't. When God gave him that strength he also gave him a lot of wit. It was lucky for Sammy that he did. Don't ever talk yourself down or call yourself stupid when you don't know what life has in store for you. There are lots of guys who have left this school who weren't great readers but they earn more money than I do. And the reason they do is because they are better at what they do than I would be.'

A lot of what I did was about building belief and self-confidence. I was forever telling them success stories about ex-pupils, stories that, in most cases, were absolutely true. Because of their academic shortcomings they often had an increasing air of fearfulness and doubt as they got older and nearer to leaving. It was perhaps ironic that when I was with a number of the senior boys, it was they who gave me a confidence and reassured my self-doubts.

★

As careers teacher I often brought a number of leavers to different career events and industrial visits. On one occasion in the middle of Belfast city centre, a company of eight lads and I were stopped by a squad of soldiers. We were ordered to line up against a hoarding with our hands raised. I protested and explained that I was a teacher and my companions were pupils. When I think about it now and ponder how we must have looked, I can understand their scepticism. There were no school uniforms and at least three of the boys, including Tommy, looked like potential combatants. Even my obvious authority, breeding and impressive appearance held little conviction! Realising that further argument was useless, I told the boys to do as ordered. I turned and put my hands above my head and placed them on the hoarding. Quite unintentionally I slipped and my hands smacked down one after the other quite loudly. Tommy immediately did likewise. The boys took this as a cue and followed suit. To my horror I realised that they were intent on beating out a tattoo of resistance. Only a very emphatic order to desist saved us from a prolonged detention.

After one visit to a city centre YMCA it happened that Tommy and I were the last of the class to leave. As we descended in the lift in the company of five trainees from another school, the lift came to an abrupt halt. The emergency buttons failed to get any response. Tommy began warning that as it was a Friday afternoon and most of the people had left the building it was possible we would be trapped for days. He was only joking of course, but I fell in with his mischief.

Tommy turned to a slightly overweight trainee. 'Well if we have to start eating each other… I don't fancy your chances, big lad!'

His mates laughed but as the minutes passed and nothing appeared to be happening, the laughter died and tremors of terror started to spread. It became uncomfortably warm and sweat started to appear on our faces. It probably lasted only ten minutes or so but it seemed a lot longer before the lift started to move and we could hear the mooted voices of the security men. Terrifyingly, the lift stopped between floors and the doors opened to show ground level roughly at our waist levels.

'Let's go for it,' suggested someone.

The possible scenario of the lift starting to move again and bodies being guillotined in the attempt of escape was horrific but some remained unconvinced.

Luckily it was Tommy who convinced them.

'Go ahead if you want but you'd be a right idiot. I want to go home in one piece tonight.'

That bought us enough time for the doors to close and the lift to be reactivated. Tommy left school that summer and I missed his presence greatly.

★

Many years later, I returned home after our staff Christmas 'do'. It was the days before overpriced and overcooked evening meals (with special DJ included for free) and our Christmas outing consisted of heading for the pub and becoming quickly inebriated. As I came through the front door the phone rang and a voice asked, 'I'm not sure I've got the right number so I'm trying a whole lot but would you be Mr Rooney that used to teach in St. Cuthbert's?'

'Guilty as charged,' I slurred.

'This is Tommy H. How are you?'

I was delighted. He told me he was married, was working steadily and had a baby and he would love to meet up again. We chatted for a while and I took his number and promised to get back to him to arrange a visit. However, due to my less than sober state when I tried to remember where or on what I had scribbled his number I failed totally. In vain I searched the phonebook but he was ex-directory. If you ever read this Tommy, you'll recognise yourself, give me a ring. I promise this time I won't screw it up!

CON AND DERMOT

The Braniffs were twins, but not identical either in looks or personality. Con was feisty and confident, unflappable and unconcerned with a shock of blond hair and lively eyes over an incipient pale moustache. He wasn't afraid to answer back or assert his thoughts but never in a cheeky or aggressive manner. Dermot was quieter and more thoughtful. He shared the blond hair but he had a thinner face. He was always better groomed but he was much less confident.

He also lacked his brother's proliferation of freckles but his pale skin only appeared to heighten the intense honesty in his eyes. He used glasses for reading and they were timidly perched at the end of his nose, as if closer contact would render them useless. They were both well-built, strong, physically adept with a terrific work ethic which compensated them for very considerable reading problems. Despite their undoubted intelligence and effort they were very clearly dyslexic and my attempts to help with their reading problems were ineffectual.

Jim and I decided to invest the vast bulk of our requisition on an expensive course of phonic teaching aids. They came in an impressive-looking briefcase and contained a full range of tapes and workbooks. We worked diligently through it but while we had a number of successes we eventually called defeat with a number of others, including the twins. I concentrated my efforts in trying to build self-confidence and stressing the more important qualities than literacy. They lived quite close to me in the west of the city and fell into the habit of coming to the house nearly every day after school. Con enjoyed the sanctuary of my greenhouse as he could smoke his cigarettes away from parental sanctions and Dermot fell head over heels in love with the girl next door.

We had only moved into the house the previous autumn and the gardens resembled the aftermath of a World War One battle. Now that the inside of the house had been painted, I turned my attention to the mud outside. With all the ambition of a first-time house owner I was very determined and keen to have a good lawn, a decent vegetable garden, a rose bed, rockeries, sweet peas tossing luxuriantly over an extensive fence… all the things that I'd never had before.

With enthusiasm, energy and a singular lack of knowledge I threw myself into the task. The twins watched as I ham-fistedly began work. It wasn't long before they joined in and showed more energy and probably more ability than I had. We jointly discovered all sorts of magical things: how to mix concrete; how to build walls; how to dig drains; how to efficiently bandage gashed fingers, etc. They became part of the family and even when we couldn't work outside because of the rain, they turned up and sat around the house. I would be barely home when they would arrive and often when I came home, I would find Dermot chatting up the girl next door while Con would almost be invisible in the greenhouse under a fog of smoke.

I was conscious of the fact that their mother might have concerns over this unpaid labour but she continually thanked me for 'looking after them'. They were not particularly streetwise and she was concerned with the deteriorating Troubles, they could easily become embroiled in problems like so many others of that age. They would play with our baby daughter, Paula, with good humour and patience and they were unfailingly pleasant and polite. Often Eileen would ask them to stay for dinner but they had obviously been warned by Mum not to do so. The parental caution stopped there however, for they could clear a French patisserie of sweet biscuits.

Over the course of the next year we concreted posts, attached fences, dug French drains, built walls and patios and transformed the mud of Flanders into the gardens of Versailles (well not quite). They learnt quickly and were eager and interested. Had I not had their help, the task would have taken very much longer.

I recall one day in June when I had taken them and the

rest of the class out in my father's van. We had gone fishing to Maghery and afterwards we went to Loughall to see where the Orange order was founded. It was nearly six o'clock by the time we arrived back in the city and then dropped off some of the boys in the city before leaving those local to West Belfast at a number of different spots. The journey back was a nightmare as I was suffering badly from hay fever and was continually sneezing and rubbing my inflamed eyes. Arriving back in the clammy heat of an unusually hot spell, I saw to my horror that ten tons of top soil which I had ordered some days before had been dumped in my driveway. I felt limp and useless. There was absolutely no way I was going to do anything about it so I suggested that the boys might give me a hand the following day after school to move it to the back garden. Eileen had taken Paula to her parents' home in Armagh overnight so without her ministering kindness, I pulled the curtains and lay down on the sofa. I was sweating badly, my eyes had been rubbed sore and my nose ran like a dripping tap. As anyone who suffers badly from hay fever knows the only relief is to lie in the dark, fall asleep and dream of winter.

It was well after eleven when the door of the living room opened and Dermot came in with a pot of tea and numerous rounds of toast. They were filthy and the sweat had carved little pale rivulets down their faces. They had gone home as I told them but told their mother that I needed them and borrowing another wheelbarrow, they returned and moved all the soil to the back.

'We'll hose down the drive, tomorrow,' they added.

As it was now dark I walked them home and conveyed my gratitude to their mother.

'Aye they're good boys,' she agreed.

They were due to leave school a few weeks later. As one of my responsibilities was career guidance I was delighted to get them accepted into one of the better government training schemes. Unfortunately, the course didn't begin until September. Living as we did in Andersonstown with the Troubles at their height, I would often escort the boys home if we were working late. Because of their size, similar looks and blond hair they were hard to miss and with every change of army regiment, they were stopped and searched. My presence didn't stop us from being searched but it helped ensure Con didn't respond aggressively to any taunting. I once had to shake my head fiercely at him when he was accused of being a 'blond fucking Provo'. I later lodged a complaint at the local police barracks.

★

Their mother was aware of the potential for the boys to become 'involved' in one way or another. She was concerned that with the entire summer stretching out, before their course started in September, they could get sucked into the mayhem that was raging around them. She rang me the day after they had left school in the middle of a brutal and sustained period of killings, bombings and maimings, worried about what they could do in the long days before their course began. I suggested that, if she could afford it, she should buy them a Flymo and they could earn a couple of pounds cutting grass and tidying up gardens. With her husband having recently died the £43 involved was a lot of money to her, but she agreed. With my borrowed wheelbarrow and a few basic tools they began working in local gardens. To the chagrin of neighbours they invariably began at 8 am and worked until the last light flickered from the sky. Together we worked out a reasonable fee for their efforts and within three weeks they had repaid the Flymo cost to their mum. That summer was warm and reasonably dry, which meant that they were 'on the go' every day. Their customer base increased to such an extent that when the time came for them to begin their work placement, they decided to continue with the gardening and forget about any other training placement. As the days shortened, their shoulders broadened.

One day they asked me to help them hire a Rotovator, which I did. The shop owner who hired out the equipment was unpleasant and fussy. He lectured us on the correct procedures and repeatedly warned us of the dire consequences of returning his precious tool either late or damaged. It was almost inevitable that later that day Con and Dermot arrived at the house with the machine, which now had a broken steel rotating cog. Dermot was visibly worried, as I was.

I examined it but it was obviously beyond fixing.

'Don't worry, lads. We'll take it back and explain.'

Con looked at me and smiled. 'I'm not going to worry over a stupid old thing like that.'

The difference in their demeanours was amazing. 'You'll never die of a heart attack,' I laughed.

Glancing at Dermot I added, 'I wish I was as sure about either of us.'

Returning to the shop I realised how much Con's imperturbability and confidence had affected me. We were positively bullish as we returned the damaged item and explained that his unfit-for-purpose, second-hand machinery had let us down and caused us a lot of grief!

As their work increased, an older brother who had been training as a chef resigned from his course and managed the business side of the operation. They tackled everything from building garden walls to laying down patios and general labouring. I saw less and less of them as the months passed but their business thrived, with the brother organising the bookings, paperwork, payments, etc. One afternoon two years later they arrived at the house in a Land Rover with their name emblazoned on the side; 'Braniff Brothers – Landscape

Gardeners'. They went on to employ a number of other people and gained contracts for maintaining the grounds of different organisations. They also had a contract to maintain some stretches of the banks beside the motorway. With their new affluence, they moved from their rented Housing Executive house and bought a fine bungalow. With increasing prosperity they then bought a substantial farm on the outskirts of the city. In addition to a number of vehicles they bought or rented a JCB and Con spent months working for farmers, removing hedges and digging drains. They had come a long way from working in the garden of my small semi.

★

However their story had a tragic ending. Following an argument with someone, Dermot was threatened with being shot. I don't know how serious the threat was but perhaps because of the all-enveloping violence, it had a shattering effect on him. He returned home and drank Paraquat, a particularly lethal poison. His suicide devastated me. There wasn't a big crowd at the funeral and I was almost angry that there wasn't more grief. It seemed to me that there should be crowds screaming about the injustice of life; people should be lining the streets crying over the waste. How could such a gentle, hard-working, affable life be snuffed out so suddenly? I still get very emotional when I think about him. I had felt a part in his success and I had rejoiced and boasted to others about how he and Con had triumphed over what life had thrown at them. Dermot's gentle nature lacked his brother's hard-headedness and he found the problem too much. I didn't want to know the details or the reasoning behind his death. It was enough to grieve for a young man who had overcome his learning difficulties and found his place in the sun. When someone in class would suggest that they didn't have much chance of a job or 'making it' I would quote their success to other pupils when we talked about overcoming problems in employment. But I would never finish the story: in my world they continued to thrive intact, healthy, wealthy and successful.

DARRAGH

My first memory of Darragh was when he was in the class below mine. I had been interviewing him on his own about his future ambitions in employment. Appreciating that a number of the pupils would fail to get work after leaving was depressing but I always balanced it with the number who had, despite the odds, got steady jobs. To keep up morale we would explore all the avenues as if we were interviewing first-class honours degree chaps for civil service entry.

With his ginger hair, his face was typically Irish, accelerating at the first sign of summer sun from sepulchral white to violent puce without stopping at any of the intermediate phases. He was neatly dressed with an open, sincere look with piercing blue eyes. His short sleeved shirt revealed arms that were muscled in the Popeye style. He stood with his hands clasped behind his back, waiting for an invitation to sit. He was extremely well mannered to an unusual degree and chatted openly and honestly. In my preamble, I commented on the heavy rain that beat on the upper floor windows adding, 'It's a terrible day!'

I was somewhat disconcerted when he looked at me and said, 'I like days like that… I feel very close to God… it's as if the rain is a direct line to him.'

'Really?' (Well, what else was I to say?)

During the course of the next hour I discovered a fascinating personality who in turns intrigued and disturbed me. I was unsure to categorise him as either a fanatic or a saint. He didn't preach to others and had a quiet air of self-assuredness but he was certainly deeply religious. The religion that I practiced was full of doubts and I envied his certitude. I would always have said that the dividing line between sanctity and sanity was dangerously thinly drawn but there was nothing crazy about Darragh.

I don't think I ever taught a more determined pupil. Like others he had major literacy problems but he tackled everything with earnest endeavour. His single-mindedness extended to everything. In football his flaming orange head whizzed about vigorously and he would scythe down opposing players with a total lack of malice. Despite his specific reading difficulty he worked assiduously at any work set. Had life and nature been fair, the amount of effort he expended would have placed him well above the norm. He was interested in every subject and particularly enjoyed religion or what passed for it during our 'gather round the desk' daily mission. I never remember him missing a single day at school. His family were poor working-class people but his mother always ensured he arrived in school neatly dressed with an ironed shirt and a tie.

He would confide to me frequently that he wanted to be a priest. Realising that with his reading problems this wasn't practical, I would steer him towards being a religious brother in a monastic order. My cousin was a Cistercian monk in Roscrea and I was very impressed by the character, personality and lifestyle of both the priests and brothers. Darragh would always listen politely but would invariably conclude that he still wanted to be a priest. The best advice that he accepted was that he should perhaps first get himself some experience in the real world of work.

In school he was one boy that others looked up to. At the first sign of anyone being annoyed he would immediately enter the lists on their behalf. Normally protection of someone would have taken the form of, 'If you touch him I'll dig your head in!' With Darragh there was no threat but rather, a gentle rebuke indicating that what was said or threatened 'wasn't very nice' or 'it was not very fair'. Despite his placid entreatments and peacemaking character, his combative nature in the gym ensured that others were well aware of his physical prowess. This generally ensured a quiet acquiescence of his suggested recommendations. I often suspected that beneath that quiet, peaceful exterior there was a boy who, if pushed hard enough, had the strength and determination to finish any fight.

★

Each year the school took part in an inter-schools' gala. Every so often we would be able to assemble a squad that could compete successfully. Trying to ensure that nobody would be suspended before the day was a major concern. As it happened, one year my top, certain winner in the backstroke was suspended after a serious altercation with another staff member. The unfortunate teacher had just returned to school after a minor operation and was not best pleased when, after an altercation with my best swimmer, he was told that he would be returned to hospital, only 'this time you won't fucking get out'.

At very short notice I realised that the only senior who could reasonably approximate a backstroke was Darragh. Apart from his rather erratic stroke, his problem was in breathing… or more accurately, the lack of it. He would speed down the pool but stop about three times to place his feet on the bottom and take a deep breath before launching a fresh assault. But, I reckoned, if he wasn't disqualified he would at least gain us a single point for finishing. My pep talk was marginally less worthy than that of an Alex Ferguson.

'Listen, Darragh… it's important you breathe when you're swimming… so just do your best. What would be really brilliant is if you didn't stop to do it!'

Darragh flew away at the start with his arms spinning like gale-force windmills, eyes fierce with determination, the face reddening with effort. At fifteen metres he was still ahead but his face had become contorted, his colour more deeply red, the neck veins throbbing. I realised with admiration that he was determined to win at all costs and if the only factor that could prevent that was breathing, then he simply wouldn't breath. At twenty metres my admiration had turned to concern as his face had turned purple and the veins rose like furrows in a ploughed field. Over the last five metres I was screaming at him, 'Breathe! Darragh, for God's sake breathe!… Please.'

He declined and his right arm struck the finishing tiles with such force that I thought he must have broken it. He stood waist high in the water, looking dazed, gasping for the interrupted oxygen as his face and veins slowly returned to normal. He finished second but the points meant he had done enough to ensure the team victory.

★

As one of the more mature pupils he travelled on tickets and not school transport. As we were leaving one day, a boy on the bus was shouting at him, 'Bet you won't win today!'

I discovered that on most days Darragh would save his bus ticket and race the school bus into town. The finishing line was the bottom of the Antrim Road about two miles away. Because of heavy traffic and a number of traffic lights, he often won the race.

It was obvious when I talked to him that he had a great affection for his mother. His father was only mentioned to me once when he confided, 'My father and I don't really get on.' (Darragh was the only boy I knew who ever referred to his dad as 'father'). How badly they got on was clear when one summer evening when I was at home cutting the grass,

Darragh arrived sweating and panting, in obvious distress. He had phoned one of the Brannif twins who had given him my address. He had run right across the city, a distance of at least four miles. We immediately brought him in and tried to calm him down. He drank his tea nervously but eventually calmed somewhat. We were distressed to see that the insides of his wrists were lightly scarred with self-inflicted cuts and welts. Apparently his father had been arguing with his mother and Darragh had intervened. He had arued with his father and ran out of the house. He told Eileen and me about his general unhappiness with his relationship with his father and how much he loved his mother. After a couple of hours, he wanted to go back home and I brought him by car. He was adamant that I shouldn't go into the house and assured me that everything would be fine.

I thought hard about what, if anything, I should do. I felt powerless to do anything to help. Social services wouldn't feel that they could interfere in a domestic matter where there was no evidence of a minor being physically maltreated. My only similar previous contact with social services was when I had asked them to quietly investigate marks on a child's back. I was less than pleased when the father arrived at school complaining that I had told social services that he had been beating his son. It turned out the marks were the result of his son's new interest in a martial arts club. It seemed likely that any interference or their intervention now would only result in trouble for both the mother and Darragh. Nevertheless I was relieved when he arrived in school the next day with his customary good humour. I kept a close eye for any more self-harm. On many occasions, thereafter whenever I would ask him how things were at home, he would smile and assure me that everything was fine. I didn't believe him.

★

He was very keen on gardening. Most of the jobs in the class were rotated but it mattered little who was supposed to be looking after the classroom plants; Darragh ensured they were well looked after. He would often chide others for giving too little or too much water and also dictated when they were fed with BabyBio. As his leaving date approached I was keen to have him placed somewhere where his literacy problems would be mitigated by his cheerful, helpful personality and his determined work ethic. There was considerable discrimination against Catholics within the city council and it was more in hope than expectation that I filled in an application for the gardening section of Belfast Parks and Cemeteries Department. I was delighted to be told that he had been successful. I knew that Darragh would win over even the hardest bigot and, in my mind's eye, I saw him working as a labourer/gardener. About a month after he began work he arrived at my house one evening with a bag containing books. He asked if I could help him. It was with shock and then horror that I realised that there had been a mix-up in the application process and Darragh had been registered as an indentured apprentice nurseryman. His books carried titles such as *The Royal Horticultural Society Guide to Flowers and Plants*; *A Beginner's Guide to Latin Etymology*; *The Professional Groundsman*, etc. It was an Everest for a lad with serious literacy problems. Latin plant nomenclature would only ensure illiteracy in two languages. I tried to be as gentle as I could about the difficulties ahead and tentatively suggested that he transfer to the more mundane but entirely feasible ground staff. I should have known better than to gainsay his determination. He told me that he was also obliged to attend the technical college for classes every Tuesday. I was extremely concerned that his problems with literacy would have left him as an outsider within his group. I left it a couple of weeks before I went to see the nursery superintendent.

Feigning ignorance of the Tuesday classes, I told him that

Darragh was an ex-pupil and as I was passing I thought I would call in and see how he was getting on. The superintendent welcomed me. He was a well-educated, gentle man with twinkling, warm eyes and a ready smile. As things were slack he offered a cup of coffee and we chatted easily about the centre. He proudly showed me around the gardens and he was fascinating to listen to. I was interested in plants but my attention was feigned as I sought an opening to discuss Darragh's problems.

'How's he getting on?' I enquired as casually as I could.

He looked at me intently and leaning forward in a conspiratorial whisper asked, 'Did you know that he has difficulties with reading?'

I accepted the diagnosis. 'Does that mean you can't keep him?'

He looked at me and paused. 'Let me show you something.' He got up and moved to a desk buried under paper. He rooted round and produced to my horror a question paper with Darragh's name scrawled across the top of it.

'The first question was to identify a picture of a chrysanthemum... This is the answer.'

He pointed at a two upper case letter answer 'CR'.

'I have a couple of lazy sods with GCEs who didn't know that. I knew what Darragh meant and as long as I can decipher his answers, and he continues to be the hardest working apprentice I've ever had... he stays!'

His enthusiasm was encouraging my frankness. 'But he must find the work incredibly difficult... he told me he studies three or four hours every night.'

'Isn't that incredible?' he beamed. 'And you think that I would let someone like that go?'

'But the exams... surely he can't possibly get through them?'

He paused. 'Well, that depends on the examiner.'

'But who marks them?' I probed.

He looked at me, winked and smiled. 'If I have anything to do with it he'll do OK.'

'That's brilliant… I'm delighted, because if ever someone earned a break it's him.'

I left the centre on top of the world.

A few weeks later Darragh phoned me and asked me to come and pick up some herbaceous plants that were surplus to requirements. I was assured that they were more kosher than Gobie's cigarettes or Dan's whisky. With the benediction of the supervisor I loaded the boot with a number of plants. As I write this thirty years later, I can look out and see an Irish Yew – the only remaining survivor of Darragh's generosity. Over the next few years he kept in touch. He had become very friendly with a lecturer at the university and tended his garden after hours. I knew him from my time at Queen's and knew him to be a warm and compassionate man. After his apprenticeship, he helped get Darragh work at a teachers' training college where he became a groundsman and played football with a minor but important football team. He returned a number of times and would visit us on each occasion but as we moved house we eventually, regrettably, lost touch. I often wondered if he had been able to maintain that innocent sanctity with the same determination that he applied to everything else. In an ever-increasingly cynical world it is rare to meet anyone who encapsulates goodness and total selflessness but Darragh was such a person. It was a privilege to have known him.

BARNEY

Barney was the sort of pupil who was hard to motivate. He excelled in making irrelevant and unwelcome interruptions but generally there was a vein of humour in most of his comments that bought him a begrudging clemency. He was a big, well-built boy but he had no interest in physical activity. He could always be depended on to have forgotten his gym gear and on the occasions when he had left them in school he would be struck down with an illness which, despite its apparent life-threatening potential, only lasted until the PE period was over. He had a regular mop of dirty brown hair that topped his tanned face and he was invariably smiling to reveal a lower set of teeth that resembled tombstones in a vandalised cemetery.

His favourite time of the day was first thing in the morning. The buses carrying the boys to school came from different parts of the city and there were also taxis that came from further away. In addition, in order to encourage independence in the older boys, the education board provided bus tickets. Nearly every day some group would be delayed because of bombs or bomb scares. So Jim and I would encourage the early arrivals to gather round the desk and chat. It was fascinating and gave us a real insight into what life was like in certain areas. We were told who had been beaten up: who had been kneecapped and why; who got involved in a riot; who got shot; whose house had been raided by the army or police; who had got drunk; left home voluntarily or otherwise, etc. Barney was our own town crier. Where he gathered his information I never discovered but he was the archetypical gossip and, like most gossips, he enjoyed an audience. When they finally returned to their desks and began the work that had been organised, the real fun of the day had gone for Barney.

To be fair he always tried initially to 'get on with it' but a leaf passing the window was sufficient distraction to put him into a dreamlike trance, staring out the window. I remember describing in graphic detail how leprosy affected victims, or at least what I fondly imagined could be the worst effects. I would describe in gory detail how, if affected, your leg would suddenly fall off or if you were picking your nose your finger might disappear into the nasal cavity. I was thoroughly enjoying my tour de force and was gratified to see Barney staring at me intently. When I had finished, Barney stuck his hand up.

'Can pigs see the wind, Sir?'

'What are you talking about?' I asked, exasperated.

'I asked Mr Bailie if I could become a teacher and he said, "Aye, when pigs see the wind".'

My Oscar-winning performance was as naught compared to this great imponderable. So much for my theatrics!

★

He loved stories and poems and any activity where he could sit back, relax his face and dream was a preferable option to the more mundane aspects of education, which involved effort. His cheery face would stare benignly up at me but whether there was anyone home, I doubt. Everybody liked Barney. Part of his charm was that he would talk to everyone as if he was their best friend. The fact that he was immensely likeable didn't hide the fact that he could be very frustrating. One day, Jim had had an argument with Barney and was complaining to me about what a nuisance he was. It was unlike him to be so worked up by someone who essentially was 'only messing'. I assumed that he was in pain from his gallstones, which were becoming uncomfortably acute. I was in a giddy mood.

'Barney, come on up here a minute.'

He had obviously been scolded severely by Jim and he came like a docile dog, eyes flicking upwards, testing the ground.

'Look. Professor Humdinger, I vill show you ze reason vhy zis Barney voz, how you zay, acting zee maggot.'

I got Barney to stand sideways between us and pretended to peer through his ear. 'You must understand, Professor, I can zee you. Zer ist nothing but ze big empty tunnel straight through.'

Some of the other boys laughed and Barney's face suddenly reverted to normal service. 'Sir, your head's full of wee white mice.'

Jim stretched out his hand and apologised for shouting at him and Barney reciprocated with his own apology which consisted of 'No problem, Sir.' That was how the school day finished.

Barney was one of the senior boys who travelled on tickets rather than the school buses so he collected his ticket and left. On my way home, I stopped at a local bank to withdraw some cash. At that time there was an ad running on the TV with the comedian Frank Carson promoting a bank where he ended by shouting in a strong Belfast accent, 'Will you take a cheque?'

As I queued in the rather sombre surroundings the silence was loudly punctuated by Barney pushing open the front door and screaming down the floor, 'Will you take a cheque?'

A few of the customers smiled while others tutted. I remained outwardly oblivious but inside I mused on Barney's indefatigable resilience.

*

March 20th 1973. It was only another shooting on the *Ten O'Clock News*.

A group of young men had been standing on a corner on the periphery of a Catholic area when a stolen car opened fire and disappeared into the Loyalist Sandy Row.

'One of the young men was reported to have been shot dead while another was in a serious condition. There are no further details at this point.'

It was about two hours later that my brother-in-law rang to ask me if I knew the dead boy as the midnight news had said he attended our school. The name of the boy was given and I can still remember the numbness and shock as I realised it was Barney.

One of the longest nights of my life followed while he flitted in and out of a broken sleep.

When I arrived at school the next morning I almost screamed when another teacher said, 'Trust that bloody idiot to be hanging around there.' That appeared to be the sum of his feelings. Perhaps I judge him unfairly. I'm sure, on reflection, he was upset too but couldn't find the appropriate phrase. As the boys drifted in one could feel the quiet tension as the word spread. Again I was numb, knowing I would be unable to speak without crying. Jim took control brilliantly. He had suffered the death of a young daughter and age and experience had given him better coping skills. He put his arm round my shoulder and said, 'Thank God you made me shake his hand yesterday before he left school.'

Eventually we gathered them round the desk and Jim spoke movingly about friendship and responsibility. We prayed a rosary for him. The rest of the day dragged by with a resigned interminability. Nowadays we would be smothered with grief counsellors but then we were left with our taunting demons. That mood lasted throughout the rest of the next day as well. I asked if any of the boys wanted to come with me after school to his house to pay our respects and was gratified that only the more mature pupils who travelled independently were able and wanted to go with me by car. Tommy, Joe, Ciaran and Paul accompanied me. The terraced house was only about fifty yards from where he had been murdered and his family had heard the shots and were, indeed, among the first on the scene.

A straggle of neighbours hung around the door quietly smoking and nodding acknowledgements. There was a smell of drink from the man who opened the door and the father seemed almost entranced with the scene as he shuffled around uncomfortably, shaking hands, thanking us for coming, and offering us cups of tea. The room had been cleared of all the furniture apart from a line of kitchen chairs ringing the walls and in the centre, Barney's corpse. Laid out in a white shirt and tie his face had obviously been manicured by the undertaker. The unruly and tattered hair had been wetted and plastered down over his forehead. On his face a childhood scar showed which I had never noticed before. His skin was waxy cold. A phrase from Owen, *'the pallor of girls' brows'*, darted through my mind. He had indeed died like cattle, like so many before him and so many to come. He had never been so tidy in life. There was no obvious bruising and without the mischievous eyes flickering, he was totally innocent and naive. The endearing stammer, the cheeky response, the joy of laughter, the essential goodness were all gone. His hands were folded over his chest and a set of rosary beads was draped over his fingers. Beneath the nails the customary crescents of dirt had been manicured away. The fingers showed the blue blush of cyanosis. Another victim, another innocent, unlucky enough to be in the wrong place at the wrong time. The five of us were caught in an almost timeless web as if everything was hushed and all I could think of was Barney shouting down the bank hall and all I could see was the grin and the laughing inconsequence of it all. I wanted to leave but I couldn't. I stretched my hand out and placed it on top of Barney's waxy fingers. The cold clammy touch sent me over the edge. I was aware I was sobbing. Everything was so final, undeserved, inhuman, evil. Somewhere someone was gloating at this scene; others were condemning but making excuses, the 'whataboutery' of Ulster life. Somewhere too, someone else was planning revenge... there were plenty of other Barneys. I turned to the father to leave but I couldn't speak.

'He liked you, Mr Rooney. He used to talk about how you carried on in the class.'

I was trying desperately to control my blubbing and then, quite remarkably in that moment of desperation something astounding happened. Tommy and Joe each took an arm and gently led me out. Their look had no reproach or even embarrassment but a genuine desire to help and comfort. They had coped much better than I. Outside the house I leant against the red brick wall and dried my eyes with tissues. They looked at me and Joe said, 'Are you all right, Sir?' He leant forward and gently, almost tenderly, like a caring mother brushed some of the brick dust from my jacket. The moment is indelibly imprinted in my mind. It was a couple of moments before I could speak.

'I'm fine lads, I'll be OK, you just get yourselves off home… and be careful.' As they turned unsurely, almost reverentially I choked… 'Thanks lads.'

I never really discovered whether it was because Barney was one of the first or if it was because of the force of his personality that I was so affected. I can't even read or think about him today but that I'm aware I'm close to tears. The tragic fact was that over the next twenty years there were many other pupils' and ex-pupils' funerals. One was blown to pieces by a car bomb while attending a Republican funeral; another was blown up planting a bomb; three others were shot dead. Some disappeared and some committed suicide. Some died accidentally like one boy who had left school and was blown off a lorry on the motorway. Another one was shot dead and he gained fame by becoming one of 'The Disappeared'. They were all tragic, undeserved and in large part innocent. For some, a lack of common sense was their only crime. Some put themselves in dangerous situations and their naivety cost them dearly.

Yet Barney still affected me most. He never quite left the class. For years, every so often, when the class was working quietly a stillness would descend and I would look up to see him twirling his hair and staring out into the unknown with that silly, vacuous smile.

The Three Musketeers – ALAN, JAKE and MORGAN

I like to think that I influenced a number of pupils (hopefully for the better), but no matter how much that might have happened it was minor compared to the influence that these three boys had on me. They were all contemporaries and their presence filled me with hope for the day. They could always be relied upon to support enthusiastically my every action and embrace any innovative topic.

As I indicated earlier, the school's reputation lay somewhere on the list between Bash Street Primary and Strangeways. It was only when after visiting it or getting involved that one realised how unfair that reputation was. In that third-year class, I was lucky enough to be the class teacher for three memorable boys. I owe a great deal of gratitude to them and that group of fourteen-year-olds. Within the group were a number of boys who apart from some learning difficulties, were capable of soaking up new ideas and knowledge like a damp sponge.

The Principal had recently introduced a new approach to teaching called ITA. This Initial Teaching Alphabet was the brainchild of Sir James Pitman in the early 1960s. Essentially it was a simplified writing system designed to help people to read using a phonetic alphabet, which did away with most of the eccentric traditional spelling. It had forty-four characters and each symbol represented a single English sound including affricates and diphthongs. 'Dou you faulloe... itz raellee simpil when you get the hang auf it.'

My main problem with it was the fact that only half the boys were to be taught it while the rest continued with TO (traditional orthography). That meant that I had a vertical line dividing my blackboard with ITA and TO on either side of the line. It had a reasonable degree of success.

Certainly with Alan, Jake and Morgan it opened the door into literacy and they accelerated through the books. The theory was that after a fair degree of competence was attained the skills acquired would transfer seamlessly to ordinary English. This was not always accomplished as seamlessly as hoped for. It didn't allow for regional accents and while it was easy to learn a logical consistent spelling system, there were difficulties when one moved to an illogical and inconsistent one. Another major problem I found was the lack of other support materials. There were no comics, books or newspapers other than the course books themselves. I imagine that the boys who learnt to read fluently through the medium would probably have learnt anyway. For whatever reason, ITA is no longer used in schools although it remains of interest in talk about possible spelling reform.

I was grateful that I had at least four pupils who could read competently and were hungry for new experiences. The rest of the class, with the odd exception, were also involved and interested. I began to read them abridged versions of the classics: *Call of the Wild*, *Oliver Twist*, *Treasure Island*, *White Fang*, *The Count of Monte Cristo*, etc. I was a good mimic and enjoyed peopling the characters with John Wayne or James Stewart voices. Every day was a real joy. I had never been happier. That third-year class were like devoted acolytes. They embraced everything novel and challenging. The greatest buzz I got was when I started to read poetry. I had been fortunate enough to have had Seamus Heaney and Michael McLaverty, the well-known, respected writer, lecture us during our post-graduate training.

McLaverty had asked us to build up a collection of poems suitable for differing age ranges… an exercise I only appreciated some years later. I redrafted it and it became a sort of bible. I found the most successful way to deal with a poem was to explain it all beforehand so, that the ideas were accessible as the language could be difficult. It would have been grotesque to change the words of the poem so, if they were to be moved by it, they didn't need to be confused with strange words or ideas. Housman's 'A Shropshire Lad' was a particular favourite as was Robert Service's 'Songs of a Sourdough'. I always recall the gusto I employed, my face contorted in lunacy, growling *'I burrowed a hole, in the burning coal, and stuffed in Sam McGee'*. 'The Man from God Knows Where' was always worth a retelling.

We spent months talking about the First World War and I read them the poems of Wilfred Owen, Siegfried Sassoon and others. Perhaps the greatest measure of my success was when a number of pupils attempted to write their own poetry. Morgan and Alan sat together and worked as a team. They were both very creative and while Alan was a wordsmith, Morgan was a highly talented artist. For years I had a collection of their poems and drawings in a book they made. I live in hope that it will one day turn up again in a box in my attic. They were particularly enthused with the more serious stuff and I remember clearly one of their joint productions where Alan's poem included the lines:

'As I lie here in this deserted battlefield
I hear the rats picking at the bones of the lost-hearted men.'

It was accompanied by Morgan's pastel drawing of a soldier with an emaciated face and a look of resigned acceptance. It was moments like that which made your day and gave you a glow of satisfaction. These were twelve-year-old boys whom the system determined were 'educationally sub-normal'! I never discovered why they had been placed in the school.

Like some of the others they would not have been out of place in 'normal' school. In any event, I was grateful for their company and enthusiasm. As 'The Three Musketeers' (as I thought of them privately) moved through the school I was lucky enough to move with them, and after a short hiatus we were reunited in their last year. Alan had become fascinated by local politics and we would often discuss the latest political developments. It was a fascinating, if terrifying, time in Northern Ireland and he had a better, more intelligent grasp of what was happening than many of the staff.

★

Alan and a number of other pupils lived near my home and when my wife and I were asked out one evening, I hesitatingly suggested if he and Jake could babysit. Eileen was more than a little unsure but I convinced her. After all, the house we were going to had a phone (I know… but in those days not every house had!) and our two daughters at that time usually slept through the night. They were also familiar with the boys as they had been in the house a number of times. As we left Eileen showed them the snacks she had left and we told them to help themselves to anything they fancied from the fridge. They took up this generous offer and when we returned we discovered they had each finished two cans of beer. Compared to most sixteen-year-olds nowadays that would merely have been a pre-session tipple but they weren't that used to drink and they had convinced themselves they were completely drunk.

We poured coffee and food into them envisaging *Sun* headlines: *'Teachers entice two children into drunken stupor while babies slept upstairs.'*

Eventually, satisfying ourselves that their parents would suspect nothing I drove them home, with them chewing frantically on a third packet of Polo mints.

Jake always lived in an optimistic bubble. I rarely saw him

in bad form and he tackled every subject with enthusiasm. His blond hair hung untidily over a complexion burnt by the outdoors. His blue eyes were searching and animated and he loved nothing more than to talk confidentially about… well… anything really. He had very good hands and while he enjoyed drawing and painting, he really excelled in woodwork. It was with some pride that he gave me a wooden coffee table he had made in the woodwork class. His teacher added that it was the best anyone had ever produced. Years later Jake invited my wife and me to his wedding in Dublin. He had joined the Irish army. I felt a sense of shared pride as he stood escorted by his comrades in smart military uniform outside the church. He told me that he had been selected to shoot for his unit in an international competition. I wondered had he stayed in Belfast in those troubled days, would he have ended up shooting at more than bits of paper? He also served in the Officers' Mess and I jokingly counselled him not to repeat his interpretation of 'helping himself to anything in the fridge'.

★

Alan's interest in poetry and literature was progressive and he and Morgan continued to collaborate in their own efforts. It was an exceptional group of boys that unusually had come together in one class. Normally there were one or two who stretched the rest and where progress was noticeable rather than attritional but fortune had given me an accidental gathering of bright knowledge-thirsting minds. Every day was a true pleasure. Poetry was very special. World War One poetry continued to influence them heavily. Graphic imagery and the total, pitiful waste of life concentrated all our imaginations. Sassoon's 'Died of Wounds' and Rosenberg's 'Break of Day', along with a lot of Owen, were favourites.

One particular memory involved 'As the Team's Head-

Brass' by Edward Thomas. It had started to snow and a restless afternoon was transformed into a quiet observance of the tumbling flakes. I had explained and read the poem two or three times some weeks before. As the class dreamily watched the football field turn to white, Danny, a pupil whom I don't recall ever evincing anything but boredom during the poetry sessions asked, 'Sir, read that poem about the man watching the horses going up and down the field.'

Somewhere the timelessness and wonderment of falling snow awakened a stirring. I never discovered the trigger but he had sensed a mood and I responded. I don't think I raised my voice much above a whisper as once again I set the scene, painted the background and slowly read the poem. There wasn't a sound as they listened. It was almost as if some elusive spell, an intense shared bond would be broken if someone spoke and broke the narrative and the following silence.

Everyone stared dreamily out the window, many with their heads resting on their crossed arms on the desks as they watched, trance-like, the meandering flakes slowly whiten the world outside. The silence was only broken when Michael, another boy whom I had considered to be immune to the beauty of poetry, said, 'Sir, read it again.' There were times like that when one realised the power a teacher sometimes has; a power to enthuse, to lead out from the mundane, to open a door to a new excitement. The class was a unit which could be moulded in a created mood with powerful emotions. One became a privileged omnipotent.

POSTSCRIPT

When I began this book I was very reluctant to identify the school by name and concocted St Cuthbert's. However, anyone who lived in Belfast during that period and was gifted with half a brain and the deductive powers of Sherlock Holmes' cat can readily identify it. Unfortunately it had a certain 'reputation' and that baggage might be an unwelcome attachment to many of its past pupils. For that reason the names of most of the pupils have been altered. A lot of children, particularly those with 'ascertained' learning difficulties, while they enjoy and profit from attending 'special' schools, are embarrassed and unsure about how that has placed them in the world and how they are viewed.

There is absolutely no possible justification for educating children with any sort of difficulty in separate schools unless they can actually profit from a better education both socially and academically than what is available in the 'ordinary' sector. Sadly, it is the case that they do. The present education system, driven by successive governments to see academic achievement as the ultimate *raison d'être* for education, doesn't allow for the financial and personnel considerations involved to support true integration.

However there has been progress. A lot of the pupils that

I taught in the 1970s and 80s would not be placed in special schools now. The truth of that is evidenced by the true portraits of some of the boys I write about. Some of them were placed there because they were considered to have behaviour problems or had some quirk of personality that caused them to be designated as being in need of 'remediation'.

Whatever the reasons for their placement, I profited from the eclectic mix that resulted. I had twenty years that were challenging, exciting and vibrant. The hard times were rarely dull and the dispiriting ones were infrequent and short lived. I taught many boys with whom I developed a bond.

I have no false modesty about the success I enjoyed. As I re-read the narrative I realise how immature and naïve a lot of my behaviour was but even during that terrible violence the world was also a lot more innocent than now. Experience sandpapered any of the rough edges and I became your round peg in a round hole. I owe them all a debt of gratitude. While I may have taught them something, they taught me a lot more. I wouldn't be so rash as to claim I liked them all... there was the odd one whose leaving was greeted with relief: but that number is overwhelmingly surpassed by the number of boys I enjoyed teaching and being with.

As I write I wonder, 'Was it all really that good, that enjoyable? Has distance leant enchantment to that dirty green mobile? Did I really feel that enthusiasm and happiness?'

I believe some of the happiest moments in my life were when I would be in that hut with a quiet buzz of activity; the boys working, to-ing and fro-ing to my desk for help or me moving purposely amongst them. I was doing something that was rewarding for all of us; life had a pleasure and a purpose and I was cocky enough to know I was able to do it better than most.

I also became increasingly aware of the limitations imposed by inability. It was important that targets were achievable and desirable. I knew a very dedicated teacher who failed to understand this and ended up depressed and frustrated by his failure to produce an educational alchemy.

I wrote of him in a poem that included the lines;

> *'If he were God, he would dance the moon among the stars*
> *Increase eternity, extend the universe, accept no bars*
> *I feel no like need for confrontations*
> *I sighed and shaved my expectations.*
> *I'm not inclined to shred my soul*
> *Because of God's own limitations.'*

As I get older my dreams are increasingly filled with memories both real and imaginary of those times. Faces and personalities flit between the hours of sleep.

I am, once again, in front of a class, or gathered round the desk with a miscellany of pupils in an assortment of garbs, differing sizes physically, some younger, widely different in maturity and understanding; emotionally and intellectually disparate. Jim is beside me, pinching my arm, entreating me to listen. Con's face is twisted in concentration and effort as he attempts to master the mystery that is literacy; Morgan is painting a colourful scene to accompany another of Alan's poems; Francie is quietly leaving his seat to put on the kettle; Tommy and others are regaling me with various local incidents and Barney is always there with that same, vacant, empty goodness.

Robert Rooney
August 2013